black **power,**
white **blood**

Also by Lori Andrews

The Clone Age: Adventures in the New World of
Reproductive Technology

black POWER, white BLOOD

The Life and Times of Johnny Spain

With a new epilogue by the author

Lori Andrews

Temple University Press   Philadelphia

Temple University Press, Philadelphia 19122
Copyright ©1999 by Lori B. Andrews
All rights reserved

Published 1999

First published in 1996 by Pantheon Books
Printed in the United States of America

∞ The paper used in this publication meets the requirements
of the American National Standard for
Information Sciences—Permanence of Paper for
Printed Library Materials, ANSI Z39.48-1984

Cataloging-in-Publication Data available from the Library of Congress

For Amanda Urban,
agent extraordinaire—
and for Michael, Bryan,
and Sahara

Sometimes I think this whole world
Is one big prison yard.
Some of us are prisoners
The rest of us are guards.
Lord, Lord,
They cut George Jackson down.
Lord, Lord,
They laid him in the ground.

BOB DYLAN

contents

black **power,**
white **blood**

prologue

Johnny Larry Spain crossed the grassy plaza of San Quentin with the measured steps necessitated by his leg irons. The soft umbrella of his Afro shaded his face from the July sun's glare. His hands were cuffed in front of him, attached to his waist chain by heavy links of soldered metal. A few prisoners from the mainline excitedly caught sight of him and raised their fists in the Black Power salute. It was a brave gesture—greeting Spain in any way could subject them to weeks in solitary confinement.

The guard behind him gave a tug on the chain attached to the dog collar around Spain's neck, directing him to the nearby van. One by one, Spain and the other members of the San Quentin Six boarded. They were Fleeta Drumgo, Hugo Pinell, Willie Tate, David Johnson, and Luis Talamantez—strong black and brown men who had come of age in the California prison system, and whose actions had set it on its head. The escort cars from the police and sheriff's departments took their place. As they headed down Highway 101, Johnny could hear a whir of helicopter blades. Johnny turned to Fleeta, on the seat behind him.

"We've got more security than the president," he said.

It was July 28, 1975, the opening day of their trial, and the whale-shaped Marin County Civic Center was surrounded by demonstrators. We're no longer some fringe element, or some ghetto gang, thought Johnny. The size of the crowd made that clear. As the van sped through the parking lot, Johnny eyed the Black Panthers in their uniforms of black pants, powder blue shirts, black leather jackets, and black berets. With them were movement whites, men with long hair and women with short skirts, the clothes he noticed in the television coverage of anti-war demonstrations. Shit, our ideas could *work!* People *believe* in us.

Everyone who wanted to attend the trial—spectators, reporters, and even the defendants' attorneys—had to sign their names, provide identification, be photographed, pass through two metal detectors, and be frisked. A cadre of security officers was checking for bombs. Angela Davis, tall and sleek, with jeans taut across her hips, approached the first metal detector. The prison matrons ran their fingers through her hair, searching for contraband. It's as if all of us are also on trial, she thought to herself. We are suspect by virtue of the fact that we want to witness the proceedings.

The van stopped at a back entrance and the defendants were hustled into the holding cell. There was a long metal strip in the center of the floor, with six hooks along its length. Johnny and the others were shackled to the hooks by their neck chains, like elephants at a circus. The chains were not long enough to allow them to stand erect.

Johnny tried to find a comfortable way to sit on one of the two cement benches in the room. His wrists were raw from the cuffs and his back pinched from the twenty-five pounds of shackles. So far today he'd only worn the chains for two hours. He knew they'd be on for at least sixteen more. His muscles tightened, like those of a man being beaten.

A half hour later, two guards released him from the elephant hook and escorted him into the empty courtroom. There they secured his waist chain to his chair, which was bolted to the floor. Before the jurors and spectators were admitted, the other defendants were likewise molded into the furniture.

My day in court, Johnny thought. A ludicrous concept. Based on the pretrial hearings, he knew how the day would go. First, the cramp in his shoulder blades would vie for attention with the numbness of his legs. By early afternoon, the waist cinch would wear away the skin over his bottom rib. Toward the end of the courtroom session, the ache in his head would drown out anything the witnesses had to say.

The courtroom doors opened, and the audience took its place behind the bulletproof glass which separated the San Quentin Six from any people who might try violence to free them. Davis mouthed a greeting of support to Johnny through the thick glass which distorted his features.

The spectator section swelled with people who had spent the late 1960s and early 1970s riding the crest of ideas to change the world. They had lived their beliefs, in the streets and the courts, and their revolutionary ideals had been countered by desperate, violent measures of the F.B.I. The prison had killed George Jackson, who had given voice to the oppressed in his best-selling *Soledad Brother.* Now the government was after Johnny Spain, his Black Panther partner.

Many had traveled lengthy distances to attend the trial, but none had spent as long getting here as Johnny. His journey to this spot had begun at the moment of his birth, some twenty-six years earlier and thousands of miles away.

chapter
one

At the Catholic hospital in Jackson, Mississippi, Ann Armstrong bore down and struggled, but the baby did not appear. Her strawberry blond hair was matted with sweat across her pale forehead. Contractions wracked her body and the pain seemed endless. Just as she thought she was too exhausted for even one more push, a tiny head with black silky hair began to crown. With her next contraction, she watched as she delivered a butterscotch-colored boy.

A nun at the hospital entered Ann's room that night as she was nursing the infant.

"What have you decided to do about the boy?" she asked Ann, nodding her head in the baby's direction.

Ann squinted at the curve of the nun's cap, not comprehending the question.

"Perhaps," said the nun gently, "you could give the boy away, and tell your husband he was stillborn."

Ann jerked her head back so forcefully that a drop of the translucent milk spilled on her belly.

"It would be better for the boy," continued the nun. "What good can come of this? What kind of life will he have?"

As Ann looked down at the suckling infant, she found it hard to imagine breaking the bond. She considered her

7

options, which were few. The only promising one was to lie.
He wasn't that dark. His hair was straight.

Ann's sister, Margaret Smith, visited the next day. "How
are you feeling?" she asked, but Ann's reply was interrupted
by a nurse bringing the baby in. He appeared to have been
carried into the white ward in disguise, swaddling cloths covering everything except his eyes and nose.

Margaret pulled the cotton wrapping back to reveal the
baby's face. She gasped, turned away, but did not speak.

The baby struggled to escape his bindings. His arm poked
through and a tiny hand wrapped around Margaret's finger.
She took him from the nurse, holding his small hand in
hers.

"I may need some money," said Ann.

Margaret watched as the baby's long fingers reached
toward her cheek. "I've got a little money set aside, and I
could talk to Mama."

The following afternoon, Ann told the nurse how to fill in
the birth certificate, her child's passport into Southern life.
When asked who the baby's father was, Ann firmly replied
with the name of her white husband, Fred Armstrong. The
baby, she said, would be known as Larry Michael Armstrong.
Ann's gaze was so intense that the nurse did not argue. She
hesitated briefly, then wrote clearly on the line for race:
White.

Ann had first noticed Arthur Cummings two years earlier, in
1947, at the cafe that she and her husband owned. She
watched him out of the corner of her eye as she served din-
ers on both sides of the wall that divided white customers
from black ones. He sat up straight, his neat shirt tucked
into the waistband of his pants without a wrinkle, reading as

he ate. The clatter, the cigarette smoke—none of it seemed to reach him.

One afternoon Arthur was taking a late lunch in the otherwise deserted restaurant. He closed his book and concentrated on the broadcast of the game. Ann approached him. "You look like an athlete. Did you ever play baseball?"

Arthur moved his right hand a few inches off the table, remembering the ripple in his arms from a good pitch. He tipped his head back to look at her. "I had a tryout scheduled for the Black Barons—you know, that team in the Negro League. But I threw out my shoulder during practice in Jacksonville."

"That's a shame."

"It's for the better," replied Arthur. "Baseball is a young man's game."

Later that week, Arthur was buried again in his books. "You're always reading," she said. "How come you like it so much?"

"You can learn a lot. Take this book— it's about what we should have done differently in the war."

"Do you only read true stories?"

"Not always."

The next day when he finished his meal, he handed Ann a slim book of poems and left.

She opened the volume. She hadn't read a poem since high school. What could he learn from this? These poems weren't even about black people.

She read a few pages and felt the lines soothe her, the cadence of the words pushing her thoughts back and forth as if she were in a rocking chair. She wanted to read more, but couldn't risk bringing the book upstairs to the apartment where she and Fred lived with their son, Charlie.

Wrapping a towel around it, she hid it behind the flour sack in the cabinet.

The next day, Arthur looked at Ann playing solitaire when the cafe was deserted. "Do you dare play a game of gin rummy with me?" he asked.

She began to deal.

After that, Ann would pull out a deck of cards whenever they were alone in the cafe. Sometimes Arthur would set them aside, preferring just to ask her opinions about the day's events.

Ann was startled by a man's asking for her viewpoint. She found herself confiding in Arthur, sometimes thinking aloud when he was around and voicing opinions she didn't know she had.

She told him that she had always wanted to be a nurse, but wasn't sure how good she'd be at taking care of other people because she sometimes didn't take care of herself. Arthur nodded. He had noticed the occasional bruises and realized her husband beat her. "I think you'd be a fine nurse," he said. "You could do anything you put your mind to."

Ann left the cafe after the lunch shift one Saturday afternoon and drove up State Street. She turned a corner and noticed a familiar figure waiting for a bus. She rolled down her window. "Arthur, do you want a ride?"

"I don't want to take you out of your way," he replied. "Where were you going?"

"Actually, I was heading south to feed the horse my mother gave me." Her face brightened. "Would you like to come with me?"

Arthur got in and they rode to the stables. As she petted

the chestnut-colored horse and sweet-talked the animal, she seemed girlish and soft. Arthur watched from a courteous distance, until Ann motioned him over. He ran his hand over the horse's warm coat. She watched his long tapered fingers and stared into his pale brown eyes, with their bluish halo.

In the weeks that followed, they spun long conversations at the blacks' section of the cafe. He'd come in for dinner now around 8 P.M., and stay until the cafe closed at midnight, just to make sure she was safe. He no longer left his money on the counter, but instead pressed it in her hand. She lingered in his touch.

Even when there was no one else in the cafe, Arthur and Ann never thought to move to the more comfortable white section. Everywhere in Mississippi, the dividing line between races was clear. Where the pavement ended, the black neighborhoods began. In business establishments, blacks entered through a different door. On the streets they drank at a different water fountain. Separate everywhere. Never equal.

In private relations as well, blacks were cordoned off from whites. An 1890 amendment to the Mississippi constitution—still in effect—forbade marriage between the races. Scientists provided pseudogenetic support for the restrictive law, warning against the adulteration of the Caucasian blood line by inferior stock.

Others said it more succinctly: The children would be hexed.

On Halloween night, 1948, Ann drove Arthur home. They made love tenderly that night and, for the next few weeks, made a series of reckless arrangements so that they could spend time together. They even talked about going away together, perhaps to some city in the North. "We don't

have to stumble around Alabama, Mississippi, and Louisiana," he said. "There are other places to go."

But whenever Ann tried to develop a plan, it wouldn't
come into focus. Fred would never let her have Charlie if
she left, and she couldn't abandon her son.

Arthur understood, but saw no sense in staying involved
with a married woman—particularly a white woman, in
Jackson, Mississippi. He started thinking about the cities he
had visited and gave notice at the garage.

One day, Arthur stopped coming to the cafe. Ann looked
up his phone number in the Jackson directory, glancing
quickly over the "C" for colored in the left-hand margin.
When she dialed, the phone rang in an empty room. She
drove past the garage a few times, but he was never there.
She longed to ask some of the other black men what had
happened to Arthur, but she was afraid it would get back to
her husband.

A month later, she realized she was pregnant.

chapter
two

When Ann arrived home, the baby didn't seem quite as dark as he had in the glaring white of the hospital. Fred got a quizzical look in his eyes and remarked about Larry's color, but Ann smoothed it over by reminding Fred of her grandmother's dark hair and eyes.

A few months later, they sold the cafe and moved to a small blue frame house on Stokes-Robertson Road, just as if they were any young family. Across the street was an open field, with a creek a few blocks away. Plenty of places for the boys to play and, Ann noted happily, a lot of other children for them to play with.

Fred's new job—driving a beer truck—took him away for long hours on the road, leaving Ann free to pour her love into the new baby. The noise of her sewing machine could be heard at all hours as she made exquisite clothes, little dress suits that she thought would make him seem more white. It seemed to work. The neighbors smiled and cooed over him as she pushed him in the buggy, Charlie walking alongside her. Ann's sister, Margaret, never brought the matter up. Only Fred was occasionally distant and skeptical.

For the first two years, Larry passed. His skin appeared tanned by the Mississippi sun. But then his fine baby hair grew out, replaced by wiry tufts. No matter how much Ann combed it, the kinks stayed in. After his second birthday, when they took their walks around the neighborhood, people stared ahead without greeting them.

The women Ann knew from church stopped dropping in. A black maid approached Ann and Larry in the grocery store and asked him where his mama was.

When Ann took Larry for his booster shots, she entered the main door of the doctor's office and gave her name to the nurse. The woman frowned at the child and pointed Ann to the colored waiting room, with its hard wooden chairs. "You'll have to wait in there," she said.

Ann raised her chin, ready to protest. There was plenty of room here on the couch, where she had waited for the doctor in the past. She opened her mouth to speak, but the nurse crossed her arms in front of her and prepared to hold her ground. Ann guided Larry into the next room and watched him as he examined the keyhole and knob. Like the sky before an October rain, he seemed to blacken before her eyes.

After that, Ann pushed her sewing machine even harder, trying to close the skin-color gap between the brothers by dressing them like twins. Identical cowboy outfits. Tiny Budweiser uniforms, their names sewn above the shirt pockets. She talked Fred into taking the uniformed brothers along in his truck to make deliveries.

Margaret marveled that Ann stayed married after Larry's birth. At rare moments a look of passion would pass between Fred and Ann, but most of the time their relationship was fueled by rage, their lust sometimes following the pounding of blows. Ann didn't know when those moments were coming, but her body kept a calendar: Broken ribs. Black eyes. Split shin.

After one of their fights, they made love hungrily, despite her bruises. Ann got pregnant, and spent the following months hoping that a new baby would take Fred's mind off Larry.

One night, when Ann was five months along, she sang softly to Larry as she pulled the Davy Crockett blanket up to his pale brown chin, then whispered good night to five-year-old Charlie and quietly made her way to her bedroom. She could hear Fred's key in the door at last. That afternoon his boss had taken him aside. "You've got to do something about the nigger," the man said. "Your little boy can still ride in the truck, but the nigger got to go." Afterward, Fred had tried to wash the words away with a river of beer.

The perfume bottle on the dresser shook as the front door slammed. Fred charged into the bedroom, talking to Ann as he walked.

"Who was he?" Fred demanded.

"Who was who?" Ann replied evenly, not wanting to upset her husband when he was drunk.

Fred grabbed Ann's hair and pulled her toward him. "The dirty nigger who knocked you up."

Ann slipped free. "I've told you a dozen times, Larry is your son," she said. "He gets his dark coloring from my grandmother."

She turned to the closet to avoid Fred's gaze.

"Even the other drivers can tell," said Fred. "My boss told me today that I better do something about the nigger boy."

Ann felt the new baby, Fred's baby, kick inside her. She turned to face his reproachful eyes. "His name is Arthur Cummings," she acknowledged at last.

Fred crossed his arms in front of him, as if waiting for an explanation. How easy it would be to tell him she'd been raped. Instead, she confessed, "I did it of my own free will."

Fred jerked Ann by the shoulders. "Where can I find him?"

"I don't know."

Fred flung her on the bed, pressing his hands on her throat. "I'm going to ask you one more time."

Ann choked. "He worked at Fruehauf's."

Fred stalked to the hall closet and loaded his gun.

"Are you Cummings?" he asked the first black he saw at the truck garage.

The man shook his head, trying not to move his glance down to the outline of a gun in the raging white man's pocket. "He moved to Chicago a couple of years ago."

Fred turned sharply and drove quickly home. Ann was waiting in the darkened kitchen. Her hands shook and tears rolled down her cheeks.

"Take that nigger baby and get out of here!" he roared.

She thought of her two children, and the third on the way. "This is my house, too, Fred."

He cracked the pistol across her left shoulder. She crumpled to the floor. Fred sat down at the table, tipped his head into the pillow of his folded arms, and passed out. Ann rolled over on her right side, pushing herself to a sitting position. She reached for his pistol with her right hand, her shoulder screaming with pain. Trembling, she aimed at Fred's head, trying to steady her shaking hand. Then she thought about her sons, dropped the gun, and wept.

chapter
three

I t was nearly dusk when five-year-old Larry heard the Budweiser truck pull into the driveway. Larry looked for a place to hide, again choosing the hall closet. He pulled the door behind him, and imagined that the musty odor of the wool coats was the smell of a cave. He was Davy Crockett, hiding out from a wild animal. The cramped darkness frightened him at first, but then became a comfortable blanket he drew up around him. He touched the thick stiff wool of his mother's coat, the skin of a buffalo he'd killed.

He heard his father click on the radio and wondered if it was safe to go out and pee. Half-crouching, he inched the door open, moving as quietly as Davy Crockett. He was halfway to the bathroom when he heard a flush and Fred appeared in front of him.

Larry stood in place, a mixture of panic and bravado gluing him to the floor. At 6 feet 2 inches tall and nearly 300 pounds, Fred was a huge man—big shoulders, big gut, big nose. His eyes were etched red from a palette of beer. The color shone like the fires of an immense hate.

Fred took a breath, and raised his hand.

"Fred, leave the boy alone!" Ann called from the kitchen. Larry turned and ran toward her voice.

"You can't protect him forever," Fred yelled after him.

"Everything is alright," Ann whispered, as Larry wrapped his arms around her legs.

He shook his head. "Why doesn't Dad love me like Charlie or Lissie?"

"He does," she said. "You just don't understand."

On some nights, Larry lay awake in the room he shared with Charlie. He would hear his dad saying "that nigger baby" and his mom shushing him. Sometimes they'd yell loud enough to wake Charlie. "GET OUT!" his dad would scream at his mom. Larry's muscles would tighten as he listened to hear whether the front door would slam and his mother would go. But she never did. Charlie assured him she would stay and take care of them—not just Charlie and Larry, but Lissie, who'd been born when Larry was three, and the new baby, a boy named Ray.

Even when his parents' room was silent, Larry slept fitfully. He dreaded the early mornings. First he'd tiptoe around to avoid his father. Then he'd watch as Charlie got ready to go off to school. Larry desperately wanted to go with him.

After Charlie left, Larry took out his brother's old school books. He took a piece of lined paper and traced the letters from the book onto the page. He concentrated intently, and produced the shapes crisply. Then he wrote the numbers 1 to 100 from memory. He showed it off to Lissie in her playpen, and then told her a story about a princess named Lissie who made the sun rise.

It was almost summer vacation, time to register children for the next school year. Ann had thought she could admit Larry on the strength of his birth certificate, but she knew now that his hair would cause them a problem. No matter how closely it was cut, the truth about his father poked through. Now the white barbers were refusing to cut it altogether.

What were her choices? There were schools for black children in the Delta, but the school year there was just a few months long. The schools did not open until late in the fall, after the cotton crop was picked, and they closed early in the spring, in time for planting.

It had been over a year now since the U.S. Supreme Court, in *Brown* v. *Board of Education*, had given black children the right to go to school with white children. Ann had seen an editorial in the *Jackson Clarion Ledger* mourning that "May 17, 1954, may be recorded as a black day of tragedy for the South." Mississippi politicians called the day of the decision "Black Monday" and vowed that educational integration would never be accepted. Mobs of violent whites would retaliate against any black child who tried to attend a white public school, or that child's parents.

Just two months ago, on May 31, 1955, the Supreme Court had handed down another decision, ordering schools to be integrated "with all deliberate speed." A week later Mississippi's Education Advisory Committee announced it would "never compromise on racial segregation."

The previous January, an office of the National Association for the Advancement of Colored People had opened in Jackson. That same month, the Mississippi constitution was amended to raise voting requirements to exclude most blacks. A U.S. senator from Mississippi, Theodore Bilbo, had previously warned a crowd of whites in a Mississippi town square of the dangers of letting down even slightly the bars of segregation: "The best way to keep a nigger from the polls on election day is to visit him the night before."

Ann rarely saw blacks now that she lived on Stokes-Robertson, but she knew from the news that tensions were mounting in Mississippi. That past spring, an NAACP leader, the Reverend George E. Lee, had been killed in Belzoni, Mississippi, by a shotgun blast from a carload of whites after he dared to register Negroes to vote. The killers had not even been prosecuted. It was like that man from the NAACP, Medgar Evers, had said: "A Negro in Mississippi is always in danger, if only of starving to death."

chapter
four

The summer of 1955 flew by with Ann never admitting to Larry that he would not be able to go to school, never talking to him about the issue of race. On a muggy August day, Larry and Charlie darted between the trees in the shadow of their faded blue house. Larry was the scout, helping his cowboy brother chase after Indians. Larry shimmied up a tree and made his way out on the limb without a snap.

"Here they come," Larry announced.

Three boys Charlie's age rode up. "Do you want to ride bikes with us?" one asked Charlie.

"Can I come too?" said Larry.

The boy looked up to see where the question was coming from. Then he motioned to his friends and started riding away. "We don't play with no niggers," he yelled over his shoulder.

"Don't call him that," Charlie shouted, running after the boys. "He's not that. He's my brother."

Larry clung tightly to the limb, trying not to cry. He couldn't understand why the boys from the block didn't want to be friends with him. Charlie liked him, and Lissie, and Ray, and his mom. But the neighborhood boys seemed only to want to make fun of him or hurt him. He thought about how when he was three, the dark-haired one had shot him in the knee with an arrow. The boy claimed it was an accident, but Larry had watched the boy's eyes as he aimed right toward him. A few months later, Larry was on his tricycle and Charlie was on his bike when another boy threw a rock and hit Larry over the eye. Charlie had gotten a small axe and chased the bigger boy around the neighborhood.

Charlie told Larry to climb down from the tree, that it was time to go inside now, that Mama wanted him to help with Ray and Lissie. He didn't tell Larry what he had heard. As the boys were pedaling off, one of them had said he was going home for a rifle. "My father told me about shooting niggers. I'm going to get myself a nigger."

Charlie walked Larry into the house, then sneaked into his parents' room and quietly loaded Fred's pistol. Back outside, he stood behind the tree for the next half hour, but the boys did not return.

That night Larry lay awake, thinking of the boys and their chants. "Nigger! Nigger! Nigger!" The words seem to grow louder and louder in his head—until he realized they were coming from the front yard. He looked over at Charlie sleeping in the other bed, and wondered if he should wake him. Just then, a loud thump shook the house, followed by the sounds of shattering glass. Charlie leaped out of bed and the two boys ran to the broken living room window. Flames shot out from a wooden cross on the lawn, leaping nearly to the front door.

"Get back," yelled Ann, pushing the boys back toward their room. She closed her eyes to erase the sight of her neighbor's truck pulling away from the curb and veering around the corner to his house.

. . .

Fred did nothing to confront the neighbor the next day. But he did start thinking of a plan. Larry's face haunted his long drive as he delivered beer to the bars and honky-tonks in and around Jackson.

His delivery route that August day took him out of the city, west on Route 18 to a small town called Utica. His stop there was the Corner Grill, a night club and restaurant managed by Iris "Shorty" Davis and her husband, Johnnie Davis. They were the first blacks to own a business on Depot Street, and they catered to both blacks and whites. Iris called it "the best eat business in town."

"How come you let whites eat here when we can't eat in their places?" a black asked Iris.

"Their money in the drawer is as good as yours," she retorted. The register rang often, and those earnings were supplemented by Johnnie's winnings at poker and skin, another card game that was popular in the South. The Davis children, twin sons and a daughter, had more toys than many of the white children in Mississippi.

Fred called Iris over as he unloaded a keg of beer in the club. "I got this child at home, he can't go to school with the rest of the children," he said. "You can tell he's a colored child. Can he come live with you?"

Iris was silent as their eyes met.

"He's smarter than my kids," Fred continued, recalling the papers he'd found with Larry's writing on them. "I just can't keep him. I have to pick up and send him somewhere."

He took out a picture of Larry and showed it to her.

"I'll tell you what," said Iris. "I can't keep no child here. But Johnnie's got a cousin in California. She hasn't been able to have a child of her own. I'll see if she can take him."

That night, Iris called Helen Spain to ask if she wanted to adopt a six-year-old boy. "I pined for a baby for years," replied Helen, "but now I'm forty-seven years old, too old for a child that young."

"Oh, Helen, you're really not that old. And this is a *beautiful* child."

"It just wouldn't work. Johnny and I have settled into our own ways. We both have our jobs. There's no room in our lives for a child."

"Think about what you're saying. Here's an opportunity you've always wanted. Think of how much you love my two boys."

"Shorty, you're an angel to think of us, but it's not right for me."

Late that evening, while Iris was thinking about what she would tell Fred when he made his rounds the next Monday, Helen called back. "When Johnny came home from work, I told him about your call," she explained. "He told me to call back and get that little boy."

Iris could sense the hesitation in Helen's voice, and knew that Helen had been pressured into making the call. But Iris didn't say anything. The boy couldn't continue on with a white family in *Mississippi*, for heaven's sake.

Fred explained to Ann that the Spains were willing to adopt Larry. "You can't protect him from the whole world," he argued. Ann knew he was right. The phone calls were getting worse, harassing her about her "nigger baby." Next time it wouldn't be just a cross on the lawn. The whole house might go up in flames. She had to think of her other children too.

Ann spent the next week nervously sewing clothes for Larry and pulling together his favorite toys.

"Would you like to go to California?" Ann finally sum-

moned up her courage to ask Larry the day before he was
due to leave. "You could go to school there."

"Why can't I stay here and go to school with Charlie?"

"You could get hurt if you stayed here," Ann told Larry.
"You see, everybody is not the same in the world. They are a
little different in how they look. Bad people here can't
accept the difference in other people and try to hurt them."

Then Ann told him he was going away to live with "a nice
Negro family in California."

There was more—Ann trying to explain in her own way
about racism. But Larry didn't hear the words.

He ran to his bed and dived under the covers without
even taking off his shoes. He reached over for his stuffed
dog and pressed its face against his nose, as if to read some
explanation in the button eyes. He wished Charlie were
home from school now so he could ask him what was going
on.

Ann came in a few minutes later, sat on the edge of the
bed, and held her son against her shoulder. Then Ray
started crying to be fed and she left the room. Charlie
arrived from school a half hour later, but she didn't fill him
in on the plan.

"C'mon, Larry," Charlie said, "let's go out in the yard."

Larry thought about it for a minute, then decided that his
mother's hug must have meant that she'd changed her
mind. He tucked his dog under the covers and followed
Charlie into the yard.

The next morning, as Larry walked toward the kitchen for
breakfast, he saw a small brown suitcase next to the door. He
snuck up to it, unfastened the clasps, and confirmed his
fears as he saw the neatly folded cowboy shirt and matching
pants. Clothes. His clothes. He thought of hiding them
under the couch or throwing them into the trash. Doing

something, anything, to be able to stay here. But he couldn't move. Could hardly breathe.

Ann, in the meantime, was telling the other children what was happening. "Your brother's going away," she said. "He's going to live with a nice family in California."

"No!" shouted Charlie.

"Yes," said Ann, her nostrils flaring. "And I don't want any back talk from you!"

Charlie started crying, which scared the baby, igniting his tears, too. Lissie began bawling as well.

Larry heard the sobs, ran to the bedroom, and began to cry and shriek.

Ann hugged and patted them until they calmed down, then left them alone for a while. Larry kissed Ray and Lissie and hugged Charlie. Then their mother came in with his little suitcase and his stuffed dog and told Larry, "It's time to go."

chapter
five

"I've got so much to do," Helen Spain said to her mother. "I've got to get a room ready for him, give notice at my job. And how in the world are we going to get that little boy from Mississippi to California?"

Mary Davis had already thought the whole thing through. "I'll go to Mississippi and pick him up," she said calmly.

In the life of 23rd Street in South Central Los Angeles, Mary Davis was a major character. A dark-skinned black woman in her late sixties, she wore floral print dresses and a small hat with a half veil. Everyone in the neighborhood, even the winos who slept in back of the liquor store, called her Miz Davis. She walked with her head high, dispensing her sound advice only if asked. She could look right into children's hearts. If an infant was crying in the neighborhood, she would pluck him from his mother and have him smiling and cooing within seconds.

Although gossip pulsed from porch to porch, no one asked anything outright about Miz Davis's past. Some guessed that a half century earlier, when she lived in Mississippi, she'd gotten pregnant by a white man. Her daughter, Helen, had straight black hair and a small, Caucasian nose. Helen had married a tall and gentle black from Louisiana, Johnny Spain. He hadn't finished high school, but, thanks to Helen's help and urging, he had become a licensed electrician, with his own electrical business. Helen had helped him through his exams, and now she kept the books in addition to her regular job.

For Southern blacks like Johnny and Helen, Los Angeles was a magnet, drawing them with the promise of the much-touted tolerance of the North without the spirit-chilling winters of Detroit or Chicago. Rather than being herded together in tenement rooms, a black family in Watts could aspire to a small house, perhaps even with an avocado tree in the yard.

Helen and Johnny owned such a home, a small, sand-colored bungalow set in a yard splashed with red and yellow flowers. But by the time they got the call about Larry, their dreams were dusty. Helen had been a nightclub dancer in the 1930s, but her dancing couldn't take her beyond the black clubs, and as she aged into her late thirties, she no longer had a place even there. In the decade since then, her satin dresses had hung in the attic as she made her way each day to clean and cook for white entertainers and producers across town in Beverly Hills.

Helen drank to blunt her desire for more, and found comfort in the order and predictability of her life at home. She was not at all sure how a boy of six would fit in, nor what she would do with him once he got there. Mary Davis, though, felt pride in her daughter, son-in-law, and the little house they had built for her in their cramped backyard. Add a grandson and her life would be just about perfect.

A week later, Mary Davis was sipping iced tea at the Corner Grill in Utica, Mississippi. When she heard the car pull up, she moved toward the window. The first words she heard from the boy's mouth were, "I don't want to go to nobody's California!"

As Ann, Charlie, and Larry entered the Corner Grill, the

young boy stayed close to his brother. Ann had picked the
day carefully. Her mother and sister, Margaret, were on vacation in Florida, so she wouldn't have to put up with their
questions. When they returned, Larry would simply be gone.
She would say that she had sent him to live with his Negro
father.

Mary eyed the clock, and pointed out that they would
need to leave soon for the train station. Ann separated the
boys and moved Charlie back into the car. From the stoop
outside the Corner Grill, Larry yelled, "Charlie, help me!"

Charlie opened the car door, but his mother pulled him
back on the seat and slapped him. He punched her back—
the first time he had ever hit his mother. As the car sped
away, Charlie could hear his brother crying and yelling his
name.

When they boarded the segregated Pullman, Larry's eyes
darted from seat to seat. He'd never seen so many black
faces.

The lady he was with tried to pull him up on her lap, but
he moved away. He sat stiffly, staring out the window without
speaking.

The ride stretched on for hours, then days, but Larry
slept only in brief snatches. If he closed his eyes for long,
who knew what might happen or where he'd end up? Or
who with?

This is going to end, he thought finally. The train is going
to turn around. It's going to stop. I'm going to be back with
Charlie and Ray and Lissie and Mama.

"You'll like California," Mary tried to assure him. "That's
where Davy Crockett lives."

When they reached the Los Angeles station, Mary told
Larry that the Spains would be meeting them and taking

him home. There were lots of people in the station, and
Larry grudgingly let Mary take his hand as they moved up
toward the gate and into the main lobby. In his other hand,
he held his stuffed dog. A well-built black man, over six feet
tall and with gentle eyes, greeted him. "Hi Larry," he said.
His tiny wife was at his side.

"Hello," Helen said gently, "I'm your new mother."

I don't want a new mother, he thought. I want my old one.

Helen extended her hand, but Larry recoiled, turned
sharply, and bolted out into the street.

Mary grabbed him as a car swerved to miss him. She
didn't let go until they were safely inside the Spains' car. An
hour later, Larry followed Helen Spain into his new home.

He had expected to see toys scattered around the living
room, as they had been in Mississippi. Here there was plas-
tic on the couch and there didn't seem to be anything to
play with.

Helen showed him to his room. He'd often thought how
great it would be to have a room of his own, but now as he
stared at the single bed, he remembered how much fun it
was to whisper over at Charlie in the middle of the night.

"I want to play outside," Larry said.

"Okay," said Helen, "but don't get too dirty and don't
cross any streets."

Larry peeked at the yard, eyeing the little house in the
back where Mary Davis lived. Then he came around to the
front. He took to the sidewalk tentatively, his shoulders
slumped. He thought about everything he had done the
week before he left Mississippi. What had he done that was
so horrible that they sent him away? He'd played catch
with Charlie, told stories to Ray and Lissie. He must've done
something.

Maybe it was 'cause he and Charlie had trampled the

turnip greens in Mrs. Fortinberry's yard. Mom yelled, but she kissed and hugged him that night, same as always.

Maybe it's just me. Maybe I'm a monster.

That night, just after dinner, he said he was tired and wanted to sleep. He went to the strange new room and found his pajamas already unpacked in one of the drawers. The bed felt stiff as he lay down, and he could feel the tightness in his chest. He pulled the big pillow over his head so that no one would hear him cry.

Weeks passed, and one day Larry realized that he could no longer call up Ann's face in his mind. Other traces of her teased his memory, though. The way she smelled. The softness of her inner arms as she held him. A little song she'd hum as she cooked.

This other lady, Helen, didn't do any of those things. Sometimes she'd look at him as if she wondered why he was there.

"Did you write to your first mother?" she would ask. Ann had sent a few letters, the first of which Larry had answered.

But now Larry didn't want to think about Ann. He missed her in a desperate, choking, hard-to-catch-his-breath way. He tried to push Ann out of his memories, but she'd pop back in, like that game where you try not to think of an elephant.

When it got to be too much for him, Larry would sneak into Johnny's backyard toolshed. He felt free to cry there, sometimes howling with tears, until he felt the shed would collapse from his sobs.

"Larry, what's the matter?"

He turned to see Mary Davis in the doorway of the shed.

"I hurt my finger," he lied. He had taught himself not to

cry, no matter what anyone did to him, except in this private place.

"Let me look at it, child."

"No, it'll be all right."

She took his other hand and led him back to her house. She sat down in her rocking chair and pulled him up on her lap, one hand supporting his neck.

"I know you don't understand all this and that it's hurting you," Mary said, "but you're going to be okay."

He pressed his head against her chest, closed his eyes, and felt the sway of the rocking chair. She smelled good, like cookies or vanilla ice cream. He fell asleep as she hummed and rocked.

That Saturday, Mary took him on her weekend errands. They boarded a bus and took a seat behind a white woman and a light-brown-skinned boy who looked to be about four years old. Larry rested his hand on the back of the seat in front of him and noticed that the color of his arm matched the color of the boy's neck.

The white woman leaned over to the boy and kissed him lightly on the cheek.

"Mama, can we go play in the ocean sometime?"

She smiled down at him. "Ask your daddy."

The boy reached a chubby arm across the aisle, touching a dark black man who grinned widely at him. "Daddy, can we?"

The man reached over and lifted the boy to his lap. "Sure, big guy, we'll get your cousins and all go down to the ocean."

When Larry and Mary arrived home, Larry walked into the bathroom. He closed the lid of the toilet, stood on top of it, and looked at his face and arms in the mirror. He stared at the long, light brown fingers, then turned his hands over to reflect the white palms. He bent his head to look at his hair, so different from Ann's or Fred's. He turned to look at the side of his face.

That night Larry could hardly sleep. It was the first time he realized that Fred Armstrong could not be his father. Fred, like his mother, was white. He hoped his real father was on his way to California to get him.

chapter
six

The following Monday, Larry adjusted the jacket of his Catholic school uniform and walked out the front door. When he first came to Los Angeles, Helen had asked him, "Are you Catholic or Protestant?" He had no idea what she meant and said the first thing that popped into his mind, "Catholic." And so she sent him to a Catholic school.

Most of the children on his block went to the neighborhood public school. Dressed in his never-changing uniform, Larry would trail them in the morning, but when they turned into the schoolyard, he kept walking, another four blocks up and then a mile east. On this particular morning, on 26th Street, he heard voices behind him and turned to see three other uniformed boys. He retraced his steps, approaching them expectantly.

"Look at that yellow boy!" one said.

"Yeah," added the tallest, "he's got piss skin."

Tears formed in Larry's eyes, which egged them on further.

"Yellow boy! Yellow boy!" they chanted.

In Mississippi, Larry had been taunted for being too dark; now he was too light. The heat of his anger dried his tears. He stood firmly in front of the boys, pulling himself to his full four-foot height. In his finest Southern accent, he said,

"You *black* niggah." He had heard it in Mississippi and he knew it must be bad.

On his way home from school that day, he crumpled up his jacket and carried it under his arm. He lingered, as he often did, at the fence of El Santo Niño, the local activity center of the Catholic Youth Organization, to watch the children play basketball. The CYO center was just a block away from the Spains' house, and he preferred to stay there and watch rather than go home and face Helen.

He was startled by a voice from the other side of the fence.

"Why aren't you playing?" asked the black man. "Don't you know how to play these games they're playing?"

"Yeah, I do," lied Larry, who had never played basketball.

"Then why don't you play with them?"

"I don't want to."

"Why not?"

"I don't like those kids," he said, even though he had never met them.

"Well, I'm Shelby Bacon, the coach here. Why don't you come on back tomorrow?"

The following day, the man handed Larry the basketball. It was heavier than Larry had expected when he'd watched the other boys play. Larry threw the ball down on the concrete, but it responded with only a weak bounce.

"Here, let me show you." The man dribbled left-handed as he drove toward the basket. He leaped, shifted the ball to his right hand, flicked with his wrist. *Swish.*

"I want to learn how to do that," said Larry.

Larry came back the following day, and the day after that. At first he felt like he was all clumsy thumbs, but Shelby urged him on anytime he came close to getting a basket. Over the next few weeks, he mastered both free throws and layups. By the time summer vacation began, Larry had joined one of the CYO teams.

Most of the other kids treated Shelby like they treated their teachers at school. When he asked for attention, they would sometimes keep on talking and fooling around. Not Larry. He was right there listening, practically right under Shelby's mouth, because he believed that a coach could give you some secret fundamental, some clue to what you needed to win.

That summer, the highlight of each week was the Saturday game, when they played teams from other youth groups. Most of the other kids' parents would come on that day.

"Why don't you ever invite your parents?" Shelby asked Larry.

He immediately regretted the question when he saw the boy's shoulders tighten and his head drop. The following Saturday, when Larry was once again there alone, Shelby made an effort to pay him a little extra attention.

The Spains never did come to see him play. But sometimes Miz Davis would stand by the fence when they practiced, deliberately routing herself past El Santo Niño whenever she needed to do an errand.

"Larry, your grandma's here," the other boys would yell. He would keep playing, but there would be more of a snap in his dribble, more confidence in his free throw, for the time she stood near the fence.

In school that fall, Larry listened closely to his teacher as she read books aloud to the class. She put so much drama in her voice as she took on the role of the various characters that he felt like he was part of the story. Mama used to read like that, he thought. Helen never did. The nun urged him on, taught him to write his own stories and poems, and he applied himself eagerly to please her. But in the afternoons, he would wait impatiently until the 3:00 P.M. bell, when he could rush off to El Santo Niño. He felt his best on the basketball court. No matter whether his teammates gave him grief about his light skin or not, once they were on the court the rules were clear. They had to pass the ball to him, because he was good.

By the time he was nine, he still wasn't tall enough to be consistently assigned to play center, his favorite position, but whatever position he played, he loved the rush he got as he ran down the court, controlling the direction of the ball, outmaneuvering opponents as if he'd hypnotized them. He was the only kid on a CYO team who could dribble with his off hand, and his balance allowed him to bend his upper body in unlikely angles to make a shot.

For Larry, though, it was not enough to be on a winning team, to be one of the best. He had to feel he was *the* best. He was playing as much against his team members as against the other team.

"Team ball!" the coach yelled at him between halves. "You've got to play with the team."

But Larry lusted to be better than the others. And near the end of one game, when his team was six points behind, Shelby pulled him aside. "Go out there and do your thing."

Larry cared less and less about fitting in at his Catholic school, now that he had found a home at El Santo Niño. When someone would taunt him at school, he'd respond with his fists.

A few times, the nuns called Helen and she'd try to shame Larry into acting differently. But Larry could have cared less what Helen thought. Mary was a different matter, though.

"I know you probably had a good reason to hit the boy,"

she told him. "But you've got to be careful, baby. There'll be enough trouble out there in the world for you without you searching it out on your own."

When a boy named Bobby started playing for an opposing team, Larry got his first real competition. In their third game against each other, when the ball headed out of bounds and Larry needed to knock it back in, he winged it hard, right into Bobby's face. Afterward, Bobby jumped him in the alleyway. Larry got a hold of Bobby's arm and tried to flip him, like he'd seen in the old movies on television. When he didn't flip, Larry kept twisting and twisting the arm. He was thinking so intently about what he wanted to accomplish that Bobby himself seemed to disappear.

"Larry, let go," Bobby screamed. And then there was a small ripping noise as the boy's shoulder was torn out of its socket. Bobby was sidelined for months, and Larry was once again the top player.

For the next few years, the CYO team was the center of Larry's life. On some days, Shelby was not there and a white coach subbed. The kids defied and mocked him. Larry got a clear message: It was better not to identify with the part of him that was white in this totally black environment. In fact, on the few occasions when white people came to the house to visit the Spains, he would run away until they left.

When Helen went to make Larry's bed one morning, she saw the wet spot of urine in the center of the sheets. Damn it, she thought, nine years old and he still pees on the bed! At least once a week she faced the stinky sheets. No matter what she said to him, it seemed to do no good.

That evening, when Larry approached the yard, he could hear Helen say to a neighbor, "It seems like I'm always doing the laundry, what with him wetting the bed and all."

He walked past her, humiliated, as the sheets swayed on the clothesline. *Bad boy, bad boy,* they seemed to say as they fluttered back and forth in the wind.

Once he was out of sight, Mary walked over to the two women. "Don't be so hard on him," she told Helen. "He's a good child. Look how he's always saying, 'Yes, ma'am,' and 'No, ma'am.' He just needs a little love."

But Helen had so many unmet needs herself she didn't know how to love a little boy, one who clearly had no more desire to be there than she had to have him there.

By the spring of 1959, Helen had returned to work as a maid and a cook. She fretted about what she'd do with Larry that summer. Her friends adored the boy's politeness, which he pulled out around other adults, but they didn't have to live with the scrapes and torn clothes when he came home in the evenings. She wondered what damage Larry and the boys from the neighborhood might do to her pretty house that summer while she was at work. Johnny had been talking for months about maybe going to see some of his relatives in the South. Helen decided he should go that summer, and take Larry along.

"How would you like to see your mother again?" she asked Larry one night at dinner.

Larry looked up from the kitchen table, wondering what his teammates would think if Ann arrived at El Santo Niño. "Is she coming here?" he asked.

"No," said Helen, "Johnny's driving to Mississippi and thought you might like to go with him to Utica. Maybe your mother could meet you there."

It seemed to Larry that he didn't have much choice. Helen launched into a listing of what clothes he'd need to take and described how on the way he and Johnny could stop in Louisiana to visit Johnny's sister before they saw Helen's cousins, the Davises, in Utica.

A few months later, on the morning they were leaving, Mary Davis pressed some coins into his hand for a treat and whispered in his ear, "Now you be a good boy when you see your mama and do her proud."

Once they started their journey, Johnny became more talkative, as he often did outside of Helen's presence. As they rode through Texas, he taught Larry about the desert animals—the jackrabbits and coyotes. Larry liked being alone with Johnny. At home, he would sometimes sit with Johnny on the couch and listen to baseball games on the radio. He felt an invisible bond between them as the announcer, Vince Scully, transported them to the stadium, describing how the pitcher was kicking away a piece of gravel and the batter was sweating slightly under his cap.

When they crossed over into Louisiana, Johnny pulled into a filling station. Johnny paid for the gas, then bought a Coke. While his back was turned, Larry trotted into an adjoining diner and tried to get the counterman's attention. "I'd like an ice cream cone," he said.

A small sign in the window clearly said "Whites Only." In his shock at Larry's ordering, the man behind the counter went ahead and scooped out a dip. Then he followed Larry into the gas station lot.

"You'd better watch that boy," the white man told Johnny. "No tellin' what kinda trouble he could get hisself into."

Larry watched Johnny take a step back and saw fear cloud over his eyes. He'd never seen his adoptive father look like that before, his shoulders slack as if his body might crumble.

"Get right in the car," he mumbled to Larry. Once on the highway, his voice was more clear. "Don't you *ever* try anything like that again." For the rest of the drive, Johnny hardly spoke.

Larry spent the quiet hours thinking about Helen and Johnny—and Ann. He had never felt good around Helen, but he'd always held out hope that Johnny might want him. Now Johnny was freezing him out, too.

His thoughts moved involuntarily to memories of Ann. He wondered what it would be like to see her again. Maybe she wanted him back. Maybe she realized now that she had made a big mistake.

He looked at Johnny guiltily, having made a heavy decision. If Ann wanted him home, he would say yes.

chapter
seven

Larry bounded out of the car in Utica and up the narrow stairs into Iris Davis's house. He waited impatiently in the living room as Iris wandered out from her bedroom and her twin boys came in from the yard. He had expected Ann to be there waiting for him, and once he realized she wasn't, he felt a tense letdown, like when he first moved to California and would wake with the sad realization that he was no longer at home.

"Ann is coming over tonight," Iris told Johnny. "I thought maybe the boys could take Larry hunting for rabbits this afternoon."

Iris's son Joseph took him outside and handed him a .22 rifle. It felt heavier than Larry had imagined and made him a little fearful. He handled it clumsily, pointing it ahead as he walked through the woods.

"No, no," Joseph said, "point it up when you're moving."

They heard a rustle ahead. Joseph took quick aim and downed a rabbit.

"The next one's mine," said Larry.

Joseph held his fire when the next rabbit appeared. Larry aimed and was shocked at the kick of the gun, at the ease with which the rabbit jumped out of sight. He rushed after the animal and emptied his gun, but none of the bullets connected. Frustrated and angry, Larry made Joseph quit and return to the house.

Ann arrived at Iris's house near sundown. The rest of the people politely busied themselves elsewhere, leaving Ann and Larry alone on the porch. Larry stood tensely, his shoulder muscles tightening.

"Why haven't you answered my letters?" his mother asked. He was silent.

She summoned a smile. "Don't you remember all the fun we had? The pony rides? The visits to Santa?"

Larry looked out at Iris's yard, straining to get back with the other children. Finally his bitterness burst forth. "If it was such fun, why'd you send me to *them*?"

The seconds stretched on, as he waited for her to reply and ask him back into her life. But instead she asked him about school and sports and whether he needed anything. He answered in monosyllables, sometimes so quietly she couldn't hear him. He could feel a pressure in his neck grow into an ache, then spread to an explosion of pain behind his eyes.

In Los Angeles, whenever Larry had thought of Ann, his head had begun to pound. He sometimes remembered the feelings he'd known of love, warmth, and protection, but the thoughts of those times had merely brought him pain. At times, he had thought that he would die from the aching. Face to face with Ann, the pain had magnified a million times. Her presence brought back the memories of a life before, preceding the hurt.

"I knew you wouldn't like this," she said, "but I didn't have any choice." His face squeezed up as if he were going to cry, but his eyes remained dry.

Ann touched his cheek, then held him against her. But to

Larry, it was as if his body had vanished. The nerves seemed severed; he felt nothing. It was as if he'd sprung out of his body and was watching the two of them from the tree branch above.

"You're too young to understand, but I did everything I could."

She leaned down to kiss his hair, but he broke free and ran. "I did what was best!" she yelled after him. She held her chin high as she walked back to her car.

Later that night, Larry walked the few blocks into Utica and bought a firecracker. He stood in the alley next to Iris's Corner Grill, got into his best free-throw position, and threw it at a white man who walked by.

On the drive back to California, there were long stretches of silence between Johnny and Larry. By the time they reached home, Larry had shut his mother out.

That year when Ann's Christmas present arrived, Larry wouldn't open it. She subsequently sent money and he refused even that, even though he *always* wanted money. Helen pressured him to write to thank Ann anyway.

"I've been on you to write a thank-you letter to your other mother for two weeks," Helen said. "I want you to go into your room and do it right now."

Larry went into his room and closed the door. He sat at his desk with pen and paper. An hour later, when Helen came in, there were no words on the page.

"Do you plan on writing your other mother any time today?"

"No," said Larry, feeling suddenly brave, but watching anxiously to see how Helen would react.

From that day on, Larry never wrote, and Helen never brought it up again. Within a few months, Ann stopped writing to him.

One day, in the backyard workshop, Larry asked his

adoptive father, "Could I change my name so that it can be Johnny Spain, too?" Larry wanted a name that had no ties to Mississippi. The older man was proud and happy, as was Mary Davis, so even though it was expensive, they filed the papers and they took him to the courtroom, where he smiled when he heard the judge call his new name out loud: "Johnny Larry Spain." It was a far cry from the way his name would next ring out in a courtroom.

chapter
eight

When Johnny returned to school in the fall of 1959 with his new name, his toughened look stood out among the sixth graders. He had always done well in school, but it hadn't made Helen like him any better or brought Ann back. Now he tuned out completely. He talked in class, telling jokes to his classmates. He refused to take spelling tests if he already knew how to spell all the words. The nuns dealt with students like him by smacking their knuckles with a yardstick, launching them into tears. When it was Johnny's turn, though, he willed himself not to cry. He imagined himself someplace else—on the basketball court or running around the block. His teacher would hit harder and harder, a dozen times, until she appeared shocked by her own vengefulness. He just continued to stare ahead impassively.

Before the year was out, he was expelled. At the public school he transferred to, he didn't pay attention at all, since the kids were studying things he'd already learned in the fourth grade. The next year, in junior high, some of the teachers, exhausted by the demands of their large, unruly classes, stopped making him take tests, since he already knew the answers. By the time he noticed that the other kids had caught up with him, he was in the tenth grade and there were girls around to do his homework.

Only one teacher in high school gave him special attention, an English teacher who encouraged him to write a poem. Johnny was fascinated to learn that lions and tigers weren't from the same jungle. So he wrote a poem about what happened when a lion and a tiger finally met. Mary Davis exclaimed over it and taped it to her refrigerator. The teacher thought it was brilliant and entered it into a contest; it was printed in an educational magazine.

But that wasn't the sort of contest Johnny wanted to win. All that really mattered to him was sports. As the seasons changed, so did the games—football, baseball, basketball, and track. He played on his high school teams, community teams, and the teams of the Catholic Youth Organization. When no team was playing, he would run, sometimes all the way to the ocean. He ran until his calves developed spasms and his legs felt the pain of shin splints from running on concrete. When he reached the sand, his aching legs buckled under his body. Then he lay there, gasping for breath.

From the ages of ten to fifteen, basketball was still Johnny's favorite, the sport in which he felt he had the most control. But football, because it allowed him to go out there and whack people, gave him the greatest release. He was much more aggressive than the other players. After years of bottling up his emotions, he would unleash bursts of violence, like a volcano letting off gusts of steam before it erupts. It was as if fury was the price he paid for being cold, for not admitting he was hurting.

At that time, football rules did not prohibit blocking people below the waist. As Johnny's teammate ran with the ball, Johnny would rush up to within six feet of an opponent. He leaned down as if he were going to dive toward the boy's feet. Then he rolled his body toward the boy. The thrust of his back would hit the boy's shins, toppling him to the ground. Johnny would repeat this play over and over. He loved coming in fast, going down, and taking an opponent's legs out from under him. With his extraordinary balance, he didn't have to slow down as he went into his dive.

He hated it when his team lost. He would splinter bats on the fence, or start to beat up one of his opponents. When it looked as if Johnny's basketball team was going to lose, Gonzalo Cano, the Mexican-American man who directed the CYO, or one of the other coaches would move toward him to head off a fistfight at the end of the game.

Despite having teammates, he didn't really have friends in sports. The photo of his basketball team hanging up at the CYO seemed to mock him. There were seven dark boys—plus him, with his faded skin, his jersey hanging awkwardly across his thin torso. He knew he didn't belong. He didn't look like them. They hadn't gone through what he'd gone through. After the games, the boys broke off into little groups, sometimes going to each other's houses, but they didn't include him.

When Cano would start to close the CYO for the night, Johnny would try to find ways to get him to keep it open just a little longer and shoot a few hoops with him. Mary was usually asleep by that time, and Johnny preferred to avoid Helen, who always made him feel that he was disappointing her. She expected him to get A's, and so made no fuss when he did, but she flew into a tirade when he did not. And she didn't want to hear about how his team had won in overtime. All that mattered to her was that he let the door close too noisily when he entered the house.

One night when he was fifteen, as he walked home from the CYO Johnny noticed a few of the older neighborhood boys on the street corner. Some of his teammates crossed the street to avoid them, but Johnny just watched them as he walked by, listening to their deep laughter and watching them blow smoke from their cigarettes. He was jealous of the easy way these guys seemed to hang together.

A few days later, Johnny noticed that the group was larger than usual. There were a few guys there who used to play sports at El Santo Niño, giving him an excuse to go over and join the conversation. He asked one of them what happened to his arm.

"Some guy from the Watts gang jumped me," he said. "But a couple of us went back and kicked his ass. He ain't going to be bothering anyone for a long time."

The guys were going over to a taco stand and Johnny fell into step alongside them. It was like a big party there, cars with radios blasting cruising slowly by.

One of the old CYO players introduced him to the guy who seemed to be the leader, Leroy "Hutch" Hutchinson. He was darker and a head taller than Johnny, was two years older, and was dressed in an expensive white shirt, with sleeves that belled out in the latest style. Johnny was amazed at the respectful way the kids spoke about Hutch, even though he didn't play sports. He watched the man carefully, and when one of the other guys offered him a cigarette, he tried smoking it with the same deep-puff intensity as Hutch.

Johnny stayed out past 2:00 A.M., thinking, Screw Helen, as he smoked and listened. One guy was talking about how his stepfather used to beat him up—until he'd hit the old man with a beer bottle. Another talked about how he had a key that opened almost any kind of car trunk. That day, he'd stolen some eight-track tapes from one car, and slashed the spare tire in the trunk of another, just for the hell of it. Johnny felt a sense of shared exhilaration as they talked about how they'd outconned, outfought, and outsmarted outsiders.

In the nights that followed, after the CYO closed, Johnny

sought out these same guys, who called themselves the
Slausons, after a street that ran through their territory. He
joined them as they threatened strangers who strayed into
the neighborhood, who tried to cross Jefferson or Central
without Hutch's okay. It was as if suddenly all the anger
inside him had someplace to go. After years of random fist-
fights, he now could target his violence. He had no fear of
getting hurt. He'd take on much bigger guys, and get a thrill
when Hutch or the others would say about him, "That is one
bad monk."

Cano noticed when a few of the Slausons began waiting
outside the CYO for Johnny. He sensed that the boy was still
on the edge, that he was attracted to the gang but hadn't let
it take over his life, still made room for sports. He tried to
reach Johnny, ever careful not to preach, just dropping a
hint here and there about the importance of school and of
planning for the future.

Cano worried about his boys, these proud young men
he'd watched and coached for years. The white cops who
patrolled the neighborhood were hell-bent on keeping them
in their place, and Cano could sense violence brewing. A few
of the boys had complained to him about cops stopping
them for no reason, throwing them against a wall or a car,
searching them for imaginary weapons.

"Don't try to fight them," Cano would advise. "Get their
badge number and we'll complain to City Hall. But the cops
own the streets. You'll never win this one out there."

Johnny would listen intently to Cano's coaching tactics,
but saw little value in his advice about working hard for some
future goal, or taking your complaints through a system.
He'd laughed in Helen's face when she'd told him she was
campaigning for Tom Bradley, a black man, for city council.
He thought she should find someone more like Malcolm X,
who said he believed in niggers with guns.

Johnny couldn't understand the blacks Helen and Johnny Sr.'s age, why they didn't want more, demand more. Whatever Johnny wanted, he wanted immediately. His internal clock was set at the pulsing speed of competitive sports. One of the Slausons had given him the car trunk master key, and he'd move down the street—click, snap, score—taking anything that interested him. He rarely kept what he scored—hell, the Spains gave him whatever he asked for—but instead would distribute what he found to the other Slausons.

He bragged to Cano about the key. "Man," said Cano, "if you keep on living the life like you've been doing on the streets, one of these days I'm going to read about you lying on the sidewalk and the cops going to come and write chalk on the sidewalk where they picked you up."

Johnny Sr. too, was worried about Johnny. He knew that when a black male reached adolescence, there was danger on all sides—from blacks in other gangs, from whites who felt threatened. And Johnny seemed to be courting harm, with that fuck-you look and unwillingness to back down. He thought if he got Johnny involved in something new, he might be able to keep the boy out of trouble.

At breakfast one morning when Johnny was in the tenth grade, Johnny Sr. turned to the boy and said, "I could use some help at my job today. You're pretty good with your hands. Would you like to come with me?" Johnny looked up and nodded.

Johnny Sr. worked mainly for other blacks, in simple bungalows like his own. Occasionally, though, like on this Saturday, a black who'd made a little money as a physician or lawyer would hire him. The challenges were greater there—multiple types of wiring, air conditioners to hook up. On the more complicated calls, he felt every bit as professional as the men he served.

While the elder man labored, his son picked up different

tools. Johnny Sr. explained the concept of electricity and how different appliances worked. "If you learn to be an electrician," he told the boy, "you'll have something to compete with in the world—and something to fall back on."

Johnny listened patiently to his adoptive father's explanation of his work. The precision and logic of the wiring appealed to him; connecting things and making them work held his attention and challenged him, as nothing other than sports previously had. Plus he liked having a topic for dinner conversations that pulled Johnny Sr. in, at the same time it kept Helen out.

Dinners were more tense now that Mary Davis felt ill and often failed to join them. At one such dinner, Helen talked about how old and frail Mary was getting. "What if Mother falls back there without our knowing?" she said. "It would be different if she had a phone."

The next weekend Johnny wandered into his adoptive father's toolshed and picked up a 24-volt buzzer. He ran some wire from his house to Mary's, so that she could push a button and signal them if something went wrong. He tested it. But it didn't work.

He sought out the elder Johnny with a hypothetical question.

"Johnny, what would make a 24-volt buzzer burn up?"

"Well, it usually happens when you got someone who takes a 24-volt buzzer and runs it into a 110 circuit without putting a step down transformer in it."

"Oh," he said. "What's a step-down transformer?"

Johnny Sr. drew a picture, but when Johnny went back to the workshop, he saw two different items that might have been a step-down transformer.

He went looking for Johnny Sr. again. "Are either of these—"

"Both are. You have to look at these numbers in back."

He went back and tried it all again. When he was sure that it would work, he took Mary into the Spain house and said to Helen, "Go back there and you'll see a buzzer in the front part of the house and when I give you a wave, I want you to press."

When Helen pressed, the buzzer from Mary's house made a loud sound on the Spains' back porch.

Mary was startled. "What in the world was that?"

"It's for you," he said excitedly. "This way if you need anything, you can let us know."

From then on, whenever anyone came to visit Mary, she showed off the buzzer. "Let me show you what my baby did," she would say.

Mary would use the buzzer whenever she needed something. Whenever Johnny was home—usually just in the early mornings—he'd be the one to run to her house in response. One morning she looked so sick that he insisted his father call an ambulance. He felt confident that she'd pull out of it, if she could just get to a hospital. He went to school that morning and stopped at home afterward to get word of Mary's condition before going to the CYO.

The first thing he noticed was that his father's truck was there, even though it was the middle of the afternoon. Once inside, he saw Helen's red-rimmed eyes. Johnny Sr. knelt down in front of the boy, cupping his big hands around Johnny's arms.

"Your grandmother's dead," he said.

Johnny broke free and ran to the narrow backyard house. He saw the apron folded over a kitchen chair. He moved into the bedroom and sat for a long time on the corner of Mary's bed. He thought about the train trip, about how she was the only real link between Mississippi and L.A.

Then he slipped out the back gate and went on one of his endless runs.

. . .

In the late fall of 1964, a new coach joined Cano at El Santo
Niño. He was a black guy from the neighborhood, on leave
from his senior year at Arizona State University. Even kids
who didn't usually come to the center turned out for his first
day. They'd all seen his picture in the newspaper, running
the 4 x 400-meter relay. He was Ulis Williams, and he had
brought home a gold medal from the 1964 Olympics.

Most of the younger kids just hung back and whispered
among themselves, but fifteen-year-old Johnny approached
him right off and shook his hand.

"You're the World Champ, huh?" said Johnny. "I want to
race you 1,000 yards."

Ulis was taken aback at first by the boy's spunk, and tried
to put him off. But the slight, light-skinned boy insisted, and
Ulis finally agreed so that he could move on to his work.
Even though he had to exert himself a little, he readily finished before Johnny.

"Wait, we're not done yet," Johnny said. "I want to race
you around the block."

Ulis smiled. Around the block was a quarter mile, the
exact length of his event. They both took off, and again Ulis
won handily.

"Well, I bet I can do more sit-ups than you."

Now a crowd was gathering. They got in position, and
each lurched up, time and again, until even the audience
was sensing the cramps in their stomachs. Finally Johnny
stopped, his heart beating wildly. Ulis got up slowly, knowing that his stomach muscles would be sore for the next
two days.

Johnny was not about to give up. Puffing to his feet, he
said, "I bet I can shoot more foul shots than you."

Ulis smiled. He recognized the energy, zeal, and fearlessness of the kid. He had the fire that every great athlete had.

He would make Johnny his special project.

Over the following weeks, Ulis coached Johnny's basketball team as they played throughout the city. Johnny honed his skills—even to the point of becoming a championship tennis player because Ulis said it would help his footwork on the court. One evening, Ulis, Johnny, and four other players—six black guys—were riding through a Chicano neighborhood in East L.A. on the way back from a game. Johnny was in the seat of honor, the jump seat in the front of the car—riding shotgun, they called it.

They'd gone a few blocks when a car pulled up next to them. "Hey man, you're in our neighborhood," yelled a Chicano from the next car. The second car veered crazily to force Ulis's car off the road. Ulis hit the accelerator and slipped by, but the other car followed closely on their tail.

"Hang on tight, guys," warned Ulis. He pulled over and hit the brakes suddenly, then veered around in a U-turn as the other car roared past.

Barely had he pressed the accelerator to hightail it out of there when one of his players yelled, "Wait!" He turned his head slightly and realized that Johnny had leapt out of the car when he'd braked and was standing in the middle of the street.

"Okay, guys," Johnny was screaming at the other car. "If you want me, come and get me. I'm standing, not running."

"GET BACK IN HERE!" yelled Ulis as a teammate jumped out and pushed him back in. Ulis sped away with Johnny back in the jump seat, grinning and laughing.

In January, after Ulis returned to college, El Santo Niño seemed quiet and dull. Johnny's teammates were even more alienated from him now, since he'd so clearly been Ulis's pet.

Johnny began to spend less and less time at the center. One night, he was practicing basketball and didn't want to give up the ball to let Cano lock up for the 5:30 P.M. dinner break.

"Okay, I'll tell you what," said Cano. "We'll shoot ten free throws. If I come up with a better score than you, you'll give me the ball and that's it. If I lose, I'll owe you a dollar."

Cano beat Johnny, took the ball, and locked up. As Cano was getting into his car, Johnny approached him. "I want my dollar," he said.

"Johnny, you didn't beat me. I beat you."

"You owe me a buck."

Cano stared at Johnny. The boy's face was ashen and his expression told Cano that something was seriously wrong. It was one of the few times in his thirteen years on the job that Cano had felt physically at risk. He had never been touched in anger. But now it was as if there were a split in Johnny's personality, as if, for an instant, the Johnny whom Cano felt he could count on had disappeared. Years later, when the psychiatrists analyzed the incident, they recognized how Johnny had dissociated from himself, how, having suffered the loss of Ann, Mary, and now Ulis, Johnny was pushing away Cano, insulating himself from the chance that Cano would leave him, too. But at that moment, all Cano could sense was danger. Without a word he gave in and passed Johnny the dollar bill.

After that, Johnny avoided the CYO. He still played sports at school, but his off hours were spent with the Slausons. In the three years that followed Mary's death, he led a double life. He was polite to his mother's friends, even helping them carry groceries up their stairs. At school, he won various sports letters; he kept up a B minus average, mostly by having the girls he was dating do his homework. Some of his coaches told him he might win an athletic scholarship to U.C.L.A.

He read intensely, though rarely what he was assigned in school. He read whatever he could about sports, memorizing batting averages and percentage shots, who won at Wimbledon, how fast various tennis players could serve. He was thrilled when a friend of his—somehow—got a copy of the U.C.L.A. football playbook, with X's and O's diagramming the team's plays and introducing him to the secrets of a strategy called the audible system.

On the streets, he used some of his sports talents—speed, strategy—and earned the nickname Caesar as a leader of the younger members of the Slausons. When he first joined the gang, he just spent the afternoons and evenings cruising, talking with three or four other guys, facing down strangers who entered the neighborhood. But gradually the routine began to change. One night, two guys broke away from the group, walked down an alley, and robbed a guy. To Johnny, it was almost magical. One moment they were talking to him and then—voilà—a few minutes later they were back waving a couple of bills.

As with everything else, Johnny learned quickly. He began to hold up people on street corners, white people. He never did it alone, only with an audience of friends. He had no moral hesitation. He didn't even see it as particularly dangerous. Whenever he heard talk of crime from a streetmate, the narrator had gotten away with it. He was oblivious to the flow of the older boys out of the Slauson and Watts areas into the men's prisons at Chino, Tracy, and, if their crimes were particularly serious, to Folsom, Soledad, and San Quentin.

One day, Johnny was on the corner of 29th and Jefferson with some Slausons who had dropped out of school. He

spent the afternoon smoking cigarettes and then watched
the men come home from work. Sometimes he resented the
slow pace, and imagined himself running down a basketball
court. But as "Caesar" now, the leader of the younger members, his duty was to keep up with his homeboys and wait.
Wait until the boredom was uncontrollable, wait until night
came and he could find a target.

As dusk fell, the air was dense and muggy. Johnny was
feeling restless without the chance to run for miles or dance
among the cluttered gutters. He was the first to spot the
white guy approaching. He felt the blood thicken in his
chest and his legs twitch with unreleased tension.

"Look at that trash," one of the younger boys said to
Johnny.

The man tried to move quickly past the group leaning
defiantly on the brick wall. Johnny reached down and
rubbed the length of the jack handle one of his partners had
used in stripping a car a few days earlier. The feel of the
smooth metal heightened his rising adrenaline as he
blocked the man's path.

"Give me your wallet."

Instead of reaching for his pocket, the man defiantly
moved on.

"Hey man, what's your deal?" Johnny yelled, chasing him.
"You hear me?"

The man broke into a run and Johnny rushed after him.
The first blow of the jack crashed, soothingly to Johnny, in
the hard muscles of the white man's calves. The man's leg
buckled, but he somehow continued to propel himself forward. Johnny clenched his teeth as he lifted the jack into the
thickness of the summer night air and brought it down again
on the back of the man's thighs. The jack racked the man's
body as he fell, face first, into the curb, blood running from
his lips into smooth, small puddles on the sewer grate.

"C'mon, Johnny, I hear a cop car," one of the younger Slausons pleaded. Johnny could hear it, too, and the man had fallen under a streetlight where it was too bright to roll him. Johnny followed the others as they began to sprint away to the tune of the siren. He did not glance back, and not until years later would he wonder if the man moved from that street at all.

That night, Johnny thought about how the guy had refused to give in and about how he'd blown the robbery because all he had was a crappy jack. It would have been different if he had had a gun.

chapter
nine

A few weeks later, Johnny Sr. asked for some help with an electrical job. It was a Saturday morning, long before Johnny's pals would hit the street, and Johnny liked the thought of spending a few quiet hours with his father, working with his hands, and not having to try to impress anyone.

The job was not in any of the neighborhoods that Johnny Sr. usually served. As they rode in the car, the grimy South Central streets fell away and the lots grew larger and greener. The California of the postcards emerged in front of Johnny's eyes.

"It's amazing what a Negro can do these days," Johnny Sr. said. "Earl Broady's got himself a house in Beverly Hills now."

Johnny's dad had spoken of the black lawyer before, and how well he was doing. But that, thought Johnny, was one man. As he looked down the streets of Beverly Hills, the few kids he saw playing were white kids.

Broady's wife let them in and showed them to the guest house, which needed rewiring. Johnny offered to help his dad trace through the circuits. He did so by moving from room to room, opening doors and following the path of the electrical circuitry.

Most of the closets held hotel-like amenities for guests—

towels, sheets, extra soap and toilet paper. But as Johnny peered inside one closet, he saw something quite out of the ordinary: six gleaming antique guns—.14 gauge side-by-side barrel shotguns, a 30-06, a 30-30. Johnny stood and stared at them for a long time while his father was laying out his tools. The Slausons could sure use those.

Johnny thought about the guns on the drive back to West 23rd Street. He'd like to show them off to Hutch and the others—especially one of the old rifles. He'd never seen anything like it before.

When they'd first arrived, he'd overheard Broady's wife talking about their plans for the evening. By the time he'd reached home, he had it all figured out. He would borrow a car from a friend and take a couple of buddies to help him cart the guns out to the car.

The theft went smoothly. They sailed in and out of Beverly Hills, spending less than fifteen minutes in the house. Johnny was elated. Who would ever suspect them? he asked himself. No one would believe that three young blacks could have maneuvered a '54 Chevy in and out of Beverly Hills without attracting attention. They were home free!

The three took the guns to the freeway and shot them off. At first it was like his attempts in Utica, but Johnny was five years older now, and the added strength in his forearms and fingers gave him much greater control. After he and his friends had tested them, they hid the guns under a friend's house.

Helen was waiting for him when he got home. "Where did you put the guns?" she asked.

"I don't have any guns," Johnny said, his shoulders tensing. "I don't know about any guns."

"Look, Earl Broady knows that you have the guns, he just wants them back. There will be no questions asked and no charges filed."

Johnny called his friends and they decided to return the guns. True to his word, Broady didn't press charges, but because he'd reported the guns missing when he first got home, the cops picked up Johnny anyway. Since he was only fifteen, he could be taken to juvenile hall—the jail for teen offenders—under a statute governing "minors in need of supervision." Maybe if it had been a different offense they might have let him go. But in the cops' minds, there were too many young blacks in Watts with guns already. That place was like a powder keg, ready to blow.

Johnny was frustrated by his confinement, talked back to the attendants, and started fights with other boys. One boy cut him above his eyebrow, but he won the fight. The guards responded by putting him in a solitary confinement cell, known as the lockup.

Johnny Sr. came to see him. He was dressed in his good brown pants and a pale yellow shirt. Johnny expected to be yelled at—for stealing from one of his dad's best customers—but instead his adoptive father spoke with a sad softness, shaking his head when they brought Johnny in.

"You all right?" the older man asked, nodding at the cut on Johnny's face.

"Well, I'm in lockup because I had a fight with a guy."

"Did you start it?"

"No, but I finished it."

"You have to stay out of trouble if you want to get out of here," his father advised.

"Well, sometimes you don't have a choice," explained Johnny. "People will eat you up in here if you just don't do anything."

Three nights later, on August 11, 1965, the cells in juvenile hall swelled with young black men. Johnny recognized one of them as he was led past Johnny's cell.

"What's going on, Hutch?" he asked.

"Watts is burning."

Later, Hutch yelled down the tier to Johnny to fill him in on what was going on. "Man, those cops are crazy," said Hutch. Hutch had surrendered and was standing perfectly still, he said, arms up, when he saw a crazed look in the cop's eye. The cop raised his gun, and Hutch tried to dodge. The bullet grazed his hip.

Hutch had been looting, but not from black-owned businesses, only from whites. "Those whites come into our neighborhoods, charge twice as much for a TV set as you'd pay somewhere else," he said. "We were just taking back what we were owed."

The idea of some sort of racial reparation didn't register with Johnny. He just wished he'd been out there for the thrill of it, the adrenaline high, outsmarting the cops and taking what he wanted. He imagined himself plucking televisions out of shattered store windows, cruisin' with the brothers, taking on the cops. But he had to serve a few months before he would be returned to the streets. For Hutch, the wait would be longer. He was being tried as an adult, and would be sent to prison.

Johnny was sent away to a forestry youth camp, Glen Rocky, in San Dimas Canyon, to fight fires and cut trail breaks. When he was caught trying to run away, he got sent back to Los Angeles, under the domain of a community delinquent-control project worker, Howard Lambert.

Howard was white, and a social worker. He was the first person to try to understand what Johnny was going through. He asked Johnny, "Why are you doing all these things?" but Johnny didn't have any real answers. Johnny didn't know.

Johnny was a puzzle that Howard was determined to figure out. He visited Cano at El Santo Niño and probed Cano about his experiences with the boy.

"He is not without character," said Cano, "he is not without intelligence, he does not studiously go out and harm people, and there are plenty of my boys who do. It's just as if he woke up one day and understood how few restraints there are on the individual.

"You know," continued Cano, "the thing that surprised me most about the burglary is that the guns were so easily traced to him. If there is one thing I pride Johnny on, it's that he's not dumb."

Like Cano, Lambert immediately warmed to Johnny, seeing something caring and reachable under the tough exterior. He learned quickly about Johnny's sports interests and tried to expand them, telling him about new programs and camps sponsored by the park district. Johnny tried one—a tennis camp—intently blasting a shopping cart full of tennis balls across the net, then watching Wimbledon videotapes to enhance his serve.

He began almost to look forward to his weekly visits to Lambert's office. It was one of the few places where he didn't feel rage, and Lambert was one of the few people he felt he could talk to. In one of their sessions, Johnny confessed, "I hate whites."

"What about me? I'm white," responded Lambert.

Johnny looked almost shocked. "You're not a white. You're my friend."

After a few months with Lambert, Johnny felt things were looking up. He was looking forward to the fall, when he would rejoin the teams at school. But when school started, he was told that he couldn't play sports. "You failed all your classes last spring because you weren't in school enough days to qualify for a grade," the principal told him.

"If I'm not allowed to play sports, I'm going to quit school," Johnny threatened.

"This is incredible," Johnny complained to Howard Lambert after he'd talked to the principal. Lambert understood the principal's reasoning, but he was worried what would happen to Johnny if sports weren't a part of his life. He went to the Board of Education and got a special dispensation for Johnny. The board said that he would be allowed to play sports if he could pass four finals, but it would be up to his individual teachers to decide whether they were willing to give the finals.

Three teachers agreed. One said no.

The deal was off. Johnny quit school—and went back to running the streets.

The Slausons were waiting, guns everywhere. After the Watts riots, they felt that guns were a necessity, to protect them against the cops and other gangs. The Slausons talked in terms of self-defense.

They told Johnny tales of robbing cab drivers—the fun of the free cab ride, the shock on the driver's face when they'd make their demand for money. One evening Johnny and two other boys his age decided to try it.

Johnny was dressed in neatly pressed pants and a navy blue windbreaker, looking like someone who could afford the ride. In the polite tone that he used to shine on Helen's friends, he asked the driver to take him and his two friends to a destination that he knew would be deserted at that time of night. He sat on the front seat, turning slightly to look out the passenger window, mostly so that the driver wouldn't notice the bulge of the gun on his right hip.

The driver was a white man in his early fifties. He knew the area well, and took the most expeditious route. He slowed the car to a halt, then turned to Johnny with a smile, expecting his fare. The two boys in the back pricked his neck with their pistols. Johnny's breath was coming fast and he paused a moment to control the pitch of his voice, wondering if maybe this time he was in over his head. "Give me your money and get out of the cab," he demanded. "We're taking the cab. If you call the police, we'll come back and finish you off. If you do as we say, you'll find your cab on the street behind Bob's Auto Body when we're through with it."

One of Johnny's friends followed the driver out of the taxi and made him lie down on the grass. Then the friend climbed into the front seat and started the cab.

The three teens hit the freeway at eighty miles per hour, and drove out to the Santa Monica pier. There, they opened the cab doors and searched under the seats, in the trunk, in the glove compartment, and everywhere else they could think where the driver might have hidden more money. They came up empty, and divided the original take of sixty dollars and some change.

Within the next few weeks, Johnny tallied a dozen cab robberies. Amazingly, none of the drivers called the cops, even though Johnny told them where he would be driving the cab. It made him even more appreciative of the power of a gun.

As the cab robberies became routine, he looked for a new thrill. Riding an almost empty bus one night, he realized what an easy target it would be. The following weekend, two of Johnny's friends boarded a bus and moved to their places in the middle and back of the bus. At the next stop, Johnny was the lone passenger to board. The three pulled their guns simultaneously and Johnny demanded the driver's money. Then he walked icily down the aisles, telling passengers to hand over their wallets and jewelry, making anyone who looked tough cower with the pressure of a gun on the temple or behind the ear. Johnny lingered with his gun pressed on the flesh of a heavyset white man, counting the sweat beads as they blossomed on the man's forehead.

"Caesar, let's go," yelled one of his partners. Johnny grabbed the man's watch and the three bolted into the night.

There was a common thread now to Johnny's street crimes. The victims were always white. If someone had suggested his crimes were racially motivated, though, he would have laughed. To him, it was a business proposition. White people were better targets because they had more money.

chapter
ten

On the evening of Saturday, December 21, 1966, Johnny and two friends took a fifteen-minute drive from their neighborhood to Lambert's office. The occasion was a Christmas party for youth offenders. It was a little after 8:00 P.M. when they walked out of the darkness of the street and into the white glare of the office. A few couples were dancing to a Beach Boys record—peppy tales of cars and surf and blondes. White boys' music, Johnny thought. He found it hard to imagine dancing in all that light.

Lambert shook Johnny's hand and introduced him to a few of the younger black parolees. "This man's going someplace," he said of Johnny. That was Lambert for you, thought Johnny, always encouraging, always keeping the faith.

Johnny poured himself a cup of punch, nodding to some of the other white office workers whom he'd met on his visits to Lambert. The sugary liquid made his teeth ache and he was disappointed to find there was no liquor in it. Shit, he thought, Helen has stronger stuff than this for breakfast.

A secretary asked him if he had any New Year's resolutions. She was planning—it was an annual event—to stop smoking. He shook his head. Everything he wanted to change was beyond his control.

As he looked at the presents surrounding the brightly decorated tree, he felt a tug at the corner of his memory. Then a wisp of an image poked its way into his brain. A tricycle under the tree. Looking up at his mother, Aunt Margaret, his grandparents. White faces, kindly, like those in this room.

Johnny turned to a friend, "Let's find a real party."

They slipped out the door and made tracks for the friend's car. They knew there were big parties going on in Dog Town—slang for the William Meade projects. After a twenty-minute drive, they crossed the broken steps into a ground-floor apartment. In the darkness of the living room, Johnny could discern a dozen or more black figures, dancing to the lazy blare of "You've Lost That Lovin' Feeling." Other couples were making out on the couch. He grabbed some Rainier ale from a cooler, and paced the edges of the room as he drank.

One of his friends motioned him over, saying, "Let's see what's happening upstairs."

They made it to two other parties in the projects, but none of his other Slauson friends had shown up at either one. Johnny drank a few more ales and smoked half a pack of cigarettes. He danced a couple of times, mainly because it took more energy to say no to the girls who asked than just to do it. About 11:30 P.M., he thought of calling his girlfriend, then remembered she'd taken a baby-sitting job for two weeks over in Compton.

A few miles from Dog Town in a predominantly white neighborhood on the edge of downtown Los Angeles, Joe Long was helping his wife Nancy into her coat at his apartment. They were estranged and lived separately, but they had met for drinks that afternoon at the Ringside Bar to discuss how to handle Christmas for their daughter. They'd been drinking, on and off, through the evening. As they walked two blocks to the bus stop, so that Nancy could ride home, they talked about getting a Susie Homemaker oven for their daughter. Joe Long stood next to the bench, with one foot up on the edge.

Johnny and two friends left the projects by car. They were aimlessly cruising when they saw the white couple on the corner of Hill Street and Venice Boulevard. They parked the car, then came around the block and approached them.

"How far is Washington Boulevard?" Johnny asked Nancy Long.

"About three or four blocks up the street," she replied.

"Thank you," said Johnny. He and his friends kept on walking. They returned to the car and Johnny took out a nickel-plated four-barrel .22, with a rotating firing pin, which one of the Slausons had picked up in a burglary.

"No, man," said one of Johnny's partners. "Let's split."

Johnny felt restless, as though the evening had been wasted. He hadn't quite fit in at either party, and his confusion about it angered him. Now that he no longer had sports in his life, he needed to prove himself in the one remaining area in which he had control. "We've come this far," he said. "Let's see what we can get."

Johnny walked back to the bench. "Hi baby," he said to the woman, and smiled.

Her husband started to say something to Johnny.

"Look man, I wasn't talking to you."

Johnny and the husband moved behind the bench.

"Give me your money," demanded Johnny.

Long moved toward Johnny, raising his arm. Johnny couldn't believe this guy wasn't obeying, didn't seem to be scared by the pistol. Johnny himself was paralyzed for a moment, not knowing what to do as Long moved toward him. On the man's third step, the streetlight shone on his face and his bloodshot eyes glowed at Johnny. Fred Armstrong's eyes.

Johnny fired, hitting Long in the right lung. He fired again. And again. And again. Long kept coming. Johnny and his friends turned and ran.

Cops in a nearby patrol car heard shots and turned on their siren. When two cops bounded from their car, Johnny's partners bounced to a stop. Johnny sped further down the block, fled over a gravel driveway, and leaped a fence at the corner of 15th and Olive. He lost the cops, tossed his gun on a roof, and dodged into California Hospital. By now several officers were pursuing an assailant described as a light-complected Negro in a black leather coat.

Johnny saw a phone booth and began to dial the number of an old girlfriend who would pick him up and not ask any questions. Before the connection was made, a cop materialized in the hallway, knees bent, his pistol aimed at Johnny.

"Hands up."

Johnny let the phone dangle. He couldn't believe this was happening to him. The cop began to read him his rights, but the words were blocked out by a flood of sound in his head.

The cop took him back to the bus stop. A witness from a nearby street looked at Johnny and said, "That's not the man." The cop was confused. Johnny's light skin and his surname gave the impression he was Hispanic, and the cop knew they were looking for a black. But when he took Johnny down to the station, a weeping Mrs. Long identified him as the shooter.

"What happened to the guy?" Johnny asked the cop.

"He's dead."

"Oh shit." That meant he'd be screwed.

Johnny was locked up in the juvenile jail, where he'd been taken after he'd stolen the guns from Earl Broady. His mouth tasted like stale Rainier ale, and his stomach was burning. This wasn't like the last time, when he knew he'd be out soon. He'd overheard a cop say he'd probably be tried as an adult.

He lay on his cot and felt the flame in his stomach reach up to his throat. He closed his eyes and tried to summon up the image of his girlfriend. But all he saw was the big, white face of the man on the street corner, coming closer and closer toward him.

How did this happen to me? he thought.

The evening blurred through his mind—the Beach Boys music, the Dog Town party. It's not my fault, he thought. That guy wouldn't stop. He just kept coming and coming. It was self-defense.

"Hey, Mr. Bad-Ass," one of the boys down the tier yelled at him. "Heard you downed a peckerwood."

The other black inmates stared to clap and yell at the word that he'd killed a white guy. "Way to go, Caesar," yelled a kid from the Slausons.

But all Johnny wanted was to start the evening over—to walk into the parole office, drink some of the sugary punch, and stay under those bright lights until the danger passed.

The next morning, the clawing confinement of living in a cell began to set in. He couldn't smoke in there, only in the common room. Over the next week, each day was frustratingly identical. Meals at seven, noon, and five. Guards flashing a light in his face as he tried to sleep. Bigger guys eyeing him like he was a piece of meat. He choked at the realization he'd be there for months, until a trial date could be set. He didn't have the least idea what was in store for him and wouldn't meet his court-appointed attorney until the day of the trial.

On his fifth day, the routine was broken by a guard who announced, "You have a visitor. Some guy named Charles Armstrong."

Charles was waiting in the large visiting room when a white guard led Johnny out. He immediately rose, showing that he had six inches and fifty pounds on the guard, standing as ready as he had as a boy to make sure no harm came to his brother.

In the years since his brother had been taken from him, Charles had witnessed the racial animosity that had haunted them magnified statewide. In 1961, nine blacks entered Jackson's white public library, began to read, and were arrested. The next year, James Meredith enrolled in the University of Mississippi, igniting a riot that left two dead and dozens injured. In 1963, black students marched in protest down Capitol Street. They were beaten to the ground, taken to a concentration camp set up on the state fairgrounds, and detained in the filthy animal stockades. Soon after that, though, a new source of support flowed into Mississippi: white Northern college students. They were shocked to learn that they faced the same dangers as Southern blacks. Charles recalled the murders of three civil rights workers, two white, one black—Andrew Goodman, Michael Schwerner, and James Chaney—in June of 1964, killed for daring to act on their belief that things could be changed. The night that President Kennedy spoke on national television about his civil rights bill, the NAACP's Mississippi field secretary, Medgar Evers, was killed in front of his home. At the time Charles left Mississippi for his military posting in California, the Ku Klux Klan was burning crosses in Jackson, a warning to the jurors chosen to judge the white man accused of Evers's murder.

The guard seated Johnny at a card table, and motioned Charles to join him.

"What are you doing here?" Johnny asked.

"I'm in the marines now, stationed out here. I took a bus to the Spains' last night, as soon as I got my first leave, and Helen told me about all this."

Johnny lit a cigarette and tipped the pack toward Charles, who shook his head.

"God, I missed you," said Charles.

Johnny didn't reply.

"You okay?"

"I've been better," replied Johnny.

"Do you have a lawyer yet?"

"Some guy named Axel," said Johnny. "He's got the statement I gave to the cops, but he's pretty busy, doesn't have time to come here."

Charles noticed that his brother was reluctant to look directly at him, the guards, or the other visitors. Charles thought of the outgoing little boy Larry had been. Now he seemed to be withdrawing into a shell.

Charles began describing what a beautiful girl their sister Lissie was turning into, but Johnny's shoulder muscles tensed at the mention of her name. A question burned on Johnny's tongue—How's Mom?—but he couldn't bring himself to ask it. Charles offered no information about her. Charles's own anger at Ann for giving up Johnny had so festered that he couldn't stand to be in the same city as her. He hated the way she had given Johnny away and then never mentioned him, acting like he hadn't existed, while Charles thought about him every day. How could she do it? Charles wondered angrily. In the years after Johnny had left, Charles had exacted revenge, one by one, on every boy who had ever tried to hurt his brother.

A guard approached the table and told them their time was up. As the guard led Johnny back to his cell, a Slauson yelled out, "Who was that honky you were talking to?"

"My bro—" started Johnny. "No, that was nobody. Just some guy I used to know."

chapter
eleven

Johnny leaned forward in his seat at the defendant's table as the jury filed back into the courtroom. He'd taken the stand during the trial and told his side of the story. That he'd asked Mrs. Long for directions and had started flirting with her when her jealous husband came after him. It was self-defense, pure and simple. Johnny had rationalized the incident so often that in his mind his tale had become the truth.

The judge addressed the jury.

"How do you find the defendant?"

"We find the defendant guilty."

The judge ordered life imprisonment: "I feel that the defendant is definitely a menace to society and he shall be held in the State Prison as long as possible."

Afterward, the young prosecutor, Dino Fulgoni, told the jury that they had made the right decision. Johnny was a hopeless case. His mixed racial background, and the hardening that prison would cause, explained Fulgoni, meant that Johnny could never be trusted to walk among free men. Johnny's mixed racial background would work against him again later in other contacts with the legal system.

A twenty-seven-year-old juror, James Menard Jr., shifted uncomfortably in his seat as Fulgoni congratulated them. He kept thinking about the testimony of one of the witnesses. The police officer who was chasing Johnny was asked why he didn't shoot him. The officer had replied, "He was just a kid." For years, that answer would go through Menard's mind—*just a kid . . . just a kid . . . just a kid.*

Johnny was sent to the Southern Reception Guidance Center in Chino, to determine which prison he should be placed in, and under what level of security. On his intake form, Johnny responded to questions.

Q: Who are you?
A: I am Johnny Larry Spain. I am a person in a lot of trouble. I am a person who needs help.
Q: How do you wish to change?
A: I want to learn to go by the rules.
Q: What are some of your ambitions or goals in life?
A: To be a famous athlete.

Ora Tarrson, a correctional counselor, interviewed Johnny and concluded that he was salvageable. Unlike many other new prisoners, whose eyes were dull and lifeless, Johnny's eyes, though angry, still held curiosity and intelligence. He had as many questions for Tarrson as the counselor had for him.

Tarrson filed a report saying: "Spain's denial of intention to commit robbery appears to be closely related with his need to alleviate his present feelings of guilt and remorse. His underlying feelings of rejection and his ambivalent sexual and racial identification tend to provoke much anxiety related to his overwhelming self-doubt. Prior life experiences have been fraught with incidents of being rejected.

"This is a youth who will require establishment of a close relationship with an appropriately masculine empathetic figure, with whom he can establish an identity."

Tarrson stressed that Johnny needed intensive individual

psychotherapy. But the prison had no mechanism to provide it. At that time, in 1967, the California Department of Corrections ran the third largest prison system in the world. Only the Soviet Union and China incarcerated more of their citizens. Individualized treatment was not in the cards.

Johnny could have been sent to any number of facilities—Soledad, San Quentin, and Folsom being the most famous—but the assignment he drew was the lesser-known Deuel Vocational Institute in Tracy, California, a prison for young offenders too hardened for the juvenile jails.

The Gladiator School, thought Johnny when he heard his assignment, remembering what the guys in juvenile hall had called Tracy.

Tracy was in the San Joaquin Valley, ninety miles east of San Francisco. Its green buildings were long and low, looking like army barracks surrounded by barbed-wire fences and gun towers.

"This way, niggah," said the guard who met him at the entrance. "Y'all stand right thar," said another.

Johnny was disoriented at first by the accents around him. The California prisons recruited guards from Southern states—Arkansas, Texas, Mississippi. These men in uniform were grown-up versions of the boys who had tormented him in Jackson.

He was issued an extra set of prison clothes and told to stand outside his cell until the unlock time came. His stiff jeans and work shirt hung on his lean frame. His hair was buzzed short as an army recruit's, making his high cheekbones seem even more angular.

He closed his eyes to escape the bars, but the smells

reminded him where he was. Urine and rotting food. Too many bodies. The odor of fear.

"Hey, man, I'm Balance. You living here now?"

Johnny opened his eyes. He fell back into the pattern he'd developed on the streets. Give away nothing, he thought. Nothing.

"Yeah."

"I know your celly, Rog. He's cool."

Johnny watched Balance come closer. Johnny knew he had to show strength. He narrowed his eyes. Close enough, motherfucker, he thought.

"How old are you?" Balance asked, looking Johnny up and down.

"Seventeen."

"I thought so. You here on a Y number?"

"No, I'm a B," replied Johnny. A Y "youth" number would have indicated he had been tried in juvenile court. An A or B number showed he was tried as an adult.

"Damn, what you do?"

"I had, uh, a murder beef."

Johnny watched for that look to come into Balance's eyes. That look, whenever he told someone, that flicker of respect and fear. And there it was. Balance said, "You doing life?"

Johnny nodded. "You know, I haven't been doing too much. I'd like to go out and shoot some hoop or something."

Balance led him to the outdoor basketball court. The inmates played in their blue jeans and work shirts, prison ball. Not just hand checking—banging, anything they could get away with.

Johnny watched awhile, swaying with the action on the court. I'm better than those fat-asses, he thought.

The winning three stayed on. Two others stepped forward. One of them, Michael Spearman, was from the old neighborhood and knew how well Johnny could play. Spearman said, "I guess I'll take the kid."

The guys on the other team grinned. They were all taller than Johnny. The one who was guarding Johnny was the backup guard on the institutionwide team.

The first time Johnny touched the ball, he dribbled the length of the court. His man couldn't keep up. Johnny pivoted, ran his man into one of the others, and elevated. *Swish.* Two points.

Spearman scored the next one, and Johnny followed with two in succession. He was thrilled to be back on the court. His body radiated an intensity that came from having been denied this release for so long. By the second half of the game, his team was ahead 16 to 4 and a crowd was gathering.

During the next play, the man guarding him called a foul on Johnny. Spearman wanted to fight it, because everyone had seen that there had been no foul. But Johnny just calmly moved in front of the man as he prepared to make his inbounds pass. Johnny read his body, the way he was going to throw the ball, and where he was going to throw it.

Johnny decided that he was going to leap for this ball, not just kind of lean toward it and stick his hands up, but really go for it. And as the other prisoner threw the ball in, Johnny leaped and grabbed it and came down dribbling and took it right into the basket and laid it up.

Johnny's team won and the guy guarding him handed him two packs of cigarettes. Far out, thought Johnny, I didn't know we were gambling.

He could hear eight or nine voices in the crowd saying, "That's my homeboy, that's my homeboy, you know."

After the game, Johnny talked to them. They were from South Central L.A.; a few were Slausons. They were happy to see him, and asked what was new. One of the guys from the neighborhood was Fleeta Drumgo. When Fleeta was fifteen, he'd had a fight with his stepfather and fired a gun into the ceiling. His mother called the police, and he'd been imprisoned for attempting to commit murder. Released after three and a half years, he'd spent only twenty days on the street before being sent back on a burglary rap. Fleeta was barely in his twenties, but Johnny couldn't get over how prison had aged him. The skin under his eyes was puffy, like some old man's.

The conversation died out and the men began to head back to their cells. Johnny was just about to leave the gym when he heard an inmate yell, "Hey, my man!" Johnny pivoted sharply, ready to lash out, thinking the guy was making fun of him.

His fist was in midair when he stopped and grinned. There was Leroy Hutchinson. Hutch, taller, darker, and more heavily muscled than Johnny, had been the best-dressed guy on the street, and he managed to look sharp in prison as well. Hutch gave the laundry room inmates a carton of cigarettes a week to make sure that his pants were sharply creased.

They sat down on the bleachers. "You gotta watch yourself around here," Hutch told him. "It's not just the big guys who'll kill you. Little guys will kill you at the dip of a head. Start packing a piece, a weapon—a bedspring or a zip gun out of an ink pen you can fire with sulfur from match heads. If someone attacks, you either beat him till he can't stand up. Or you kill him."

Johnny puffed nervously on a cigarette, making small jerky tilts of his head to check if someone was coming up behind him. "I'm cool," he said. "I can handle it."

"This place can be dangerous. But it doesn't have to be dangerous for you. You just have to feel what's going down and what's right. What you do on that court, expand it. And let it ride."

Later that afternoon, Johnny paced off his cell. This really sucks, he thought. Two steps from the bunk beds to the right-hand wall. Three steps from the bars to the sink and toilet. He could stretch out on the bunk, but there wasn't enough room on the floor to do push-ups. Unless he wanted to put his face in the toilet. There was no chair. Johnny sat on the floor for a few minutes, got uncomfortable, stood leaning against the wall a minute, lay down, stood again. He could hear his own breath coming faster. When he heard the click of the next unlock, he stepped outside a few seconds, just to feel a little freedom.

Every half hour, there would be a fifteen-second unlock at which inmates were free to leave their cell during the day to go to the yard, the gym, the chow hall, or their jobs. Johnny tried to be out of his cell as much as possible. When he remained inside, the half hour between unlocks seemed to stretch interminably.

His third day at Tracy prison, Johnny was hurrying along the main corridor on his way to dinner. A yellow line on the floor marked off a three-feet-wide ribbon of corridor: Guards only. Johnny couldn't stand another barrier telling him where he couldn't go. He walked in a zigzag, crossing the line as often as he could. Twenty feet from the chow hall door, in a crowd, an inmate three feet ahead of him grabbed another inmate from behind, picked him up, and swung him around. A third man stabbed the guy's chest with some-thing metal, and blood poured out. The guy screamed. The attackers ran and disappeared into the swarm of identically dressed inmates.

Johnny stood frozen in front of the dead man. An older inmate grabbed him by the arm. "What the fuck's wrong with you?"

Johnny's mouth was open, his eyes wide.

"Let's go. Let's go. Let's move it," said the man, pulling him down the corridor. "You didn't see shit. You didn't see *nuthin'*."

Sitting alone at a table in the chow hall, Johnny trembled, spilling peas off his fork, bouncing them across his tray. He knew the rules on the street, but wasn't sure he could figure out what he needed to do in here. A guy at the county jail had told him a little about how to steer clear of the guards, but not how to handle the other inmates. I gotta get it together, he thought. These guys are crazy motherfuckers!

Three inmates joined him, talking excitedly. "Did you hear? Someone got iced in the hall."

Johnny opened his mouth to speak, then thought better of it.

He shook his head and then said quietly, almost to himself, "I didn't see nuthin'."

That night, after Johnny was locked in his cell, a white guard yelled at a tall black inmate on the tier, "Shoe, get in for the night."

Johnny turned to his cellmate, "That guy's called Shoe?"

"No. It's just a name they have for us. They call us nigger, coon, spade, shoe. A shoe is something meant to be walked on."

Johnny tried to sleep, but the chill of the cell, combined with the morgue-slab hardness of the bunk, made it impossible. He kept seeing the geyser of blood from the dying man's shirt. He piled his extra set of prison-issue clothes on top of the thin blanket for insulation. The noises of the tier died down and he drifted off to a strained sleep.

At 3:00 A.M., a white guard woke him with the glare of a flashlight. "Just checking that you're still with us, boy."

The guard continued walking. Johnny got up and spit in his wake.

chapter
twelve

The next day, when he thought about the murder, Johnny realized that what bothered him most was not that a man had been killed, but that he himself hadn't seen it coming. How could I have let those guys get that close to me without realizing what was up? Prison, Johnny realized, was like being in the middle of one big gang fight. Your antennae had to be up all the time. You had to recognize the danger signs.

When he left for the gym that morning, he walked rapidly. That way, if anyone wanted to come after him, they'd have to quicken their own pace, giving him a warning sign. He'd look for Hutch today, to find out more about how to survive. He tried to recall what the old guy in the county jail had told him: "When you get to prison, man, don't let them put no snitch jacket on you, don't let them do that. Whenever you got to talk to a guard, talk real loud so everybody can hear what you're talking about. That way no one can say you're snitching."

As he passed the guards' station a few weeks later, a sergeant asked, "Where are you going?"

"I'M GOING TO MY JOB."

"What you hollerin' for?"

"THIS IS HOW I TALK. I DON'T EVEN REALIZE I'M TALKING LOUD."

Johnny continued walking. Outside of his housing wing, F Wing, he turned right on the main corridor and walked briskly past six other housing wings, then past the higher-security L Wing, which was known as the Adjustment Center. There were double doors to the corridor blocking what went on in there, making it all the more threatening. Guys with a lot of disciplinary write-ups got locked up in there—beat up, he figured. The beatings didn't scare him as much as the thought of being in a cell twenty-three or twenty-four hours a day. Meals through a slot like a chimpanzee. No sports.

After the A.C. came Control, the nerve center for the guards. Through a small glass window he could see tools, keys, radios, riot helmets, and billy clubs that shot tear gas. It looked like a fucking army headquarters.

He turned left off the main corridor and headed for his job in one of the four chow halls. He'd asked for a job as an electrician, but those jobs went to whites. Instead, he was assigned an unpaid job in a chow hall.

He hated "T.C.," as they called it—table cleaning. He hated mopping the floor. He hated serving other inmates and emptying the garbage cans. He hated the stupid uniforms, looking like white surgical garb, with the zip-up pants and the V-necked pullover top.

He reached a decision point. If he turned left he would enter the field house and be AWOL on his required kitchen duty. If he turned right, he would be at Chow Hall 2. Oh well, it was right before dinner. There probably wouldn't be much action in the gym. He decided he would go to work.

Dinner that night was Hungarian goulash. Like the rest of prison life, kitchen work was subject to a tangle of rules and regulations. Johnny could be disciplined, for example, if he gave a prisoner more than one serving of food.

An old-timer—twenty-four or twenty-five years old—came through the line and Johnny gave him a dipper full of goulash.

"Give me another dipper full."

"Here," Johnny said, "you take the dipper and get it yourself."

The other prisoner slowly drew his gaze down the contours of Johnny's body, finally staring at the zipper in the white prison pants. "No, you give it to me."

Johnny sized him up. Tinkerbell outweighed him by at least thirty pounds and clearly lifted weights. He wore a dirty denim jacket, creased and marked where the dumbbell smacked against it. Other prisoners had warned Johnny not to mess with him. But Hutch had warned Johnny that if an older guy came on to you, it was better to have your butt beat than to back down.

The man's eyes met his. "You, young pretty motherfucker, you better give me another dip."

"Come back in the pot room," he replied slowly, "and you can get all the dick you want."

When Johnny had finished serving, he went back into the pot storage room and pulled a large wooden stirrer out of one of the giant pots. It was about four feet long and looked like a two-by-four, but it was made of lighter wood. Johnny crawled in behind some pots and waited. When he heard footsteps, he waited. And waited. Then he jumped up and hit the older man in the chest, knocked his ass flat. And stood over him, with his weapon, a giant fucking spoon, thinking, Want another dip now? How about another dip now?

On his way back to his cell, Johnny knew the other con

wouldn't turn him in. The Code was clear. No matter what went down, no one ratted out another con. But what if Tinkerbell rounded up some of his faggot buddies and came calling? No problem. There were more Slausons in Tracy than any other gang; Johnny was well connected. No problem. How about another dip now?

A few weeks later, he was walking with Hutch through a far tier when he heard an alarm he hadn't heard before and the grille gates on the tier started to close.

"Shit," said Hutch, "this is no place to be." They were in a white cell block.

The unannounced closing of the gates probably meant that a race riot had broken out in a remote part of the prison. The guards responded to such instances by automatically locking the grille gates to cut the prison down into small sections. This way, a handful of men would be trapped in each tier, not enough to start a generalized riot.

Johnny and Hutch were trapped. Three white guys started coming at them. "Do as much damage to the closest ones as you can," Hutch told him. "Just don't fall—or else it's all over."

Johnny rushed at one of the attacking inmates. He ran close, then dropped to the floor, rolled toward him in a classic football move, and knocked the guy's legs out from under him. The startled white careened backward, hitting his head against the wall.

Johnny pushed himself back up to his feet, just as Hutch knocked over a domino table, broke off two legs, and threw one to him.

He turned so that his back was up against Hutch's. Like a multilimbed centipede, they edged down the tier, bashing, kicking, covering for each other. When the unlock came, blacks from the other side of the gate swarmed in and helped get them out alive.

The next night, Johnny and Hutch were in the television room on F Wing watching the news. Six white guys approached the TV and changed it to something else.

"Motherfuckers," said Johnny. He and Hutch moved to the front of the room. A dozen other blacks joined them. The program flipped back and forth, back and forth, as heads bobbed, fists connected, and men fell. Four white guards with tear gas cannisters ran in and fired at the black inmates.

Johnny doubled over in pain, coughing and rubbing his eyes. His lids felt seared, his lungs on fire. His testicles were shot through with pain. In the background, a picture of Huey Newton flashed on the screen. He had just been arrested for killing a cop.

Huey Newton and Bobby Seale were heroes to the blacks inside prison. Earlier that year, in Oakland, California, they had formed the Black Panther Party for Self-Defense to counter the racist actions of the Oakland police. The police were almost all white and hostile to blacks; many had been recruited from the Southern states specifically to keep Oakland's growing postwar black population in line. They often pulled black drivers aside and frisked them without any cause. When Huey Newton saw these incidents happen, he would jump out of his own car, usually carrying a gun, and open a law book to advise the cowering black of his rights. In an action that presaged the much later Rodney King incident, Newton would sometimes carry a tape recorder to document what the police were doing. Newton and Seale established provocative patrols of young black men in black leather jackets and berets, carrying shotguns and .38s. With law books, tape recorders—and the unsettling possibility of violence if necessary—these Black Panthers took to the streets to prevent police from harassing and brutalizing the black population of Oakland.

Johnny had first heard about them in the spring of 1967, when he was at Chino awaiting his prison assignment. On May 2, 1967, a group of thirty Black Panthers carrying every type of gun and rifle imaginable entered the floor of the California legislature to protest a bill—aimed directly at Newton's actions—which would ban the display of loaded weapons. Johnny remembered the newspaper photo of them on the steps of the California Capitol, ammo strapped across their chests, guns in one hand, the other arm raised in the Black Power salute. These armed urban guerrillas had held their ground at the legislature and read a statement written by Newton, a parolee and college student: "Black people have begged, prayed, petitioned and demonstrated, among other things, to get the racist power structure of America to right the wrongs which have been perpetrated against black people. All of these efforts have been answered by more repression, deceit, and hypocrisy. . . . A people who have suffered so much for so long at the hands of a racist society must draw the line somewhere. We believe that the black communities of America must rise up as one man to halt the progression of a trend that leads inevitably to their total destruction."

In the months that followed, membership in the Panthers had grown from a handful of blacks to over five thousand, with chapters in more than a dozen cities. Newton and Seale focused recruiting on what they called the "lumpen" (short for the Marxist term "lumpenproletariat")—ex-convicts, prostitutes, gang members, prisoners, and other people otherwise ignored by social movements. Newton himself was on parole from a knifing incident. Eldridge Cleaver, the ex-convict and celebrated author of *Soul on Ice*, became their minister of information.

On October 28, 1967, Newton was driving through Oakland, celebrating his release from parole, when the cops flagged him down. He was used to this sort of harassment. The Oakland police had a list of Panther vehicle license plates and they would stop members of the Party. Newton himself had been pulled aside more than forty times. This time, though, the outcome was different. Shots were exchanged. Officer John Frey was killed and Newton was wounded. Now Newton was in a hospital, where a cop guarding him said, "You goddamn nigger, we're going to cut off this tube and save the state the trouble of gassing you."

In the months that followed, Hutch and Johnny followed the media coverage of the Newton case whenever they could gain control in the TV room. They were amazed at how Newton's attorneys, Charles Garry and Fay Stender, were transforming the case into a teach-in on racism and Newton into a cult figure. Garry put Newton on the witness stand and asked him what the black liberation movement was.

"The black liberation movement is a movement to free blacks from exploitation and oppression," Newton replied. "Black power is the means by which blacks will free themselves from the oppression of the ruling class in North America."

In response to a later question, Newton explained, "The black panther does not attack anyone. It will back up first, but if attacked it will certainly use self-defense."

At the end of Newton's trial, Garry told the jury that Newton had been framed. "This case is a diabolical attempt to put an innocent man into jail or the gas chamber," he told the jury. He also argued that whites needed to take responsibility. "White America listen: the answer is not to put Huey and his organization in jail. The answer is not more police. The answer is to wipe out the miserable conditions in the ghetto so that black brothers and sisters can live with dignity, so they can walk down the street with pride."

Although Newton had been indicted for murder, the Newton jury came back with a verdict of voluntary manslaughter, a lesser offense. His lawyers went to work immediately on the appeal of the case. "Free Huey" buttons and posters dotted the cities.

Hutch began inflaming black prisoners with the details of Newton's case and proselytizing to get them to join the Panthers. Already, the inmates had begun to use the word the Panthers had coined for the cops—"pig"—to refer to the guards and prison administration. The Tracy officials took note, and decided that Hutch was too dangerous to keep at Tracy. They decided to transfer him to the more secure Soledad. Hutch sought out Johnny for a final conversation before he left.

"Johnny, my man, think about what you're doing," said Hutch. Johnny was more hotheaded than the other inmates his age. His disciplinary write-ups were piling up, and Hutch knew they'd be trouble for him if he ever asked for parole. Hutch urged Johnny to cool it, to just go along with some of the petty things that the guards requested and to hold his temper in check, especially with other blacks. Hutch saved his own anger for those things he felt were important—like making sure the administration allowed meetings among the various black brothers. But Johnny felt like he had to wear his aggression boldly or he might be hurt.

"You are just playing into the guards' hands by fighting with the brothers in the gym or in the yard," said Hutch. "Can't you see that the guards are down our throats if we fight with a white guy but just look the other way if we're beating on a brother? They don't give a shit if we kill each other. We've got to find another way."

Johnny just looked away.

"Johnny, don't fight it," Hutch told him. "You're going to do at least seven years no matter what. It's just time. It goes by. It's just time."

But Johnny was young and bent on taking on every rule. Seven years, one hundred years. What the fuck was the difference?

The day after Hutch left, Johnny asked a guard, "Can I get a write-up for what I think?"

"Well, no, you can think whatever you want."

"I think you're a real asshole."

Another write-up entered Johnny's file.

chapter
thirteen

In the year after Hutch left Tracy, Johnny piled up a load of disciplinaries and was linked to some of the most violent incidents there—nothing proven, of course, since the other cons "never saw anything." He was still young, not yet twenty, but he was on the tough side for Tracy, a bad influence on the seventeen- and eighteen-year-olds who seemed to be arriving in greater numbers. It was time for a transfer to a higher-security prison. The prisoners had a name for it: "bus therapy."

On July 21, 1969, they put him on a bus to Soledad, telling him he'd gotten too sophisticated for Tracy. He brought with him five orange crates of his possessions. Three held plaques and trophies he'd won in Tracy sports.

Johnny was handcuffed on the bus, and was sitting a few seats behind the driver. Between them was a metal fence. Standing on the driver's side of the fence was a guard with a machine gun.

Johnny had not been outside of prison since his assignment to Tracy more than two years earlier. Officials had denied his request for a leave to attend Johnny Sr.'s recent funeral, despite the fact that it was in their power to grant it. As the bus traveled down California Highway 101, Johnny stared out the window at the Salinas Valley, with its fields of lettuce, corn, and alfalfa.

When the bus approached Soledad, Johnny could see the silhouette of the gun towers over a squat, three-story beige building. The driver looked over his shoulder. "They call Tracy the Gladiator School, but it's pussy school next to Soledad."

A line of guards crowded around Johnny and the others as they exited the bus. One of the guards led him inside and locked him in a receiving cell in the gunmetal-colored corridor.

"Fish on the line," the guard announced, telling the world that a new inmate had arrived at Soledad.

Johnny gazed out of the cage. About every fifty yards, the corridor slanted down slightly, allowing him to see to the end of its vast quarter-mile expanse. Unlike at Tracy, where the receiving area for new prisoners looked out invitingly into the open yard, with its Olympic weight pit and fancy field house, this cell had a view of only the sweep down the corridor.

Here there were no clusters of inmates horsing around. The inmates looked grim in navy watch caps, prison blues, and big construction boots. The guards looked more hostile, fiercer than they had at Tracy. Everyone seemed on edge.

In his time at Tracy, Johnny had learned how far he could take things. He knew which buttons to push—and which not to push—on which guards and inmates. Now he had to start all over, with higher stakes. He decided he would spend the next day searching for Hutch, who'd been banished to Soledad a year earlier. If I don't learn what this place is about, he thought, I'm not going to make it. Learn about it. Live.

Hutch had a lot to say. "You can't do this one on your own. They don't play games here."

Johnny and Hutch sat at a wooden card table a few feet down the tier from Johnny's cell. The oppressive heat in the wing had pushed most inmates outside, so the two men had a little privacy. Johnny looked at Hutch. His boots were new and shiny. He must have paid some inmate a lot of cigarettes for those boots.

Hutch's voice had the same honeyed sound as before, but his eyes were less soulful. They had a new determination, a razor-sharp focus.

A black with crooked teeth approached. Johnny was up in a flash, recognizing him as a rival from the Watts gang.

"Cool it," said Hutch, motioning Johnny back into his chair.

"We on tonight?" asked the man.

"Same as last week," said Hutch.

Johnny watched the man continue down the tier, then asked Hutch, "Why are you talking to that asshole? He's from Watts."

"Watts, Slausons, Outlaws—the gangs don't count anymore. The only way blacks will survive in here is if we all get it together. There's some guys in here, W. L. Nolen and George Jackson, who are organizing all the brothers. You should come tonight."

Years later Johnny would realize that those words were the key to his ability to survive, but right now he wasn't ready to listen.

"I do it my way, on my own," he told Hutch.

"That's bullshit. It won't work here. The administration is setting us up. They're giving white cons knives and car jacks to come after us. They don't play games here. You got to recognize reality, because the brothers' lives depend on it, too."

"Are you packing?" asked Johnny, wondering if Hutch had a knife or other weapon.

"It's not like Tracy; they search us all the time." He looked down at his callused hands. "I pound these against the concrete to toughen them. They're the only weapons we have."

Johnny leaned his chair back, but had nothing more to say. The men sat in silence for a moment, the quiet punctuated by the clack of dominoes a few tables over. Finally Hutch said, "Come on, I'll show you around."

They walked out the doors in the middle of Johnny's housing wing into the quarter-mile corridor. Hutch pointed out the various other housing wings that veered off from the corridor. Each was U-shaped, with the base of the U backing up against the corridor. Each had three tiers of two-man cells. The men on the lowest tier, like Johnny, were generally newcomers under observation. They had to lock up at night by 7:30 P.M. The second-level inmates could be out of their cells until 9:30 P.M. A third-tier assignment brought an even later curfew, 11:30 P.M. But blacks had difficulty moving up. Prison authorities would not allow a black to move to a higher-tier cell that had been occupied by a white. Since whites got the majority of the better cells, even acquiescent black prisoners were often stuck on the restricted lower tiers.

Johnny and Hutch came to a locked red steel door.

"O Wing," Hutch said, nodding at the door. "It's where they've got W. L."

"W. L.?"

"The brother I told you about. He's a big strong motherfucker, won a prison boxing title. He got a lot of the brothers to put down their grudges and shit and come together. The pigs would like to burn his black ass. They've got him locked in solitary twenty-four hours a day."

Johnny stood staring at the door, trying to picture the boxer in his cell on the other side.

"The administration tried to set W. L. up a couple of times," said Hutch. "The last time, they gave a white con a knife to kill him. He took the goddamn knife away, beat the guy's face into a bloody mess, and then slid the knife under the grille gate to the guards."

Hutch smiled as he came to the punch line. "W. L. told the pigs, 'You sent a punk. Next time you better send somebody better than this.'"

Hutch and Johnny continued walking. Hutch told him how, on O Wing, the most political or violent of blacks were housed in cages alongside the most violent of whites, members of the Aryan Brotherhood. Although no two inmates were supposed to be allowed out of their cells at the same time, sometimes the guards "accidentally" let a few whites out at a time when a single black was alone in the corridor. And whites were ahead in the psychological warfare, since the white inmate tier tenders who passed out meals would put feces or cigarette butts in black inmates' food.

In the fall of 1969, Nolen and three other black Soledad inmates would file a handwritten legal motion asking for an injunction against guards who were keeping them locked up continuously, making up false disciplinary reports to quash their chances of release, and organizing and encouraging white prisoners to brutalize them. In court papers, Nolen would say that Soledad officials were "willfully creating and maintaining situations that create and pose danger to plaintiff [Nolen] and other members of his race." He "feared for his life."

Hutch and Johnny continued through a set of double doors, out into the main yard. They passed the weight pit and approached a cluster of tables. Hutch raised his fist in

the Black Power salute. Johnny looked over in the direction
that his fist had signaled. He saw a muscular black man
sitting at a table, surrounded by five or six other black
inmates. The man was lighter-skinned, just slightly darker
than Johnny, and had reddish hair. His intense gaze bore
into the person he was talking to, and his overdeveloped
arms punctuated each point. His shirt strained against his
chest muscles. When he smiled, his face glowed. But when
the smile disappeared, Johnny could read the message in his
eyes: The man was a killer.

"Who's he?" Johnny asked.

"George Jackson. They call him 'Comrade.' He's running
the show now that W. L.'s in the hole. He doesn't take any
shit from anybody. Kicked a lieutenant once and nearly
broke the pig's back."

Hutch sat down at an empty table and Johnny followed
suit.

"Any questions?" Hutch asked.

"Yeah, where's the gym?"

Hutch wasn't the only one talking about George Jackson.
Over the next few weeks, it seemed like every inmate Johnny
met had something to say about him. George this. George
that. How George did a thousand fingertip push-ups a day.
How he'd been moved to Soledad after starting a riot by
refusing to sit on the back-of-the-room benches for blacks in
the Tracy TV room.

Johnny pieced together the details of George's past. In
1960, he'd been sentenced for a year to life for a seventy-
one-dollar gas station holdup. Such a beef usually meant an
early release. At his 1966 parole hearing, Jackson had been
told that if he stayed clean, he would be released after his
December 1967 appearance. He complied, but when he

reminded them of that deal a year later, he was told, "We never make deals like that."

"No black will ever leave this place if he has any violence in his past, until they see that thing in his eyes," George later wrote in a letter. "And you can't fake it, resignation—defeat, it must be stamped clearly across the face."

George was now twenty-eight years old and had been at Soledad eight years. He'd been denied parole eight times, even though his crime partner had been released years earlier.

"Do you want to meet Jackson?" Hutch asked Johnny a month after he arrived at Soledad.

"Nah," replied Johnny. "Who gives a shit about him? Everyone acts like he walks on water."

A few days later, Johnny walked over to the gym after dinner. He passed the sand pit, where inmates worked out with the weight-lifting equipment. It was color-coded by the prison administration to indicate which race could use which equipment. The older, worn barbells had a red dot, signifying they were for use by blacks.

Unlike the one at Tracy, the gym at Soledad didn't look anything like a gym, just another building. The large rectangular room on the inside was a basketball court, with baskets that could be lowered to turn the room into a volleyball court or to set up a boxing ring. The floor was concrete, not the polished wood of even the poorest L.A. high school gyms.

Johnny blended into the never-ending basketball game. As he drove downcourt, he noticed George Jackson in the bleachers surrounded by a dozen brothers, including Hutch. Rather than watching the game, the men were listening to George. Fuck him, Johnny thought. Between periods, he looked over again. George was a big guy—had to be over six feet tall, more than two hundred pounds. He was wearing glasses, but they didn't make him look weak. His shoulders hunched forward powerfully. His hand was raised. He was talking. Moving. Talking.

As he sat during a break in the game, Johnny could hear part of the conversation.

"We've been locked up for political reasons," George was saying. "It's in our best interests to know how to defend ourselves against a knife, to know how to defend ourselves against multiple opponents. We've got to have a plan of attack.

"Nonviolence won't work," continued George, "because it presumes the existence of mercy in the heart of the oppressor."

After the game, sweaty and needing to pee, Johnny entered a large bathroom just off the basketball court. George was practicing martial arts there with some of his men. "Join us, Comrade," said George.

"Man, I don't need to," said Johnny. "I can defend myself just fine."

"Show me," said George.

"Nah, I don't have time for this."

"C'mon, throw a jab."

Johnny looked at him like, I could do it, but I don't want to hurt you.

"C'mon, give it a try."

Finally, it became a challenge. Johnny decided to hit the guy once and then go back to his cell.

He tried a left jab, but George flicked it away without moving his elbows from his side. George's body was relaxed, open to Johnny, lulling Johnny into a fight by his calm.

I can hit this guy, thought Johnny. He tried again.

George's body shifted slightly and he deflected the blow. He smiled slightly.

He's pretty good, thought Johnny, but he doesn't know what I can do.

Johnny tried a right cross, but George flicked it away.

Shit, I'm going to hit you now. But the uppercut never connected. Guy's incredible, thought Johnny. So goddamn fast for someone with those muscles.

"See, homeboy?" Hutch piped up. "See what I was telling you?"

Later that night, Johnny asked Hutch, "Uh, when are you going to practice that karate?"

"It's not karate. It's Iron Palm."

The next afternoon, Johnny joined them.

The men paired off to begin their *katas*. Martial arts were forbidden in prison, so an inmate stood outside the door, watching for guards.

Instead of making a fist, George bent his fingers back at the first knuckles, exposing his palm and creating a piercing wedge with his extended knuckles. George feigned a punch to Johnny's right cheek and Johnny responded with a jab to George's ribs.

"No, no, no, man," said George. "Let the other guy's energy work for you. If he's throwing a punch at you, get right into that punch and turn it back on him. Now go for my jaw."

Johnny lurched forward to punch, but was cut off as George whacked Johnny's approaching forearm.

"Now," said George, "come up behind me."

Johnny grabbed George around the neck and George pivoted lightly, throwing Johnny off balance as he rammed Johnny in the neck with the wedge of his fingers.

"Not bad," said George, "but you left yourself totally unprotected on your right side. If another guy came up, you'd be dead.

"You've got to keep control of the whole area," continued George, motioning over three other inmates. "Now watch this."

George pushed aside one attacker, shifted his weight to his back leg, spun a quarter turn, and thrust his arm up to pressure the carotid artery of a second inmate. Then George half-stepped to the side, getting so close to the third attacker that the man couldn't follow through with his punch. George cracked the man's arm back.

Johnny thought about what George had done. He'd moved like a snake, slithering around his attackers, always completely balanced. At the same time, he had managed to throw his attackers off balance and to turn the energy of their blows back against them.

"How can I learn that?" asked Johnny.

"There's only one way," advised George. "Think about your worst fears and fight against them."

Johnny watched the rest of the men as they went through their *katas*. They were like a group of dancers, each one listening to different music. One man's worst fear was a knife attack in the shower. He rehearsed how he would stand, turn, and respond, in relation to the wall and the water. Another dove from an imaginary blow with a metal dinner tray.

Johnny thought about his own demons. He felt comfortable using his old fighting skills when the attacks were one-on-one. What he lost sleep about was rat packing. He began to choreograph combinations of strategies, imagining people coming at him from different directions, in different parts of the prison.

He started his own *kata*.

chapter
fourteen

A few weeks after he'd begun Iron Palm, Johnny caught sight of George across the yard. George raised his hand to him in the Black Power salute. Johnny saw how nervous the gesture made a guard a few feet away. The man's hand patted the side of his khaki pants, as if he wished he had a holster. Johnny shot his arm up, made a fist, and saluted back.

Johnny was on his way to basketball practice. The next day they were playing a visiting college team. George was headed in the same direction. Johnny expected George to ask him about the game, but instead he launched into a discussion of a revolutionary South American group, the Tupamaros.

"Why do you give a shit what's going on out there when you're in here?" Johnny asked him.

"I *always* have outside thoughts. It's the one thing they can't take away. *You* let yourself be pacified by the few crumbs they'll throw you, like the chance to play basketball. But I'm honing my rage into a weapon."

Johnny was angered at the insinuation that he was being tricked by the administration, but he didn't know how to respond. Besides, they were at the gym, and the men who had been waiting for George had come over and begun to surround him.

Johnny went looking for his coach, a civilian, only to find out that he was sick and basketball practice had been canceled. He looked over at George, Hutch, and others in the bleachers, walked toward them and sat down, casually, on the fringes of the group, intending to stay for a few minutes, just to see what was happening. He had nothing to do.

"You've been dubbed a criminal," George was saying to the men. "But the fact is you've never enslaved anyone. You haven't done the things to anyone that the white pigs have done. Here's a case in history where anywhere from thirty thousand to seventy thousand black people were killed on the way to this country from Africa. Not the ones who got here, but the ones who didn't make it. You've never committed any atrocities like that. How dare these people call you the criminal, the villain."

"Yeah," said one of the men, "the *whites* say what's a crime, the *whites* sit on the jury, and the *whites* lock us up. We're not criminals. We're just trying to even the score."

Johnny hadn't intended to speak. At one level, he could accept crimes against whites because of the hatred whites had toward him, but Hutch was constantly harping on him to show respect for other blacks. "Aren't you a criminal if you steal from a brother?" he asked.

"Black-on-black crime—fighting each other—this is the epitome of stupidity," said George. "But it's not a crime. You've been sucked into the whole idiotic system of self-hatred and that's what's driving people. If you look at African society, it's a better society—communitarian, not capitalistic. It isn't blacks' way to fight over material things.

"The people who enslaved blacks went about the task of making the slaves feel they were inferior. It wasn't the case of you being inferior. It was a matter of *conditioning*. You started thinking of yourself in the worst terms and then started fighting other brothers just to prove you were better than someone."

Johnny watched George's eyes behind the glasses. They seemed like two black snakes curled up and ready to strike. His whole body was like that.

Johnny was surprised by how he talked. George was kind of like a teacher, but more complicated. He'd noticed that in Iron Palm George would sometimes speak in a puzzle, and the men would compete to figure him out.

"The question I've asked myself over the years runs this way: Who has done most of the dying? Most of the work? Most of the time in prison, on max row? Who is the hindmost in every aspect of social, political, and economic life?" asked George.

"Racism is a matter of ingrained traditional attitudes conditioned through institutions," he said. "For some, it is as natural a reflex as breathing."

Johnny looked at the other men. They were listening, their faces open with interest, not at all like their jivin' smart-ass selves.

As George talked, Johnny thought of the electrical wiring he'd seen with John Spain. You connected A to B and all of a sudden—zap—you had power. George did that with the men, making new connections, creating a force, a power.

"Look what it's done to you," continued George. "You were made subservient. You began to think of yourselves as inferior. Because of the nature of oppression, you've only been made to think of yourself as worthless. You're *not* worthless!"

Johnny noticed the other men were sitting up straighter now, their chins thrust out, heads high. "They can't stand any black with any power or freedom of thought," continued

George. "But their hatred is their weakness. They are so used to walking all over us that they won't know how to retaliate once the Black Panthers start taking over."

Johnny didn't speak. It seemed far-fetched to him.

"It's possible, it's possible," George said. "The Cubans are doing it, the Tupamaros in Uruguay, the Palestinian Liberation Organization, the Baader-Meinhof Gang in Germany.

"The brothers in Vietnam have picked up guns and they're saying to the American army, we don't care about your tanks, we don't care how many bombs you can drop, because you cannot defeat the spirit and the will of the people. The Vietnamese are small in stature, but giants in technique. They are knocking B-52 bombers out of the sky, they are fighting tanks with Coke cans.

"The Panthers are doing the same thing, employing guerrilla tactics in this country. Huey Newton. Bobby Seale. These are guys who are really doing something about their oppression. Our struggle in here is the same as theirs out there. We're in the same revolution."

After the session, George said to Johnny, "That was a good question, Comrade." He handed him a paperback book, Calvin Hernton's *Sex and Racism in America.* "I think you'll find some answers in here."

Johnny took the book back to his cell and sat on his bed. He flipped the pages. Hmm, pretty long, 180 pages. He wondered what it was about. He thought it was pretty odd that it had "sex" in the title.

His cellmate was out, so it was a good time to take a look at the book. Not that he planned to read it all, but it wouldn't hurt to look at a few pages, just to let George know he had. He flipped to the end of the book. Maybe if he just read the conclusion he could act like he'd read it all.

"Racism is a man-made, man-enforced phenomenon," he read. "Nobody, not even the Southerner, is *born* a racist. . . . People learn to discriminate, learn to segregate, learn to believe that whites are better than blacks, learn to think and fear that Negroes want to rape white women, learn to think of and to treat black females as though they were animals. When people live in a society where such things are formally and informally taught and learned, and are practiced, it is inescapable that the ideology of racism does become a functional institution, organically interwoven with every other ideology and institution of that society. Thus, racism in America is as much a part of the 'American way of life' as Protestantism or Big Business. I am referring to our social structure; our economic and political system; and the way power, jobs, and life opportunities are distributed in America on the basis of physical characteristics."

Hey, thought Johnny, this sounds a lot like George. But here it is all printed up in a book. He turned back to the beginning and began to read.

The next morning, Johnny went to Y Wing to talk to George about the book. His first impression of George's cell was that it looked as if someone had set off a bomb in a library. Every imaginable surface was covered with books and papers—the floor, the sink behind the faucet, the foot of the bed. Tilting over the toilet was a tottering tower of white—Xeroxed copies of books that were not out in paperback. Hardcover books were forbidden because of their potential as weapons, so an inmate could only receive photocopies of them.

"Done already?" George asked, looking at the book in Johnny's hand. "You're just like my brother."

Johnny frowned. He knew that George's brother Jonathan was young, just sixteen, almost four years Johnny's junior.

"No, no, he's cool," continued George. "He really understands. He's reading the same books I am, as fast as I suggest them, and lecturing his teachers about Marx. He could be a chemist, or a surgeon, or someone else who could make a contribution to the revolution.

"So what did you think of the book?"

"It made me feel how much the whites hate us."

"Yeah, but we don't have to be the floor mat of the world. Look at what the Black Panthers are doing."

Johnny picked up George's makeshift punching bag, a burlap flour bag filled with concrete chunks. He hit it a few times while he thought about what George had said.

"I've got two goals right now," said George. "One is to train men in here so that they can go out and be part of the Panther revolution. The second is to get W. L. and the brothers out of O Wing."

George told Johnny that he and W. L. went way back. They'd met in San Quentin in 1966, when George worked in the prison hospital. Nolen had been beaten up by white racists, but wanted to settle the score in his own way, without alerting anyone in the administration. George gave Nolen morphine and a tetanus shot, and tried his best to sew a wound in his back, so that the prison doctor would not have to be called in. They later practiced self-defense maneuvers together—Nolen using his boxing movements and Jackson martial arts—and formed a surreptitious Marxist reading group. Now George was trying to get Nolen released to the mainline.

George was twisting in one direction, then another, moving piles of paper in the crowded cell. He found what he was looking for, Che Guevara's *Reminiscences of the Cuban Revolutionary War*. "Get back to me after you've read this," he said.

"There's no way Cuba relates to my life," argued Johnny.

"Wrong," corrected George. "There are events all over the world that are right on with what's happening here inside."

Johnny read the book that evening. "I believe in the armed struggle as the only solution for those peoples who fight to free themselves, and I am consistent with my beliefs," wrote Che. "Wherever death may surprise us, it will be welcome, provided that this, our battle cry, reach some receptive ear, that another hand stretch out to take up weapons and that other men come forward to intone our funeral dirge with the staccato of machine guns and new cries of battle and victory."

A few days later, George asked him what he thought of the book. "I don't know all of the other people involved in this revolution, but from these accounts, this guy appears to be the reason Cuba won that revolutionary war."

George brightened. "You're the first person I talked to in here who's read that and came to that analysis."

"The way I see him, he believed in certain things and he would fight for them," said Johnny. "He believed in study in order to justify your fighting stance—that you needed knowledge to define what you are fighting for, so that what you are fighting for is clearly understood by you and those you are against."

"Right, Comrade," said George. "Not to study and fight is just to fight anybody for any reason. There's no direction in it, a waste of energy. It's like Iron Palm. You must have a clear understanding of how that energy is moving and, in order to do that, you have to watch it carefully, study it, and then make it commit to a certain point."

Over the next four months, George loaned Johnny other books. With Nolen locked away in O Wing, George was hungry for someone to talk to. He told Johnny that he'd spent two months the previous year in complete silence because he was tired of the mediocrity, disloyalty, self-hatred, and cowardliness of the other inmates.

Johnny read Marx and Mao. He was unlike the other young prisoners who discussed what they read with George. Johnny kept up with him intellectually. If George brought something up that he didn't understand, he would read further to find out more about it. Other inmates, if they debated George, never bothered with follow-up. They would either blindly accept what he said or equally blindly reject it. Johnny would always want to know for himself, Why is this position right or wrong? What other priniciples are at work here? And George respected that.

At first, Johnny read at night, after his basketball games, when no one was watching. He hid the books under his mattress during the day. After a few weeks, though, these isolated works blended together into a much bigger story, and he began to read during the days, skipping basketball games and sometimes even meals.

The books talked right to him, explaining why his life had led him to this point. Until then, Johnny thought he was in prison due to a single act. He hadn't thought about institutional racism, or about the effects of poverty, or about welfare for the poor and subsidy for the rich. Now Johnny was beginning to believe that he was where he was, not because he was a monster, but because he was black.

Johnny watched as George wrote long letters to his family about the racism and his view that blacks should fight back. Johnny emulated George, writing a few letters to Helen about those things, but even more to his coach from El Santo Niño, Gonzalo Cano. "The few who control this country have set the 'what is' and 'what is not' crime," wrote Johnny. "To us, *any means* necessary in obtaining justice is justice, and is *not* to be considered a 'crime'! When I come out I will be armed and able; Volume I of Marx or Lenin under one arm, my assault carbine in the other."

Under George's tutelage, Johnny read voraciously about revolutionaries around the world: the Baader-Meinhof Gang in Germany, the Tupamaros in Uruguay, the Palestine Liberation Organization. He absorbed guerrilla plans as readily as he had basketball plays. The term "armed struggle" dotted his sentences.

The revolutionaries Johnny admired used violence to make a point. They were willing to kidnap, or maim, or kill someone for whom they felt no personal animosity, but who served as a symbol of a government or social system that oppressed people. The concept excited him. Some of the other men talked about his murder of Joe Long as a blow against white tyranny.

George showed Johnny a magazine interview in which a Black Panther said that black people could not possibly achieve civil rights out of the present structure of the U.S. government. "So," said the Panther, "we realized that civil rights was a foolishness, that civil rights was a dead end, so that led to a brother by the name of Malcolm X who preached the necessity for armed guerrilla struggle, and we are the historical progeny of Malcolm X."

George and Johnny felt a solidarity with Black Panther leader Huey Newton, then imprisoned in San Luis Obispo, California. They joined the Panther Party, recruited fifty other Soledad prisoners to the party, and pored over issues of *Black Panther* which had been smuggled into Soledad. Newton's ideas were elevating their imprisonment to a form of political martyrdom. About black prisoners who were routinely tried in front of white juries, Newton said, "They have learned to see themselves as political prisoners in the classic, colonial sense: they were not tried before juries of their peers or a cross-section of the community, but by juries wholly unfamiliar with any aspect of their lives."

Johnny was learning a lot from George and from the Panther newspaper. He was learning to organize his rage—to direct it not against himself or against other prisoners, but at the rulers: the prison administration and the government. He'd copied the Panthers' Ten Point Program from one of their issues:

What we want, what we believe:

(1) We want freedom. We want power to determine the destiny of our Black Community.

(2) We want full employment for our people.

(3) We want an end to the robbery by the white man of our Black Community.

(4) We want decent housing, fit for shelter of human beings.

(5) We want education for our people that exposes the true nature of this decadent American society. We want education that teaches us our true history and our role in the present-day society.

(6) We want all Black men to be exempt from military service.

(7) We want an immediate end to POLICE BRUTAL-ITY and MURDER of Black people.

(8) We want freedom for all Black men held in federal, state, county and city prisons and jails.

(9) We want all Black people when brought to trial to be tried in court by a jury of their peer group or people from their Black Communities, as defined by the Constitution of the United States.

(10) We want land, bread, housing, education, clothing, justice and peace.

Johnny took an increasingly prominent role in George's meetings. One night, a prisoner was discussing Franz

Fanon's *The Wretched of the Earth.* "Fanon says violence is okay," the prisoner said.

George looked over at Johnny. "I don't think Comrade John got that interpretation."

"Fanon isn't saying violence is okay," Johnny explained. "He's saying that given the established set of conditions that exist, if people are going to survive, they must adopt this philosophy. They are not at the negotiating table.

"But violence is corrupting," continued Johnny, pointing out other sections of the book where Fanon demonstrated how violence corrupted the oppressor.

George nodded at his prize student, then they broke for the night.

George and Johnny's view of the world was shaped almost entirely by the stories in the Black Panther paper that was smuggled into prison by visitors. From the reporting there, it seemed that the outside world had changed dramatically since their incarcerations and that the rules of prison were now the rules of the world. Violence seemed rampant and oppression undisguised. In the summer of 1969, they watched the news accounts of government assaults on Panthers and Panther strongholds.

In August 1969, the F.B.I. arrested Black Panther Party cofounder Bobby Seale and charged him with the April 1969 New Haven murder of Alex Rackley, a New York Panther thought to be a police informant. Seale's only possible connection to the event was a speaking engagement at Yale University two days before the murder. Other Panthers had confessed to the murder, and the chief of New Haven police later admitted there was no real evidence against Seale. Nevertheless, prosecutors decided to jail Seale on the ostensible grounds that he had ordered Rackley's murder. This meant that both Panther founders—Newton and Seale— were out of commission behind bars. The incident caused

Yale president Kingman Brewster to express publicly his doubt that a black revolutionary "could get a fair trial anywhere in the United States."

In Chicago, the charismatic leader of the Illinois Black Panthers, Fred Hampton, was succeeding in attracting hundreds of gang members to the Chicago chapter. His followers were devoted to him, waking early in the cold Chicago winter to exercise to his chants of "I ain't going to die slipping on no ice. I ain't going to die in no airplane crash. I'm going to die for the People. 'Cause I love the People. Power to the People! Power to the People!"

The F.B.I. paid Hampton's bodyguard, William O'Neal, to provide the Bureau with a detailed floor plan of Hampton's apartment, indicating where Hampton slept. On December 3, 1969, police fired at least ninety rounds into the apartment, dozens right into Hampton's bed, spilling his blood over his pregnant girlfriend. Only one shot was fired out in response to the police attack. Hampton died, as well as Panther defense captain Mark Clark. The police beat and arrested the surviving Panthers.

Four days after the Chicago raid, police descended upon the Los Angeles office of the Black Panther Party, again in the middle of the night. One big difference was that the Los Angeles Panthers fought back. Blacks from the community heard the shots and flowed into the street to bear witness to the police action. When Panthers inside the headquarters were arrested and charged with conspiracy to assault police officers, over a thousand people gathered at City Hall in protest.

To George and Johnny, the developments outside prison underscored what they had been reading and discussing: Somehow, some way, you had to be prepared to fight back.

chapter
fifteen

On January 13, 1970, Johnny watched as a white inmate with a tool box fixed a light fixture farther down the tier. He thought about how when he'd arrived at Soledad, he had again asked for a job as an electrician, and had been assigned to the laundry instead. The electrical jobs were open only to whites.

The unlock came and Johnny walked to the laundry room. Although it was the middle of winter, it was like a furnace in there, hot beyond anything he'd felt in Los Angeles, reminding him of his early Mississippi summers. He sneaked a clean towel from the dryer to wipe the sweat off his forehead, then hid it under the counter where he worked. Tonight he would join George, Hutch, and a few others at a strategy meeting. They were pressuring the administration to have a Black Culture Night, to allow Black Panthers and white radicals from the outside to visit the prison. And they were continuing to push the administration to free W. L. Nolen from O Wing.

As Johnny fell into the rhythm of folding T-shirts—sleeves turned in, bottoms turned up—guards on O Wing asked the maximum-security inmates to strip down, get their towels, and get ready to go to the yard. After months of sitting in their cells, the inmates would be allowed outside. Twelve black inmates and twelve white inmates would exercise together. They were led into the sally port, a completely barred, double-locked cage at the end of the tier. Each one was strip searched to assure that he carried no weapons.

Johnny pulled the contraband towel out and mopped his forehead, then grabbed a pile of work shirts to fold. Most of the shirts were in bad shape, with sweat stains under the arms that never seemed to disappear. But there was one in this batch that was newer than the rest. Johnny was thinking about trying to smuggle it out to Hutch when a rifle shot echoed through the air.

Bam! Bam! Bam! More shots.

He dropped the shirt and ran to the window.

In the distance, in the O Wing exercise yard, black inmates were gathered around three black bodies on the ground. One was clearly dead, but two seemed to be bleeding and alive. Other blacks were rushing toward them.

"Stay in your places or I'll shoot," shouted a gun tower guard.

"We've got to help them!" an inmate shouted back. "They'll die!"

Blood poured out of the wounded inmates, and they bled to death before help was summoned. The three bodies were loaded onto gurneys—Cleveland Edwards, Alvin Miller, and W. L. Nolen.

Guards started yelling for the mainline inmates to get away from the windows and lock up. As his cell door closed behind him, Johnny thought about how he'd seen prisoners maim, mutilate, and murder other prisoners. He had seen a sort of insanity that had mostly been inspired by racial antagonisms. But the violence he had witnessed that day scared him more than anything had before. The Soledad Prison administration had murdered people in their care. They had finally gotten their "prize," W. L. Nolen.

It's clear, thought Johnny, that the people who are in control of my life, the keepers, are hunters.

Johnny slept no more than three hours a night in the two days after the Nolen incident. The scene in the yard, freeze-framed in his mind, haunted his thoughts. Everything that had happened in prison before that seemed like silly schoolboy games. Knifings—killings—he'd seen plenty of those at Tracy and Soledad, but they'd all seemed to be individual, independent acts, battles between inmates. After the administration killed Nolen, Johnny went back over those earlier incidents. Maybe the administration was behind them, too, pulling the strings, creating opportunities for violence, failing to step in quickly enough when hostilities began to boil over.

"We've got to get people to see what's going on here," Johnny said to Hutch. "The administration *killed* people, and they're still in power."

"I heard the D.A.'s been here, investigating," replied Hutch.

In the days that followed Nolen's death, the black prisoners went on hunger strikes and burned furniture. Fist fights between black inmates and white inmates erupted throughout the prison. Whenever he left his cell, Johnny stuffed a magazine under his shirt to provide a little protection against knife thrusts.

Three days after the shooting, on January 16, 1970, Johnny, George, and the other blacks crowded to the front of the television rooms on the various tiers to hear the news report of the Monterey County district attorney's investiga-

tion. The gun-rail guard who had killed the black prisoners,
O. G. Miller, claimed that a fight had broken out between
black and white inmates and that he had fired into the scuf-
fle to separate the warring factions. This didn't make sense
to Johnny. The inmates were unarmed and unlikely to do
serious damage to each other. And Johnny had seen where
the bodies had fallen. They were spread out around the
yard, undercutting any claim that they had been felled by
shots aimed into a single fight.

The profile of the district attorney appeared on the
screen. Although the investigation was not over, he said, he
personally felt that the killings of the unarmed black men
had been "probable justifiable homicide by a public officer
in the performance of his duty."

That night, a Soledad guard, Officer John V. Mills, was
thrown to his death from the highest tier in Y Wing. As he
hit the ground, inmates clapped. "They got the pig! They
got the pig!"

Near Mills's body, guards found a note: "One down, two
to go."

The word spread quickly to Johnny's wing, E Wing. He sat
on his cot and closed his eyes. It must have been George, he
thought. The revolution had begun. And when it came time
to choose sides, it was clear to Johnny where he'd be.

Johnny wrote a letter to the mothers of the three slain
black men, which was published in the Black Panther newspaper:

"Mothers of Many Sons!" it began, "Why is it that you shed
tears? Why is there a wistful tone in your voice? Do you not
hear *me*—your son calling out to you, calling out with words
of wisdom? Your first sons have not been lost. On the con-
trary, you have gained ten Alvins, ten Clevelands and ten
W. L.'s and, what's more, hundreds and hundreds lay in

wait to fill our spots if the air rings with the sound of the oppressor. . . ."

Then he sent Cano a note: "This shit is real. You have to take it seriously. The pigs are killing people. If there's going to be killing, we should die fighting back. Don't let just black blood run. Let white blood run, too. Let white pigs' blood run."

chapter
sixteen

A few days after Mills's death, some of the black prisoners wanted to make a hit on the Aryan Brotherhood. Hutch advised caution. "Let's ask George about it," he said. At that point, George was locked up in O Wing, awaiting transfer to San Quentin.

That night, Hutch gathered up the ingredients for Pruno, a rot-gut prison moonshine that the men made in their cells. He took care to make it so potent that the odor wafted down the tier. The guards naturally smelled it, busted him, and threw him into O Wing. It was exactly what he'd wanted.

"Comrade," he said to George, "some of the brothers want to take out some Aryans."

"No," said George, "they're not the ones to blame. Our beef is with the Man. Put a stop to it."

The next day, a black on O Wing was released to the mainline. George sent word back to Johnny, to pass on to the other prisoners, that it was the guards who were the enemy, not the white prisoners.

A few days later, the dead body of William Shull, a forty-year-old white guard, was found in a sports equipment storage shack of the north mainline yard. He'd been slashed apart in forty-two stab wounds. His assailants had left a note: "Two down, one to go."

It took a few weeks before a hit was made on a third guard, Officer Robert McCarthy. He had made the mistake of passing the solitary confinement cell of Hugo Pinell, a Nicaraguan who sided with the blacks. Pinell whispered to the guard. When the officer bent down near the food tray slot to better hear what Pinell was saying, Pinell thrust his arm out of the slot and sliced the guard's throat with a sharpened toothbrush. Later the guard died—due in part to a botched attempt to get him medical care. The Nicaraguan now faced trial for the assault.

Guards had been fearful after the first death, but when the tally reached three, paranoia swept through the prison. The guards walked nervously and tried to stay in pairs. They began busting members of George's group. They put Johnny in solitary confinement on X Wing, where he would be stuck in a cell all day and released only for dinner on the tier.

As Johnny left his cell for dinner the first night, he saw that a brother had been knocked down and some whites were pouring a large pot of scalding soup over him. Johnny moved forward to help him, when a white about thirty pounds heavier than Johnny moved near the victim, blocking Johnny's way.

The white lumbered forward awkwardly, slowly. He swung at Johnny's face, but the blow never connected. Instead, Johnny struck the man's wrist with his forearm and curved his leg around the man, dashing him to the floor.

Johnny turned to move on, but the white rose, using his natural bulk to charge at Johnny. Johnny drove his fist into the man's mouth, breaking and splintering teeth. Then— *pow*—he kicked the man in the ribs. The white fell. At that moment, another inmate came up behind Johnny and swung a metal food tray at Johnny's head. Johnny jumped out of the way, then grabbed him in a Chinese death lock, cutting off his circulation until his arms went limp.

By then, the first white had bounced up for another charge. Johnny shifted his position. The man was weakened and Johnny could have easily taken him out with a chop to the carotid artery. Instead, he punched to daze him. But when the open wedge of his hand connected with the man's jaw, Johnny could feel the bones in his fingers break. He stepped back in pain. A guard on a higher tier pointed his carbine at Johnny.

Johnny heard another guard say, "If he takes another step, shoot."

Hugo Pinell and the brothers on the tier hollered, "Stop walking, Johnny!"

Under normal circumstances, he would have, but the whites on the tier seemed more dangerous than the carbine. With his broken hand, he needed to seek the safety of his cell.

He looked right up into the tower guard's eyes and watched the white guard sweat as he kept walking.

The guard did not fire.

A few days after the fight, there were a number of whites on the X Wing tier, including the one who had attacked Johnny. A guard walked up to Johnny's cell and unlocked it. Then he went to the grille gate area and pulled the lever to take off the deadlock.

Johnny's cell was now open, making him a defenseless target for the Aryan Brotherhood.

Shit, thought Johnny, I'm going to have to break my hand again.

Johnny walked out on the tier. He started walking toward the white, without a plan yet. He had no idea what he would say to the guy, or if he would say anything. Maybe he would just test the water, walk on by.

He came up to him, and stopped. The guy's face looked pretty messed up, where Johnny had hit it the other day.

Then the words slipped out of his mouth. "Are you okay?" Johnny asked the white guy.

He shook his head.

Johnny held up his cast, with a pin sticking out to set his worst break. "I didn't do so great either.

"You know," continued Johnny, "we didn't win here. You're not my enemy."

The guard looked down the tier, disappointed that no one was fighting. He yelled, "Okay, everybody lock up."

chapter
seventeen

The day Johnny was sent back to the mainline, he didn't want to talk to anyone. He just wanted to run down the tiers, across the yard. X Wing had gotten to him. The month of confinement there, in a cell at least twenty-three hours a day, had made his body ache in strange places, made him feel like he'd been folded up into a small cardboard box.

He thought he'd feel better if he ran, but the crushing sense of confinement stayed with him. He passed inmates playing checkers and poker at wooden tables. They looked like old men killing time in city parks. Don't you understand what a sick, cramped world you live in? he wanted to scream at them.

He went into the field house and ran around the perimeter of the gym floor. A white basketball team was playing a black one, but from the looks of it, it was less a game than a race riot. Johnny whizzed around, breaths convulsing his body like sobs. He thought about the white he'd hurt.

George's teachings had opened Johnny's mind so he could see things in a different way. We can't just keep destroying each other, Johnny told himself. We're playing right into the pigs' hands. We've got to find some way to unite the prison.

Now that George had been moved to San Quentin, there was a chance that the Soledad group would fragment without his strong leadership or, worse yet, start infighting to see who would gain control. To avert those possibilities, George got a letter smuggled out to the group, anointing his successor.

At that time Johnny was twenty-one years old, slightly built, and hadn't done as much time as the other prisoners. But he'd "learned" prison, just as he had thrown himself into sports. After witnessing that first killing in the hallway at Tracy, he'd honed his senses, so that he was primed and could feel what was coming down around him before it happened. George recognized that capability and realized that Johnny also had the best sense of where the revolution was going.

"Listen to the kid," the letter said.

The next day, Johnny started spreading the word. He talked to blacks, whites, and Chicanos, saying, "Don't you guys see what's going on? Don't you see the administration is causing the problems we're having? Don't you know that we can't accomplish a goddamned thing in conflict? *Nothing.* You can't win and I can't win. What we need to do is put our heads together, put our voices together, put ourselves together and then say, Now what we want are these things."

Some of the black inmates went along, despite their continued hatred of whites, because it was expedient to get a large enough mass to take on the administration. There were few blacks or whites in prison who had lived outside of a segregated setting or ever had the chance to know someone of another race. For Johnny, though, it was different. He'd seen both sides.

After a few weeks, Johnny was making some headway; a loose coalition was forming. Then a gang of black weight lifters robbed four white prisoners of their canteen, the items that they would wait all month to get from the commissary. The whites put the word out: Payback was coming.

Johnny called together a few of George's other men. They got the canteen lists that the whites had taken to the commissary, so they knew exactly which items had been taken in the robberies. Johnny got the blacks on his tier to donate cartons of cigarettes. Then he asked one of them to go around the prison and trade the cigarettes for coffee, soap, toothpaste, and the other items that were on the lists. It took the inmate a whole day before he was able to return with four bags, each with a list attached to it.

Johnny took the bags to the victims. "I know this may not be what you want to hear, but I am apologizing for people doing this sort of thing. It's not right and won't be accepted. You just have to believe that."

The whites were suspicious. No one does this, they thought. No one makes amends.

Then Johnny went to the leader of the black gang. "I want to tell you that you came very close to starting a lot of bullshit in this prison, I mean, a lot of racial garbage. But it's not going to happen. It's not going to happen because the agenda that we're on here is one of solidarity, so that we don't have to duck and dodge every day worrying about some racial bullshit."

"We're not joining with any white motherfuckers," the man replied. "We want separation in the prison, just like we want the five Southern states to be given to the blacks."

"You know," said Johnny, "you really have to be absolutely crazy to even suggest some shit like that."

"Who the fuck do you think you are?"

"It's not me," replied Johnny. "I'm just here telling you what the whole prison wants. And if you go up against that, I don't think that's one you can win, right or wrong."

. . .

His threat had sounded good, Johnny realized as he walked back to his cell, but he really had no power to keep people in line. The prison officials, of course, did. They had their goon squad, an assault force who would rush in with tear gas and weapons. Well, he thought, what if I start my own goon squad? He knew just the guys to do it. Johnny quickened his pace, seeking out the cells of nine of the toughest cons he knew—three blacks, three whites, two Chicanos, and a Samoan. They were all powerful, burly men, with reputations as fighters. He brought them all to the gym and explained his plan.

"I don't want any mistakes," Johnny told them. "I don't want anybody coming up dead. I don't want you to draw blood from people and I definitely don't want anyone to die."

Johnny looked the group over. "We're delivering a message here," he said, "We're getting ready to take this prison over. We're going to run this prison, you know."

Johnny then put the word out in the prison. No more fighting or other shit. If you got into a fight, you'd have to fight again—because the goon squad would come after you.

In the next week, the squad beat up seven people—six who had been in fights and one who had tried to rape a young guy. Then a silence fell over the prison.

The reprieve from violence allowed Johnny to spend more time riling up inmates, especially the blacks. His recurring message was that prisoners should not fight each other. Their actions should be directed against the administrators, the authorities, the government.

Johnny talked to whites. "It's not just blacks. This is a new movement here, a new energy and power. It's larger than the stupidity of a race riot."

Some of the whites agreed with what Johnny was saying. A group of them came to him and said, "Let's get together and fight the Man." Soon another body was leaving Soledad on a stretcher. Kenneth Conant, a white administrator, had been stabbed to death. Two white inmates were charged.

As the fights between blacks and whites diminished, both sides found a reprieve from the crippling fear. They began trying to figure out how to do things together, how to take their protests to the administration. At first there were small strikes, where a dozen or so prisoners refused to go to work or refused to eat. The administration made some concessions—granting more yard time, approving educational programs. But more importantly, the prisoners themselves were changing. Some were talking about oppression in general, and the struggle they would take up once they were released.

The administration started looking for ways to slow Johnny down. A few times, prison officials transferred Johnny to a different cell. Johnny hated it, because guards would search his cell and make a mess of things. It took weeks for him to get his possessions, and sometimes they never arrived.

Each cell that Johnny lived in looked disorganized and cramped. He had piles of books, handwritten drafts of letters, and various items from the commissary, such as Velveeta cheese. But on closer inspection, there was a rhyme and reason to it all. He was compulsive about knowing where anything was at any moment. He even kept a correspondence log—detailing when he received a letter, and when he wrote back, and when the recipient acknowledged his response. All letters leaving the prison and coming in— other than correspondence with one's own lawyer—were censored by prison officials. If an inmate wrote a complaint about prison life, that was enough to stop the letter in its tracks. If the outsider tried to send a prisoner a message that was remotely incendiary in tone, the letter never made it through.

With the success of their protests, Johnny and some others began to plan more systematically. They prepared a list of demands. They wanted better sanitation, better food, and an end to the racism on O Wing. They wanted a change in the rule that a prisoner had to be acquainted with someone for six months before he could receive letters or be visited by that person.

The list was surreptitiously passed from inmate to inmate, and the demands grew. Johnny looked it over in his cell and copied down a phrase he particularly liked, a quote from an international treaty on human rights, the Geneva Accord.

When the document met the inmates' approval, they posted the six-page list of demands, signed by the Soledad Revolutionary Front, and went on strike. The support was astounding. One thousand inmates—nearly half the prison—participated. They boycotted their prison jobs, broke windows, set fire to furniture, and plugged the shower drains in their housing units.

Prisoners at Folsom expressed solidarity, crippling that prison with an eighteen-day work strike. Fay Stender geared up to provide legal aid to any inmates who were disciplined for their role in the strikes.

Fay was not representing just Huey Newton these days. She was George Jackson's lawyer as well. As the most likely suspect in the Mills killing, George had been put in the hole—and then transferred to San Quentin with two other suspects, John Clutchette and Johnny's old friend, Fleeta Drumgo. The three, quickly dubbed the Soledad Brothers by the media, faced the gas chamber.

Fay realized that the legal work itself was just a small component of the overall case strategy. She'd already begun traveling around the state, addressing college audiences and

community groups, trying to solicit volunteers and dona-
tions for the case. Using networks set up in the antiwar
movement, Fay was bringing numerous white activists to
the cause of prison rights. She talked luminaries Julian
Bond, Pete Seeger, Jane Fonda, Noam Chomsky, Lawrence
Ferlinghetti, Allen Ginsberg, Benjamin Spock, and Linus
Pauling into serving on the defense committee, and
attracted top students right out of law school and an array of
investigators and legal researchers. For many, helping prisoners became a symbol of breaking out of whatever box that
they themselves were confined in.

Fay was so persuasive that volunteers flocked to the committee. The dissatisfaction that people felt about the slow
progress of civil rights and America's aggressive stance in
Vietnam led them to the Soledad Brothers Defense Committee as a way to do something specific to change the system. They could attack the particularly virulent strain of
racism that infected the California prisons. Fay drew it out of
them.

At a Soledad Brothers rally in Los Angeles, she joined
Jackson's mother, Georgia, and sisters, Penny and Frances,
to raise support for the case. In her leather miniskirt and
boots, she passed out a leaflet: "The thousands of black
youth trapped in the prison systems through poverty and
racial prejudice stand before us in the persons of Fleeta
Drumgo, John Clutchette, and George Jackson. The wasted
lives, the brutal inhumanity inherent in the prisons system is
here on trial. These three young men are being routed to
the gas chamber for refusing to bow down, for trying to save
their identities and self-respect. Their lives are in jeopardy
for who they are, not for what they have done. . . ."

"Soledad," Fay told the Los Angeles audience, "is the
Dachau of America." She explained how Soledad promoted
racism, since as long as black inmates and white inmates

were killing each other, they could not join together to challenge prison authorities.

A tall, intense black woman in the audience watched Stender closely as she talked. Fay was animated, energized, coolly intelligent one moment and passionately persuasive the next. The woman, Angela Davis, talked to her after the presentation. Davis was fighting battles of her own with the system, but she was moved enough by what Stender said to make time for this one as well.

Davis had been raised in segregated Birmingham, Alabama, where her friends learned to read "Colored" and "White" before they learned "Look, Dick, look." She was four years old when her parents and a few other black families moved to Center Street in a white neighborhood. So many bombs were directed at the black homes there that the neighborhood became known as Dynamite Hill.

In 1969, the University of California regents, at the instigation of Governor Ronald Reagan, had tried to fire Davis from her job as an assistant professor of philosophy at the University of California in Los Angeles because she had joined the Black Panthers and the Communist Party. She challenged the regents' authority, insisting on due process, citing the U.S. Constitution. She was still teaching, but had learned to check her car for bombs. Sometimes Panthers with guns would escort her home from her classes.

When George Jackson next went to court for a hearing, his mother, brother, and Davis were there, too. Davis was struck by the racist language of the judge. He told the blacks in the audience to quiet down and behave. "You are not at a barbeque," he said.

As the hearing proceeded, George's brother Jonathan got increasingly depressed. Fay Stender was a fabulous lawyer, making motions to change the venue of the trial and to prevent harm to George by the guards inside San Quentin, but the judge didn't seem to want to listen. Every motion denied, Jonathan thought bitterly to himself on the drive home.

Jonathan looked up to Angela, and drew her into long discussions of Marxism and of his brother's case. He offered to be her bodyguard, and began accompanying her to rallies. Media photographers often captured them together, always looking serious, never smiling. Davis, with her large Afro which drooped over her forehead and a plain T-shirt poking out from underneath a denim jacket, marched in protest. At one rally, she carried a sign: SAVE THE SOLEDAD BROS. FROM LEGAL LYNCHING. A few steps behind her was the slender Jonathan, his pained, intelligent eyes peeking out of a face still rounded by childhood plumpness. He carried his own placard: END POLITICAL REPRESSION IN PRISONS.

Reading about the groundswell of outside support for George Jackson and other Black Panther prisoners, Johnny continued the project George had started, lobbying the Soledad administration to sponsor a Black Culture Night, to allow outside activists into prison. His efforts were underscored by pressure from Fay Stender and the many prisoners' rights groups that were springing up in response to the incarcerations of black radicals and various antiwar activists. The administration finally relented. In August 1970, Black Panthers and white militants entered the long corridor for a dinner with Johnny and other politicized prisoners. A few shuddered as they passed the red steel door of O Wing, where Nolen had been killed.

"I do not fear anything anymore," Johnny said to the visitors that evening. "Fear is what the pig has kept us down with, what can he do, kill us? Hell, he's already doing that! I don't expect to go at an old age. I'll die—that is fact, but I'll go down taking heads. If a person is afraid to live on his own terms then this person is already dead."

Their revolutionary drive had gone beyond rhetoric. A group of Black Panthers, joined by a white member of the Students for a Democratic Society, had begun guerrilla training in the Santa Cruz mountains. For everyone connected with the movement, the question of the day was, How far were they willing to go for their beliefs?

chapter
eighteen

On August 7, 1970, George Jackson's seventeen-year-old brother Jonathan walked into the Marin County Civic Center, a rolling, open, peach-colored building designed by Frank Lloyd Wright. He made his way to the Hall of Justice, a series of courtrooms in the middle of the building, and found the one where a black San Quentin inmate, James McClain, was on trial for assaulting a guard. Jonathan was a serious boy, with a facility for math and science, who in a later era might have become a computer whiz. But in this lifetime, he had been training for something else. He idolized his brother George and took seriously George's ideas about revolution. When his brother was transferred to San Quentin to await trial, Jonathan and his mother had moved to Oakland to be closer to him. Living at the Black Panther house there had helped convince him he should live the rhetoric he was hearing.

Jonathan stood quietly at the back of the room for a moment, then pulled out a .38 Browning automatic pistol.

"All right gentlemen, hold it right there," he said. "I'm taking over now."

He told an inmate witness, Ruchell Magee, to free the convicts who were waiting in a holding cell near the courtroom. Then he gave the pistol to McClain and armed himself with a .30 caliber carbine rifle which he had hidden under his trench coat. McClain held his weapon on Judge Harold Hayley.

"We want the Soledad Brothers freed or we'll kill the judge," McClain shouted. To prove his point to the courtroom hostages, he took some material and tape and attached a sawed-off shotgun against the judge's neck, pointing the muzzle at the judge's mouth. With piano wire that Jonathan had brought, McClain strung the assistant district attorney, Gary Thomas, and three female jurors together.

Jonathan and the prisoners could have escaped readily with the hostages, were it not for a newspaper photographer who had rushed to the courthouse when he heard the police radio for all available units. Instead, they stopped and posed, giving guards from nearby San Quentin enough time to arm themselves and travel to the courthouse. Unlike the local police, prison guards had a strict no-hostage policy. If they had to kill one, two, or even one hundred or two hundred innocent bystanders to keep one prisoner from escaping, they were instructed to do so.

"Tell them we want the Soledad Brothers released at twelve o'clock," McClain told the photographer.

"We are the new revolutionaries," Jonathan Jackson said.

Jackson, McClain, and two other black inmates herded the white hostages toward a rented van. By then, more than a hundred policemen and guards were assembled in the nearby parking lot and along the escape route. The sheriff told his men not to fire—because of the hostages—and readied a helicopter to trace their escape. But before the van could leave the parking lot, the San Quentin guards opened fire and the police followed suit. The shotgun fired, blasting Judge Hayley's face off his skull. Within nineteen seconds, Jackson, McClain, and another inmate were also dead.

Ruchell Magee was wounded, and prosecutor Gary Thomas paralyzed.

Investigators picked their way through the carnage in the van, confiscated the weapons, and immediately traced the serial numbers. A .38 caliber Browning automatic and a .30 caliber Plainfield carbine had been purchased by Angela Davis, who disappeared shortly after the incident.

The news of Jonathan's death passed from cell to cell at Soledad. The inmate who told Johnny said, "Comrade George is going to explode." Johnny, too, expected a violent retaliation. But George, sealed off in the Adjustment Center at San Quentin, was channeling his energy into a wider-reaching scheme.

The panic caused by Jonathan Jackson's actions reverberated through the prison system. Guards combed through cells to find any evidence of inmates' revolutionary leanings.

Johnny was at lunch when two members of the prison goon squad reached his cell. They moved aside a pile of magazines and the basketball Johnny no longer used. The two men worked rapidly, reading several dozen handwritten pages.

That afternoon, Johnny was summoned before a three-person disciplinary committee, which charged him with having "manifest militant political and social views." The proof of his guilt: his handwritten copy of a section of the Geneva Accord human rights treaty and a letter he had written to Helen.

Johnny reached for the letter, but the committee member refused to let him see it. "This is confidential," he said.

"Wait a minute," said Johnny. "Are we on the same page?

You're telling me that you don't want me to read what I wrote. I'm telling you that what I wrote was nothing and you say it was horrible. And I'm saying let me see what you find so horrible. What are we talking about here?"

"You talk about communism in this letter."

"Come on now," said Johnny. "I copied that definition right out of a junior college textbook—*Ideas in Conflict.*"

"Did you say anything else?" asked a committee member.

"Yes, I said that for some people in the United States, living in poverty, it may not be such a bad idea."

Johnny was taken to O Wing, where W. L. Nolen had been kept. Some of the inmates on the tier seemed to have gone around the bend from their time there—they were screeching hysterically, nonsensically. He sat on the bed of his new cell, watching the roaches scamper behind the toilet. He assessed his provisions. There was no soap in the cell, no towels. He started tearing off the sleeves of his jumpsuit to use as toilet paper.

He felt like an angry zoo animal, totally under control of his keepers. He was resentful—the administration wasn't even trying to keep up the appearance of playing by its rules, putting him in here just for having copied a human rights document and written a letter to his adoptive mother. Knowing he'd need all his power to survive this situation, he faded back onto his cot and started concentrating on the comings and goings on the tier. Wordlessly, he assessed each guard who went by, trying to figure out the guard's strengths and weaknesses. At night, his dreams were a series of dizzying *katas.*

For the first few days he was left alone, with no word about what was in store for him. Then, one afternoon, he saw a guard push an inmate into the wall and knee his back. Johnny pitched a cup of coffee at the guard's eyes. "You'll be

sorry," the guard said to him, with such calm relish that
Johnny wondered if he'd been set up.

That night, two guards stood outside Johnny's cell.
Pointing a tear gas canister at him, they ordered him to
undress to his underwear. Then they walked him down the
tier to the strip cell. "Welcome to the hole," one said.

The six-by-eight foot strip cell had no bed and a hole in
the floor instead of a toilet. Its barred door had a three-by-
ten-inch slot for guards to shove meals through. Except at
mealtimes, a second steel door remained shut over that, cutting off all light. Nearly naked, Johnny was not allowed to
take any of his books or possessions in the cell. Dried shit
from generations of prisoners coated the floor and parts of
the walls.

At night, unable to see the hole, Johnny groped with his
hand through the slimy filth. After just a few days, the hole
overflowed and he was unable to walk across the cell without
soiling himself. Once a week a guard would come by to hose
down the cell, but sometimes Johnny would refuse—since
the guard didn't provide scrub brushes or cleanser, the
water would never really clean it, it would just heighten the
smell for a few days.

He wondered if this was what it was like to be dead—to
live in your own shit, to have *nothing* that could redeem you
as a human being. He hallucinated. Of course, in the hole,
it really didn't matter, any more than night mattered from
day.

After a week, Johnny decided to deal with the strip cell by
refusing prison food, instead taking small sips of liquid to
keep up his strength, postponing the need to defecate. The
total blackness of the cell became like a dimmed theater for
him into which he could project his thoughts. He tried to
imagine himself outside prison as a Panther. He was weak,
but angry and focused. Slowly, he started to chant the

Panthers' Ten Point Program: "We want freedom. We want power. . . . We want land, bread, housing, education, clothing, justice and peace."

There was a legal limit to how long inmates could be kept in a strip cell, although it was not always followed. Johnny did thirty days, then went back to solitary confinement in O Wing, to an announcement that the exercise yard was open again.

He looked at the line of other men being strip-searched to exercise. Problem, he thought: There were seven blacks and one white. Four of the blacks he knew pretty well, but the other two were wild cards. It smelled like a setup. If any of the brothers approached the white, it would be an excuse for the gun rail guard to fire. Even running around in a game of handball could be interpreted by the sniper as menacing.

"Let's park it," said Johnny, sitting down in the yard. Two of his buddies joined him, as well as one of the blacks he didn't know. Soon all eight—including the white—were sitting in a circle, talking about the guards.

Johnny looked up at one of them on the gun rail, then looked over to a spot on the concrete near the punching bag. It was hard to believe that Nolen's murder had occurred there less than a year earlier. Johnny had begun to feel that Soledad was changing, but now here he was, in Nolen's shoes, like the next duck up in a carnival shooting gallery.

He turned to the men and began an animated discussion of the Cuban revolution. He was careful not to gesture with his arms, nor to make any provocative moves.

The guards called them all back in before the allotted hour was over.

. . .

As the weeks passed, the confining quarters of O Wing began to torment Johnny. He was a physical person, usually active, and his body was cramping up from being stuck in a seven-by-eight-foot cell twenty-three to twenty-four hours a day. He had no way to use the muscles that sports and Iron Palm had developed in him. In early 1971, Johnny was admitted to the prison hospital with a paralyzing headache. He blacked out, and woke up irrational and incoherent.

A psychiatrist, Dr. Frank Rundle, was at the hospital when they brought Johnny in. Johnny was delusional and writhing in pain. Rundle wrote of the incident: "What he describes as blackouts I tentatively concluded were what we would term dissociative episodes which are not a neurological epileptic sort of manifestation but are rather a defensive operation of the mind when the anxiety and tension level becomes too high to deal with."

A prison doctor administered painkillers and sent Johnny back into his bleak prison-within-a-prison. Over the next few months, Johnny's headaches took him to the institution's hospital a dozen times.

When the painkillers could no longer touch the head-aches, Johnny wrote to George, and had the letter smuggled out. He asked George to help him get a lawyer.

A few weeks after Johnny sent his letter, the guards announced that he had a visitor. They cuffed him and led him into a small room. He looked around, struck by what seemed to him to be about ninety-six layers of drab olive paint on the walls. He felt like that himself, layer after layer of prison days crusted upon him.

He wasn't in any shape to make a great impression on whoever this visitor was, he thought. He stank. He had used so much of his jumpsuit as toilet paper that only the bottom half was left. It was filthy, as were his bare feet. He wore a five-inch-wide leather strap around his waist, with his hands cuffed to the front and a lock in the back. To cover his filthy chest, he had been given a brand-new spanking-white T-shirt.

On the way to the visiting room, Johnny was stopped for a search. Usually in a search the inmate would put his hands against the wall. But Johnny's hands were cuffed to the leather belt around his waist, so he couldn't balance himself in that way. The guard pushed Johnny forward, smashing his face into the wire mesh fence.

He was wiping his bloody nose against the short sleeve of his new shirt when a guard ushered a dark-haired woman into the room. She stuck out her hand. "I'm Fay Stender."

Johnny had no idea what Fay looked like. This could be a setup. "Let's see some identification," he said.

She opened her wallet and pulled out a driver's license.

He smiled. "Hi, Fay. I'm sorry, I didn't know who you were."

"I got your letter. Are you okay?"

Johnny nodded. "What's the word from George?"

"His case is coming along. He said to tell you, 'Keep the faith. Don't let anything hold you back.' Now tell me what's happening here."

"They got me in the hole. I didn't have a write-up. They keep taking me to committee and giving me some new classification, but no write-up. The only reason I'm in the hole is I had a copy of something from the Geneva Accord. That's from the United Nations, you know. They're saying it's a crime to have something from the United Nations."

Fay's intelligent eyes were warm and supportive. "I understand the problem. But I'm gearing up for George's trial and I'm not going to be able to handle your case personally. I'll get a lawyer from my office, Elaine Wender, to try to get you moved to a less strict facility, where you could be put back on the mainline. Elaine's smart, she's on top of it, and I'll be working with her. George wants you to know I'm looking after you, too."

"George calls you his 'small and mighty mouthpiece.'"

Fay smiled. "And he tells me you don't back off, that even if the system says, 'We'll crush you,' your attitude is 'Kill me if you can, not if you want to.'"

Fay shook his cuffed hand again before she left the room. She had stopped referring to prisoners as her "clients," calling them "comrades" instead. She told friends she felt most alive when she was in prison, in drab rooms like these, confronted by the intensity of the lives unadorned. She was spending eighteen hours or more a day now on prison rights issues, using some of the resources she'd raised in the context of the Soledad Brothers case to help the other brave men who were rearing up against their oppressors. She had little patience with the petty problems of people on the outside. They meant nothing compared to the life-and-death struggle here.

She'd helped George publish a book of his poetic, enraged letters, *Soledad Brother*, which had become a best-seller in a number of countries. Sacks of mail poured in for him each day. There were now three Soledad Brothers Defense Committee offices—in San Francisco, San Jose, and Santa Cruz—operating like political campaign headquarters. Volunteers worked with the media, initiated fund-raising drives, and undertook community surveys to determine which types of people might be prejudiced against the Brothers if they served on a jury. Fay recognized that the volunteers came from two distinct camps. Half were drawn to the case because they believed that George had not killed the guard. The other half were there because they thought he had.

George and his codefendants had been moved to San Quentin, but to collect evidence, she needed to go to Soledad. She wanted to interview other inmates to start building the defense case.

The guards were chilly to her as they led her into O Wing for the first time, a few weeks after Mills' murder. Some of the inmates knew her from her work for Huey Newton, whom she had managed to get released from prison after winning the appeal in his case. Others admired her for taking George's case. "Fay!" "Fay!" "Mrs. Stender!" Various inmates were yelling at once.

She worked her way down the cell block, sticking her hands into the food slots to shake hands with each inmate.

When the guard noticed what she was doing, he rushed down to her side. "Don't!" he hissed. "They'll cut your hand off!"

She lifted her chin, walked past him, and stuck her hand in the slot of the next cell.

That was the difference between her and the guards, she thought. She felt prisoners were people.

Fay came to Soledad often to get information for George's defense, and in each of her following visits, she spent a few minutes with Johnny. She brought him books that he wanted and cajoled prison authorities to grant extended mail privileges so that outside radicals could write to him. To Johnny, she seemed to be a miracle worker.

In May 1971, the prison classification committee met to determine where Johnny should be placed next. This had happened five times in the months since Johnny had been confined in O Wing. The first two times, Johnny's hopes had been raised by the thought that he might be sent back to the mainline. As six months passed and he remained on O Wing, he began to think of the meetings as just a sham. He no longer bothered to speak. Even when he had tried to, at first, the committee members just ignored him, as if he were some beast that didn't understand human speech. Lawyers were not allowed at the hearing, so neither Fay nor her associate could attend to make his case for him.

Johnny looked at the three white committee members at the table. They were talking to each other, but watched him out of the corner of their eyes. Johnny wondered what they thought he could do. His hands were chained to the leather waist cinch, his ankles joined by leg irons. There was a wall of three guards between his chair in the corner and the table.

"What about San Quentin?" a committee member suggested.

Johnny thought that would be far-fetched. Only the real hard-core guys, like guard killers, were there. And not even all of them. Hugo Pinell was still here at Soledad. All they have on me, thought Johnny, is a few minor infractions.

Another person mentioned the prison at San Luis Obispo—called CMC, the California Men's Colony—where Huey Newton had been housed until his release just two days before the shootout at the Marin County Courthouse. All three looked annoyed that they had to deal with Johnny at all. He sensed that they wished he'd just disappear.

"Let's give it to a classification counselor for a report." The speaker nodded to the guards, who tipped Johnny out of his chair and returned him to his cell.

The counselor's subsequent report said that San Quentin was inappropriate. He warned against sending the twenty-one-year-old Johnny to a stricter facility, like the Adjustment Center at San Quentin, on the grounds that it would "in essence turn him into a long-term segregation case with no possibility for productive program involvement for a prolonged period of time." But Johnny was a Black Panther, which automatically classified him as dangerous.

Two guards approached his cell a few weeks later. "You're being transferred." They gave him something to eat and drink and then put him on the bus.

"Where you going?" asked a prisoner who had already boarded. Often the buses made several prison stops.

"CMC," replied Johnny.

The driver turned around and looked at him. "This bus only makes one more stop. You're headed for San Quentin."

chapter
nineteen

As the bus pulled up at San Quentin, Johnny was struck by how menacing the complex looked. Unlike the army-barracks appearance of Tracy or even Soledad, San Quentin was a nineteenth-century stone structure, surrounded by a twenty-five-foot-high wall, conjuring up images of dungeons and death.

There was a smirk on the escort guard's face as he took Johnny through the prison. It was late afternoon and Johnny was getting the last glimpse of the outdoors that he would get for a long time. They were walking down a path through the main prison yard, surrounded by the imposing stone wall, patrolled from three gun towers. Beyond the wall there was a twelve-foot-high chain-link fence.

The guard put a key into the door to the Adjustment Center. They entered a foyer, which was sealed off from the two ground-floor rows of tiers by a sliding barred gate. To the right of the foyer was the door to a kitchen, next to that the sergeant's office, and further on a stairway to cells on the second and third floors.

A guard inside the Adjustment Center ordered Johnny to strip down. He conducted a full body search, even though Johnny had been strip-searched before he left Soledad and again as he entered San Quentin. Johnny tried to ignore the guard's finger in his rectum and get a sense of what was going on down the tiers. The light was so bad, he could hardly see anyone in the cells.

The search completed, Johnny dressed and was led down the North Tier, the one furthest to his left. This is like a sardine can, he thought, men shoved in small cells surrounded by metal and muck. As his eyes adjusted, he could see that one inmate was using a toilet, another was setting his mattress on fire, and a third was flooding his cell. A guard had teargassed one belligerent inmate, and gas burned Johnny's lungs as he entered cell 5. He blinked his eyes several times as the two guards disappeared out the grille gate.

"Stick your hand out the food slot," a familiar voice called out of the adjoining cell.

Johnny did, and felt something cool touch his palm. He pulled his hand back into the cell and found a broken half of a contraband mirror. He stuck his hand back out and angled the mirror at his neighbor in cell 4. There was George Jackson, with his half, smiling back at Johnny's reflection.

"I'm sorry about your brother," Johnny said.

"He was a manchild, a true revolutionary," replied George. "We need hundreds more like him."

Even through the distortions of the cheap mirror, Johnny could see the sadness in George's eyes. George had always looked like someone who could soar—Johnny remembered his shock that someone George's size could match him for speed. But now gravity seemed to have more force. George carried a heavier weight.

Johnny's eyelids drooped and he stripped to his shorts for some rest. Before he had boarded the prison bus that morning for the transfer, a guard had handed him a glass of water. Twenty minutes later, on the bus, his muscles had begun to sag. Bastards! he thought, they drugged me for the trip! He hadn't wanted to give in to the trick. He'd willed his body to stay firm and walk straight. Now he was exhausted.

He laid his head back, but the noise on the tier chased sleep away. He'd gotten used to the Soledad noises, but here he couldn't identify those signaling danger from those of the routine. Well, he couldn't learn it all tonight. He picked through the pile of clothes he had dropped in the corner, pulled out his dirty socks, and looped them over his ears like earmuffs.

He drifted into sleep for about an hour, then woke in a sea of sweat from the hot cell. He snatched the socks off his ears, thinking that the wool next to his cheeks was aggravating his heat. He walked over to the sink and turned on the cold water. Sometimes if you let it run through the night it would cool a cell a fraction of a degree, enough to make it seem more tolerable. Plus, the sound of the water washed away a few of the noises on the tier.

Over the next few weeks Johnny was surprised as George started talking about growing up in Los Angeles and resenting his mother for buying into the women's-magazine view of life. He talked about Jonathan and about how much his mother had changed since Jonathan's death. A reporter had asked Mrs. Jackson, "Do you approve of this incident?"

She had replied, "I'm a black American. I'm not wanted in this country. Black and Mexican prisoners are always alone in court. George was in court three times and I didn't even know. I wasn't notified. These men stand there alone. Nobody cares whether they live or die. They bring them up five or six at a time. They run them through like a washing machine. Jonathan felt like what he did was justice. If you can't get justice one way, get it another. Nobody cares about you if you're black and poor. Jonathan did what every black man and white man should do—try to do something about it."

"She finally understands," George told Johnny.

He paused, as if waiting for Johnny to talk about his own family. "Didn't you grow up in L.A., too?"

"Yeah, near Watts." But that's not the whole story, Johnny thought. He remembered all those fights when he was a kid in Los Angeles. Shit, he thought, I probably came out of the womb with my fists up. Or at least I should have, given what I was taken home to.

And I'm still fighting, trying to get my licks in first. Not telling anyone about Ann because they might use it against me. But what about George? He might understand.

"I came to L.A. when I was six. Before that, I lived in Jackson, Mississippi."

He started talking quietly; then the words and feelings began to flow with great force. He poured out the whole story. His black father, white mother. Being given away.

He stood tensely, searching George's expression for a reaction.

George looked intently into his mirror. "People must have hassled you because of your light skin," George said to him.

Johnny turned and wrinkled his brow. "Yeah, when I was a kid." He thought about what it was like in L.A. when the other boys called him Piss Skin.

"I got shit too, especially with this red hair," said George. "I remember when I first went to court. I was fifteen and my whole family was there. The judge said how light-skinned we were and how lucky I was not to be blacker. He said, 'Families like this go farther than the real dark families. People take that into consideration.' I told my ma I wished he'd sent me to jail rather than say that."

George asked him, "How do you feel about your mother?"

Johnny looked George squarely in the eye again. "I hate her."

"Come on, you don't hate her."

"I think I do."

"You don't hate her, you really love your mother."

Johnny was pissed. How could George tell how Johnny felt about someone George had never met? But George was clever. He gave Johnny examples of how Johnny couldn't really bring himself to hate whites. "You don't really hate whites, or you wouldn't have given those canteen items back to the whites. You wouldn't have come up with other ways when our brothers suggested violence against the honkies. You can't bring yourself to hate whites because to hate whites is to hate your mother."

George was excited. His eyes glowed. "Comrade, you feel bad and you really shouldn't feel bad. You're lucky. You have one of the most unique situations that a human being could be in."

What the fuck is he talking about, lucky? thought Johnny. All the shit I've been through.

George continued. "You've been on both sides of the fence. Do you know what I would give to have been on both sides of the fence, to understand both sides?

"With that background, you can be a leader. It's not just the Panthers now. It's whites like the Weathermen and SDS. I've got to get out and be a part of it."

"How?"

"It can be done." George pulled in his mirror, signaling the end of the conversation.

What did he mean? Johnny asked himself. Release through the legal system, like Huey Newton? Or some sort of Panther-rigged escape?

Johnny tried to imagine where he'd go if he got out. Now that Johnny Sr. was dead, he had no desire to go to L.A.—he didn't need Helen's reproachful eyes, and his high school girlfriend was probably married, with a pile of kids by

now. No, he'd go to Oakland. He'd take up arms with the
Panthers. Like George was saying, revolution was just
around the corner.

"They are going to murder me," George told Johnny the
next day.

"I don't believe the state has the nerve, given your
visibility," replied Johnny.

"The obvious," replied George, "is often the most over-
looked."

The guards hated George even more now that his best-
selling book had focused outsiders' attention on the racist
treatment of black prisoners. As a result of his allegations,
the Marin County grand jury was now investigating prison
conditions.

George explained to Johnny how a few months earlier, a
white prisoner, Alan Mancino, had filed an affidavit in court
saying that prison officials had threatened to kill him unless he killed George Jackson. They had told Mancino, "We
don't want another Eldridge Cleaver," referring to a recent
parolee from Soledad who had joined the Panther Party and
given voice to black rage in a best-selling book, *Soul on Ice.*

He also told Johnny about the isolation cells in the
Adjustment Center, which could be sealed off with metal
doors so that an inmate could be sensorily deprived and cut
off from communication with others. The previous year,
guards had thrown inmate Fred Billingslea into one such air-
less cell, hurled in tear gas, and locked the metal door.
When they opened it, Billingslea was dead.

George Jackson was now a Black Panther field marshal,
and he made Johnny his lieutenant. Huey Newton issued a
statement about them: "The Panthers who are on the inside

are the leaders of this movement, because inside the oppres-
siveness is unsoftened. We, on the outside, will take our cues
from those on the inside."

Newton was not the only one who felt that way. Groups of
white radicals did as well. The progressive National Lawyers
Guild had made great strides with legal action in the civil
rights arena—pressing to desegregate the New Rochelle
school system, starting the Committee for Legal Assistance
in the South which brought forty-five civil rights cases on
behalf of blacks in Mississippi in the summer of 1964 alone,
and filing an amicus brief to help secure James Meredith's
admission to law school at the University of Mississippi. The
1971 Guild convention resolved to direct programs toward
inmate groups. At Fay Stender's urging, the guild also voted
to open its membership to prisoners who were jailhouse
lawyers.

The following year a Guild conference position paper
stated: "Prisoners are the revolutionary vanguard of our
struggle. When prisoners come out, they will lead us in the
streets because they have experienced the most blatant
oppression that the system can produce." Another Guild
convention paper pointed out that lawyers, because of their
ready access to prisons, could contribute greatly to the
prison movement. "By building organizations of revolutionary people," argued the author, "we can move forward to a
victorious revolution in this country." Other groups echoed
the sentiment. The militant Weather Underground, a spin-
off of the Students for a Democratic Society, used the slogan
"Bring the war home."

George and Johnny were reading as much as they could
in politics and economics so that they could design the new
black communes that would provide food, shelter, and self-
respect in the new order. They often quarreled about how

Johnny (then Larry Michael Armstrong) and his brother, Charles Armstrong, visit Santa in December 1949, when Johnny could still "pass."

Ann Armstrong (*right*), Ann's mother, Johnny, and his brother, Charles, in 1952.

Johnny and Charles celebrate Christmas 1952 in identical cowboy outfits made by their mother, Ann.

Johnny and Charles, also in 1952.

Helen Spain, the former dancer-turned-maid-and-cook who adopted Johnny.

Johnny's adoptive parents, Johnny Spain and Helen Spain (*left*), with a family friend, Eremina Chachere.

Johnny, at age twelve, at his confirmation in Los Angeles in 1961. The smiles that had brightened his face in Mississippi were much less frequent in Los Angeles.

Johnny (*front row, second from left*) on the basketball team of the Catholic Youth Organization in 1964. Too black to be accepted in Mississippi, he was too light-skinned to be accepted by his black teammates in California.

Johnny's cell at San Quentin Prison in 1971.

Johnny in prison, where he found a sense of belonging as part of the Black Panther Party.

Above left: Stephen Bingham, who was accused by guards of smuggling a gun into prison to George Jackson on August 21, 1971. Bingham was indicted with Johnny in the San Quentin Six case, but went underground for fifteen years. He later was acquitted. *Above right*: Bullets found in soap in Johnny's San Quentin cell on August 21, 1971.

For years, Johnny was not allowed to be a prison electrician because he was black. Finally, at Vacaville prison, he was given a chance—and invented a special lighting system that saved lives by preventing inmates from hanging themselves. (*Courtesy Morrie Camhi*)

Johnny and the other San Quentin inmates lay naked and handcuffed on the prison lawn on August 21, 1971, after George Jackson's breakout attempt. (*Courtesy AP Wide World Photos*)

Johnny's mentor, George Jackson, shot dead in the San Quentin prison yard on August 21, 1971, within a few feet of Johnny.

Johnny in chains in the courtroom during the San Quentin Six trial. He was chained in his seat every day during the seventeen-month trial.

Black Panther George Jackson introduced Johnny to martial arts, revolutionary texts, and his first sense of belonging. His fatal shooting by prison guards devastated Johnny.

Under a Black Panther banner, the casket bearing the body of George Jackson is carried to a hearse after funeral services at St. Augustine's Church in Oakland. Over a thousand mourners stood by, giving the black power salute. (*Courtesy UPI/Bettmann*)

Above: Stanford psychology professor Philip Zimbardo explains to Johnny's lawyer Charles Garry how the dehumanizing conditions in prison provoke violence in guards and prisoners alike. (*Courtesy Philip Zimbardo*)
Below: The "San Quentin Six" (*clockwise from upper left*): Fleeta Drumgo, Hugo Pinell, Luis Talamantes, Willie Tate, Davis Johnson, and Johnny Spain. (*Courtesy UPI/Bettmann*)

Beginning in 1972, Black Panther Elaine Brown was a staunch supporter and frequent visitor of Johnny's in prison. In 1974, Huey Newton designated her as chairman of the Black Panther Party. (*Courtesy Elaine Brown*)

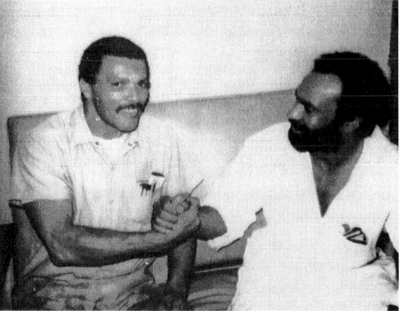

Johnny meets Huey Newton for the first time—in a prison in Vacaville, California, in 1986.

Johnny's lawyer Dennis Riordan, investigator Cathy Kornblith, and Johnny at a legal strategy meeting while the San Quentin Six case was still on appeal, in February 1988. (*Courtesy Susan Homes Schwartzbach*)

Dennis Riordan next to the growing pile of transcripts from Johnny's lengthy 1975-1976 trial. In the subsequent decade, Riordan pursued numerous appeals to the United States Supreme Court before Johnny was eventually released from prison in 1988. (*Courtesy* San Francisco Chronicle)

Johnny and his mother, Ann Armstrong, reunited while Johnny was still in prison, in May 1987.

Angela Davis rejoices with Johnny after he is freed from prison. (*Courtesy Barbara Benane*)

Above: Johnny, Dennis Riordan, and Dennis's daughter, Lisa, leaving Vacaville on March 10, 1988, the day of Johnny's release. (*Courtesy The Vacaville Reporter*) *Below*: Johnny meets his biological father, Arthur Cummings, for the first time.

Charles Armstrong,
Johnny's half-brother,
in 1990.

Johnny makes
peace with his white
mother's sister,
Margaret, after his
mother's funeral
in 1989.

Today Johnny is a community activist in San Francisco.
(*Courtesy Chris Leschinsky Photography*)

best to win the revolution. George believed in guerrilla warfare, hand-to-hand combat in the streets.

"It won't work here," argued Johnny. "People would end up getting hurt and the whole tide could be turned against you. It would be better if we attempted to immobilize processes—communication, transportation, that sort of thing."

George ordered money moved from the Soledad Brothers Defense Committee to men on the outside who he thought would help him break out. Fay Stender came to San Quentin to plead with him not to shut down the Defense Committee. They had a screaming match in the visiting room. She argued that she could free him through the legal system, as she had Newton. He ridiculed her halfway measures and ordered more direct action through the arming of a group of his comrades, like James Carr, who were now on the outside. Stender left the case, and ceded the defense to attorney John Thorne.

A few days later, George came back to his cell from the visiting room and grunted as he removed something from his rectum. He then shoved some small vials up in the doorjamb between his own cell and Johnny's. Johnny had no idea what it was, but from the caution George displayed, using his hands to soften the slamming of his cell door when he returned from a shower, Johnny guessed that it was explosives.

George announced in a *New York Times* interview that his only chance for survival was to escape. To the reporter interviewing him, the prospects must have seemed remote. The walls of the prison were twenty-five feet high and thick enough to support a gun walk on top. Around that same time, one of the guards in the Adjustment Center, Urbano Rubiaco, predicted to his girlfriend that something was going down in the Adjustment Center involving George Jackson.

In prison, surrounded by articles about the Panthers, the SDS, and the Weather Underground, Johnny felt that revolution was brewing on the streets. He expected it would ignite in the next six months, and certainly within three years the entire world would turn over because the United States would be overthrown.

Johnny felt that a complete change in the social order was not only warranted but possible. He was not bent on starting a war; in his mind, the war had already begun. College students dead at Kent State. Groups like the Students for a Democratic Society and the Weathermen springing up around the country to fight repression. He wrote about it in a poem:

> They mean business, I can tell; but so do we and
> Our business is a revolution—let's say life
> So we all understand
>
> We have to keep questioning life
> To know where and who we are
> Lest existence will be void of meaning
>
> Revolution is what we have
> To understand the past
>   change the present
>   shape the future
> With revolution
> The dead aren't dead
> But without it
> The living aren't living.

Johnny was beginning to feel the restless energy of a soldier on the verge of battle. All the signs seemed to point toward revolution, with prisoners as leaders. Other world leaders, like Mao Tse-tung, had been in prison. Johnny and George read Mao's quote:

> People who come out of prison can build up the Country.
> Misfortune is a test of People's fidelity.
> Those who protest at injustice are people of true merit.
> When the prison doors are opened, the real dragon
>   will fly out.

chapter
twenty

On August 21, 1971, Johnny noticed that George seemed nervous. It was understandable, thought Johnny. In two days, he'd begin his trial in the Soledad Brothers case. It would be quite a show. Jean-Paul Sartre and Jean Genet were expected to testify in George's behalf.

The previous day, guards had moved George from cell 4 to cell 6, from one side of Johnny's cell to the other. Generally, when an inmate was moved, his belongings were thoroughly searched. "Comrade," he had said to Johnny, "could you keep a few things in your cell while I move?"

Johnny readily agreed, and took some papers, Velveeta cheese, and Dial soap. George was so preoccupied on the twenty-first that he hadn't yet asked for them back.

"You ready for court Monday?" Johnny asked George.

"That's their idea of a plan. It's not my idea of a plan. My idea of justice isn't a trial. You don't *ask* for justice. You *take* justice."

A few minutes later, the guard at the end of the tier yelled, "Visit for Jackson."

The guard came down the tier and took George to the grille gate at the front of the Adjustment Center. George passed the guard on the other side the four expando folders of legal paper he was taking to the meeting. Then he stripped and pushed his clothes through so that the guard could shake them out and pat the seams. He spread his legs and leaned forward for the rectal search. He ruffled his Afro to demonstrate that there was no contraband hidden in his hair.

He put his clothes back on and was taken to the visiting area by Charles Breckenridge. Lean and brown-haired, at twenty-three Breckenridge was younger than most of the other guards. While many of the guards were retired military men, he was a conscientious objector, who treated the prisoners with a rare dignity. The older guards taunted him, calling him the "hippie officer."

"How's the case going?" Breckenridge asked George.

"It's going fairly well."

A few minutes later, at the end of their fifty-yard walk, Breckenridge turned George over to a black guard, Officer Edward Fleming, who patted George down. There were few black guards in prison and they tended to be extra vigilant, afraid that they'd be blamed if anything went wrong. Adjustment Center inmates were not allowed to visit in the main visiting room. Like the Death Row prisoners, they met their guest in room A or B, small cubicles divided by a partition, with half a desk jutting out on each side of the partition. The guest was led in first and locked into one side. The prisoner was led into the other side and locked in as well. For some prisoners, a grille was closed over the small opening in the partition so that items could not be passed to them by their visitor. For George that day, the screen was left open. Guards could peek in through a window, but they did not continuously monitor the room.

George's visitor was Stephen Bingham, a young white lawyer. That morning, Black Panther John Turner had asked Bingham to visit George. The visit began at 1:22 P.M. and lasted less than an hour.

Officer Fleming was too busy to search George when the visit was over. Back at the grille gate, George began unbuttoning his shirt in preparation for a strip search so that he could be returned to the Adjustment Center.

Johnny heard George coming and stuck his mirror through the bars so he could watch George come through the gate. Johnny was in cell 5; cells 1 through 4, between him and the grille gate, were empty.

What the fuck? thought Johnny.

George's hair was not its usual reddish brown color, but coal black.

George was wearing a wig.

Officer Urbano Rubiaco noticed a metallic glimmer in George's Afro. "What have you got in your hair?" he asked.

"Nothing."

"Shake your hair out."

George ran his fingers lightly over the tips of his hair, bringing his hands to the back of his neck. He pulled a nine-millimeter Spanish Astra pistol and clip out from under the Afro wig.

As he slammed the clip into the Astra, George announced, "Gentlemen, the dragon has come."

chapter
twenty-one

G eorge ordered Rubiaco to throw the switch to open the cells. Rubiaco claimed he didn't know how, but pressure from the Astra on his neck made him suddenly remember. Johnny heard the click as the lock came off cell 1, the whir as the door slid open and the clang as it came to a stop. *Dummk. Dummk. Brrr. Boom.* Cell 2 followed, then cells 3 and 4; then his own door started to slide open.

"Comrade," George yelled down to him.

Johnny ran toward George, trying to imagine what his friend was setting in motion. George had hostages now, and a modest weapon.

"Get the explosives out of the doorjamb," George told Johnny. "Be careful."

Johnny turned and walked back through the stream of other inmates being released. They had a barrage of questions for him.

"What's happening?"

"What's going on?"

"I don't know," he replied. "It's Comrade George's call."

With the pinky of his right hand stuck up into the doorjamb, Johnny nudged a vial out of its resting place. It slid down past his finger . . . he couldn't remove his hand fast enough. His heart stopped and he grabbed for the vial with his other hand, snatching it just before it hit the floor. On his second attempt he cupped his left hand underneath the hole in the jamb, then nudged his pinky back in to dislodge another vial.

With both vials in his pockets, he returned to the foyer and handed one to George. George put it in his pocket, then forced two guards, Kenneth McCray and Paul Krasenes, to lie down in front of cells 1 and 2. Other inmates flowed into the hallway; one kicked Krasenes in the face. The prone McCray lunged toward the inmate, but George crouched down, shoved the gun at McCray's temple, and said, "The next move's your last." George watched as other inmates bound the guards' hands and feet with their earphone cords and sheets.

Johnny shadowed George, expecting him to call the administration and demand to be set free. Instead, George was forcing Rubiaco to open the cells on the other hallway of the Adjustment Center. Johnny had no idea who was housed on that side. In an instant, there were ten or more inmates coming down that side of the tier, moving excitedly and jerkily, as if in a strobe light. After months of confinement in a cage, they were free to move, free to lash out. A couple were dipping in and out of the cells. A few rushed down to the foyer area, darting past the grille gate to avoid being seen through the door to the yard.

It was all happening so fast. There were so many inmates Johnny didn't know, people he had to watch out for. After over a year in solitary confinement, he couldn't stand the hyperstimulation of being jostled by the crowd. It was like the nightmares he'd had when he first came to prison, dark dreams of rat packing, of people coming at him from all directions. His stomach started to knot; then he said to himself, If you panic, you'll die. Stay with it. Stay with it.

He took cover in the Adjustment Center sergeant's office,

trying to sort out what to do next. He had no weapon, no plan. They were locked in the Adjustment Center until they could find the key to the yard door.

A rumble of voices filled the two sides of the Adjustment Center: "We are the new revolutionaries."

He heard the door to the Adjustment Center open and heard the voice of the hippie guard, Charles Breckenridge, who was bringing another Soledad Brother, John Clutchette, back from a visit. Breckenridge asked, "George, why are you doing this?"

George did not reply.

On the desk behind Johnny, the phone rang. George brought Rubiaco into the office.

"Do you know how the pigs answer the phone?" George asked Johnny.

"Yes."

George then pointed his pistol at Rubiaco's head. "He knows how the phone is answered and if you do anything wrong, I'll blow your head off."

Rubiaco reached for the black receiver. "Adjustment Center, Rubiaco," he said.

The caller asked what was holding up Officers Frank DeLeon and Charles Breckenridge. "They're down the plumbing alley somewhere," Rubiaco replied.

George motioned Rubiaco out.

When the two men left, Johnny started pulling drawers out of the desk and combing the countertops for the keys. He found a large Folger key ring, with dozens of keys. He ran to the door, praying he would find the right one before the alarm was sounded and guards with guns started pouring into the Adjustment Center.

He saw a huge smear of blood extending down the tier. The smear was heaviest where it started, on the floor outside cell 1, where Johnny had seen McCray prone. It swung slightly on the path down the tier, and got heavier again outside one of the cells. Cell 6—George's cell.

He tried a key. It didn't work. George's voice boomed down the tier. "It's time to see if this piece works." Then a shot. *Bam!*

Johnny heard the staircase door open and turned around. William Hampton, a guard from the second floor, Death Row, was peeking in.

"Hold it right there," Johnny told him.

Hampton ducked and raced back up the stairs.

Now he knew he had only seconds left. His head was thumping. There was no way they could keep control of the Adjustment Center with just one gun. Pigs would be pouring in any minute. He was a sitting duck.

George ran up to him. "This is it," said George, looking out at the yard, clear now that he was going to have to run out. His voice cracked. Gone was the self-assurance he had had when he first pulled the Astra. Voices rang down the tier. "What do we do now?" another inmate asked.

George walked back down the north side of the tier, as if to bid farewell to the prison. Johnny tried another key in the door and heard a click. He pulled the key out, flung the door wide, and fled. This is the end, he thought, running, his legs flying, running. And if it's the end, I want to be outside.

The sun's glare blinded him for an instant, but did not slow him down. He felt the fresh air for the first time in months, smelled the flowers in the yard. He felt his legs convulsing, just as they'd done on his long childhood runs to the ocean. He felt the power of every muscle propelling him forward.

He could hear George coming, hard on his heels. Maybe, thought Johnny, they would be saved. Maybe George really did have Panthers on the other side of the wall, ready to blast them out. He looked up at the wall, twenty feet of stone. He aimed himself right at it, feeling as if he could fly.

Suddenly gunshots rang out, and he could feel George lurch forward but somehow continue running. Another shot, and then a thud as George crumpled in the grass.

Johnny dove for cover in the bushes near the chapel, twisting his body slightly in midair when he realized that he still had the other vial in his pocket. Bullets flew around him, ricocheting off the dirt. Oh shit, oh shit. I'm next. Don't kill me. I'm next. He pressed against the wall.

The firing stopped. He stayed pressed against the wall, waiting for the next bullet, the one that would get him. He peeked through the bushes and saw the blood gushing from his comrade's head. They killed George, he thought. They killed George.

Then Johnny heard footsteps, and two pigs were pulling him away from the wall, unbending him. They cuffed his hands behind his back. Maybe they aren't going to kill me. Then Johnny saw one of the guards reach down and pick up the vial of amber-colored liquid which George had wrapped in black electrical tape. George! George!

"For God's sake," Johnny shouted. "Don't shake it. You'll blow us all up."

chapter
twenty-two

J ohnny lay on his stomach, his left cheek on the concrete. He saw guards with machine guns run across the yard and head into the Adjustment Center. They fired madly, then a bloody man in his underwear ran out. Johnny watched as the hippie officer, Breckenridge, stumbled and collapsed, vomiting blood. Wounds gaped open on his neck. He looked like a butchered chicken.

Officer Rubiaco ran out next, hands still cuffed behind his back. "Give me a gun and I'll kill all these motherfuckers," Rubiaco yelled.

As Breckenridge was bundled off on a stretcher, the machine guns rang out again in the Adjustment Center. Then, one by one, the Adjustment Center inmates were led into the yard. They were stripped, clubbed, cuffed, and hogtied on the lawn.

Johnny watched as dozens of guards raced into the A.C. Their faces were contorted with grief as they carried the bodies out. Three white guards were dead—Frank DeLeon, Jere Graham, and Paul Krasenes, and two white inmates—Ronald Kane and Johnny Lynn.

A guard rolled Johnny over to the grassy patch with the others from the Adjustment Center. He was the only one with his clothes still on. The guards pulled off his pants and undershorts, then tried to wrench off his gray sweatshirt. Oh fuck, thought Johnny as the shirt caught on his handcuffs. The more they pulled, the more the metal gouged into his skin, and the angrier they became. Finally, they left the balled-up shirt dangling from his wrists. He was otherwise completely naked. None of the inmates were talking. The guards surrounded them, wielding shotguns and machine guns. Johnny looked at the white prisoner next to him. He was Alan Mancino, the white inmate who swore that prison officials had tried to get him to kill George.

Mancino was completely immobilized, hog-tied with his wrists and ankles connected behind his back where his hand-cuffs were chained to his leg irons.

A shot rang out, then a scream, and Johnny saw a river of blood flow from Mancino's buttocks.

A guard yelled, "Jesus Christ, you just shot this guy. What the fuck are you doing?"

The shooting guard said coolly, "He tried to get up and escape."

They shot him, thought Johnny, to show what they would do to a white boy who helped niggers. Lord knows what they'll do to us.

This is it, thought Johnny. He lay there, waiting to be killed.

Time passed. Anywhere from a half hour to two hours; Johnny couldn't tell. The stiffness in his neck and shoulders from having his hands cuffed in back had grown into a jagged pain behind his eyes. The pressure in his head was so great that he barely noticed the three guards approaching him. They picked him up and moved toward the building.

"Why are you bothering to carry him?" yelled a guard from across the yard. The officer who had been holding the upper part of his body let go, leaving the other two to drag him, chest down, first on the grass and then across the concrete. Johnny could feel the skin being scraped off his chest. The blood flowing from the wound followed him like a shadow. As he felt the flesh tearing away, he wanted to scream, but thought, I'm not going to give them the satisfaction.

Another ten feet and he tried to holler, but no sound came out through the blazing pain.

Inside the Adjustment Center, they held Johnny upright. "Are there any more explosives?" a guard asked.

Pain shot through Johnny's head, contorting his face. He opened his mouth to speak, but he couldn't talk.

The guards had no idea that he was trying. They let go of him and he fell flat on his face.

They picked him up and repeated the question. A small *argh* came out of his lips. They dropped him on his face again, then dragged him back out into the yard.

George's body was still there. Johnny could see his dead friend from where he lay. The guards were singing, "George Jackson's body lies a-mouldering in the grave."

Johnny watched as the naked inmates were shoved in between two lines of six or seven officers. As an inmate came through, a guard would step on his leg irons; then, as he fell, another guard would hit him in the ribs with a nightstick. When it was Johnny's turn, and the guard stepped on his leg irons, he leaned forward to catch his balance. The guard with the nightstick swung, intending to knock into Johnny's ribs. Just as Johnny was recovering his balance, the stick connected with his mouth, cracking his front teeth. Blood gushed over Johnny's chin.

Fleeta Drumgo yelled, "You gonna kill us all." Johnny wished he would shut up. He didn't want Fleeta putting ideas in their heads. They didn't need any help.

Another guard pushed Johnny over. As he fell to the ground, he thought he heard George talking to him across the grass. The next day, he realized that couldn't have happened. George had died instantly. George, you crazy asshole, Johnny thought, how the hell could you think one pistol would cut a swath through a prison full of guards and gunmen? And how could someone as closely watched as you get his hands on that gun?

At 10:00 P.M., Johnny was led back into the building. Three guards held him in a chair as a fourth shaved off his Afro, nicking his scalp, unleashing rivulets of blood. Since investigators were now searching the first floor Adjustment Center cells for evidence, Johnny and the other Adjustment Center inmates were taken to cells that had been emptied on the second floor.

"No one is going to help you," a guard sneered. "You're all going to die. Every last one of you."

Johnny heard footsteps as the guards entered Hugo Pinell's cell. Then the thumps of blows as they beat him. He heard a body being pummeled against the concrete. A guard taunted Pinell, "Let's hear some revolutionary talk now."

Johnny steeled himself, waiting for them to get him next. But the phone rang at the end of the tier and they returned to the foyer area.

He closed his eyes and saw George's handsome smile, heard the laugh that lightened George's hardness. The vision was real to Johnny. A second later, he saw him dead, eyes slightly open, lips barely parted. When he collapsed into sleep, the two Georges haunted his night. He woke out of a half-sleep and cried. He had lost a father, a brother, a hero. For the past two years, he'd finally known what it was like to have a relationship with another person, to learn to use his mind, to have passion about his goals. Now it was all gone.

The next day, an inmate down the tier found some paper stuck under the mattress in the bare cell. That evening, Johnny began writing an affidavit about what was happening inside, hoping he could get it smuggled out.

Then he thought of another possibility. He stood on his toilet seat and banged the ceiling rapidly. *Boink, boink,* from Johnny. *Boink, boink,* came the reply.

He put the mattress over the toilet and pumped, clearing the water out of the pipe so that it was just a hollow tube up to the inmates on the floor above him. "How is everyone?" asked David, a Death Row inmate.

"Look, we're all alive, but the pigs beat us. They're fucking with us. We need to get word out." Johnny listed people who needed to be contacted. He hoped David would follow up, by telling his visitors or sending it in a letter to his lawyer. Legal mail was not searched.

The following day, the Soledad Brothers trial was due to begin, but the surviving brothers—Fleeta Drumgo and John Clutchette—were not allowed to make their court appearance. An affidavit smuggled out of the prison detailed the beatings the inmates were getting with blackjacks, clubs, and guns. John Thorne, George's new lawyer, screamed at the judge to do something. Thorne argued that if the court wasn't going to protect the prisoners, then "why not go out and gun them all down." The judge looked back at Thorne and said, "I don't think you have any standing in this court any longer. Your client is no longer with us . . . somehow a higher court has taken an action in this case."

Fleeta Drumgo's attorney, Richard Silver, responded, "George Jackson will never be dead in the hearts and minds of those who want justice."

The spectator section burst into applause. After further argument, the judge agreed that associate warden James Park should be required to appear and explain why Fleeta

Drumgo and John Clutchette had not been allowed to come to court.

When Drumgo and Clutchette arrived in court the following Thursday, they were scarred and barely able to walk. Drumgo ripped off his shirt and showed his wounds, screaming, "Go ahead and kill me now. They're going to kill me anyway, so kill me now and get it over with." But the judge was unwilling to do anything to protect him.

California governor Ronald Reagan issued a statement that the killing of the guards resulted from "revolutionary elements in our society intent on extending their religion of violence, hate and murder to within the walls of our prisons. . . ." He told prison officials to use "whatever steps are necessary" to halt further violence. Then he ordered the flag over the capitol flown at half staff to honor the dead guards.

The San Quentin inmates were sealed off from the outside world. Visits were canceled, and reporters were not allowed to talk to inmates. Freelance journalist Eve Pell filed suit in federal court requesting to be able to talk to Johnny. She was doing an article for *Saturday Review* about the events of August 21, but the only information she had was the prison administration's official version. She needed to talk to Johnny for the inmates' side or the article would not be credible. But, in the wake of George Jackson's popularity with the press, the California Department of Corrections had adopted a rule prohibiting journalists from interviewing the inmates of their choice. Instead, the prison could choose who, if anyone at all, a reporter could approach. The lawsuit went all the way up to the U.S. Supreme Court, but Pell was not able to force San Quentin to let her in. At other prisons, friends of George and politicized inmates were thrown into solitary confinement. At Tracy prison, Hutch spent the next eighteen months in the hole—guilty by association.

The week after the breakout attempt, Johnny and the

others were transferred back to their own cells. Johnny was feverish—probably an infection from the gouges on his chest—and fell in and out of an unsteady sleep. Sometimes he'd wake from a nightmare and speak George's name. But the cell next to him was quiet, still, looming open and empty like a wound.

chapter
twenty-three

On August 31, a black-bereted Huey Newton, leather jacket opened to reveal his white T-shirt, approached the altar at St. Augustine Episcopal Church, a small wood-frame church in Oakland. In the background, a record was playing—Nina Simone's "I Wish I Knew How It Would Feel to Be Free."

"George Jackson," said Newton, "showed us how to act. He made a statement that the unjust will be criticized by the weapon. We will raise our children to be like George Jackson, to live like George Jackson and to fight for freedom like George Jackson fought for freedom. . . . In the name of love and in the name of freedom, with love as our guide, we'll slit every throat that threatens the people and our children."

George's body was dressed in the Panther uniform he had never had a chance to wear—black trousers, sky blue turtleneck, black leather jacket and black beret; his black-fringed mahogany casket was draped in the Black Panther flag. At George's request there were no flowers, only carbines to honor him. Charles Garry was there, Fay Stender, John Thorne, and two thousand other mourners—browns, blacks, and whites—who listened over the loudspeaker to some interview tapes of George. In her brief speech, Georgia Jackson vowed, "Now we're all revolutionaries."

An unknown street thug when he'd landed in prison, through his book George had become a symbol of oppressed people everywhere. His words spurred people onto a revolutionary path. *Soledad Brother* was being read in Europe, in Vietnam, in Latin America.

The elected municipal advisory council of black East Palo Alto adopted a resolution stating that the slaying of George Jackson was an "execution" and affirming "our disgust and dismay at this atrocious act of genocide." Other groups took more direct actions. When news of George's death hit the streets on August 21, a Bank of America building in San Francisco was bombed. A letter received by the *San Francisco Chronicle* said:

> *Dear Brothers and Sisters,*
>
> *Saturday night, Aug. 21, after learning that the San Quentin pigs had murdered our beloved comrade George Jackson, we set fire to the Bank of America on Cortland St. in San Francisco and burned out one of the bank walls.*
> *This action, limited as it was, was the first of this kind for all of us. . . . Action overcomes fear.*
>
> > *Avenge George Jackson*
> > *Intensify the struggle at all levels!*
> > *All power to the people!*

Other bombings followed—in San Mateo, San Francisco, and Sacramento. Correctional offices across the state were targeted.

Johnny was cut off from the news. The guards had taken all of his possessions. They had even taken the earphone cords from the wall, so he couldn't listen to the radio. The only time he got word of what was happening on the outside was when an inmate from the mainline got transferred into the Adjustment Center.

On September 9, a week and a half after George's funeral, Johnny heard someone pounding from the floor above and pumped the water out of his toilet in response. The inmate above excitedly reported a takeover at Attica prison in New York.

The inmates there had donned black armbands to protest George's death. Their rage grew and, on September 9, over a thousand black, white, and Puerto Rican prisoners took over Attica. The first public statement they issued said, "We are MEN! We are not beasts and do not intend to be beaten or driven as such. The entire prison population has set forth to change forever the ruthless brutalization and disregard for the lives of prisoners both here and throughout the United States. What has happened here is but the sound before the fury of those who are oppressed."

A group of reporters and others were chosen to negotiate with the prisoners. After three days, though, Governor Rockefeller lost patience. He ordered the National Guard, state and local police, and armed guards to retake the prison. They let loose a deluge of bullets, slaying thirty-two inmates and wounding dozens more. Many of the prisoners were killed after the guards had regained control of the prison.

In response to the Attica massacre, the white revolutionary group the Weathermen bombed the office of the New York State commissioner of corrections, Russell Oswald. The Department of Corrections office in San Francisco was bombed as well. The attorney general of the United States, John Mitchell, vowed retaliation: "We're going to move this country so far to the right you won't recognize it."

At San Quentin, inmates waited expectantly for the rest of the revolutionary attack. They were sure that the Panther

Party, the Students for a Democratic Society, and other white radical groups would storm San Quentin and Attica in retaliation. When nothing happened, they began to feel that George had died in vain, and their anger took them in a new direction. Huey Newton had told blacks that "Politics is war without bloodshed and war is politics with bloodshed." They had watched while their brothers tried politics. Now they wanted war.

The core members of George's group were all in solitary confinement—Johnny at San Quentin, Hutch back at Tracy, others scattered throughout the prison system. The administration had locked away everyone who had challenged it, any inmate with the least tie to outside activists, any con who had organized strikes or protests against prison conditions. The blacks left on the mainline with the most power were the most racist. They wanted nothing to do with whites, and they wanted none of the Panthers' ineffective politics. They claimed that they had been spawned out of George's death. They would turn the clock back to a rule of terror among inmates, to a vice-ridden incarceration that only the fittest could survive.

Johnny thought it was wrong to target the whites rather than the administration. But, locked in the Adjustment Center, he could do nothing to stop it.

chapter
twenty-four

Johnny heard the clang of the Adjustment Center door and stuck his mirror out to see who was coming back. It was Fleeta Drumgo, back from a visit with his lawyer.

"Johnny, they fuckin' did it. The D.A. got an indictment against us—you, me, Hugo Pinell, Luis Talamantez, David Johnson, and Willie Tate—for conspiring with George to escape."

"Conspiracy? I never even saw half those guys before—how could I have conspired with them?"

"You got a lawyer? Because it's murder one we're looking at."

The escort guard pushed Fleeta along. "You know the rule. No talking among the cons."

The indictment had almost not been issued. It took a vote of at least twelve of the nineteen grand jury members to charge someone with a crime. Near the end of their two-day session reviewing the evidence from San Quentin, only eleven of the nineteen had raised their hands in favor of the indictment. The others had a hard time accepting the prosecutor's story. They wondered why no inmates had been called as witnesses, and why these six inmates in particular had been charged when there had been other inmates out on the tier.

Then the foreman of the grand jury, Milen Dempster, had decided to cast the twelfth vote in favor of indictment. "Well, let's send it along," he said. "If they're innocent, it will all come out at trial."

Over the next few days, Johnny got a few details about the case. The central legal charge, as Drumgo had said, was conspiracy. The prosecutors claimed that Stephen Bingham had smuggled a gun into San Quentin for George. They also claimed that Stephen Bingham and George Jackson and the six other inmates had conspired to escape, and therefore each of the inmates named could be held guilty for all the crimes committed as a natural consequence of that plan, including the deaths of guards who had been killed by someone else. Because Bingham had gone underground and couldn't be found, the media had dubbed it "the San Quentin Six" case, a reference to the six inmates on trial.

The *San Francisco Chronicle* had gone wild over the case, running front-page articles every day, but the rest of the country's papers were covering it relentlessly as well. For mainstream whites who had been jarred by the growing strength of the Black Power movement, this blowout at San Quentin was the last straw. If blacks in one of the nation's highest-security prisons could seize power and kill those in authority, what chance did people on the outside have? The newspapers played into this fear and into the desire for vengeance. They provided infinite details about every legal maneuver in the case. It was as if each American had been personally challenged by the twenty minutes in the killing fields of the Adjustment Center.

The trial would be heard in the same courthouse that Jonathan Jackson had ambushed. This time, though, the state was taking no chances. All spectators would be searched and passed through metal detectors. Armed guards would be stationed in the courtroom. A solid bulletproof glass wall would separate visitors from the judge, jury, lawyers, and defendants.

On the morning of his first court appearance, a guard charged down the tier in front of Johnny's cell and said, "Strip down." Johnny took off his clothes, turning his back to the guard in order not to reveal the butterfly pattern of scars on his chest from being dragged naked across the concrete on August 21. He didn't want to let them know they'd gotten to him, that they'd scored a point off of his body.

Johnny began the ritual of the strip search. He held his palms up, then turned them over to reveal the tops of his hands. He lifted his arms to show that there was nothing under them. He reached up with his right arm, went through the motion of running his finger through his hair, and then realized how absurd the gesture was. He'd been forcibly shorn on August 21, and all that had grown back were short tufts.

Johnny lifted his testicles and let them go, to show that he wasn't concealing anything. On the guard's orders, he pulled his penis and then turned around, lifting the bottoms of his feet to show that there was nothing there. He bent over, spread his cheeks, squatted, and coughed.

Through the food slot, the guard cautiously handed Johnny a pair of undershorts and a T-shirt, followed by the clothes that Johnny would wear to court, which themselves had been previously searched.

"I haven't got all day," said the guard.

When he finished dressing, Johnny turned again toward the back of the cell and stuck his hands behind his back, out the slot, so the guard could cuff them. The cell opened and Johnny was escorted to the sally port, the holding cage in the foyer area. There the guards would add the rest of his outfit—twenty-five pounds of leg irons, a belly chain, hand shackles, and a dog collar. It was the first case in the history of the country where the defendants were being continuously shackled with this much metal.

The guards there reached through the bars, took the cuffs off Johnny, put the waist chain around him, and secured his hands in the cuffs at the front of the waist chain. They opened the grille gate and put leg shackles on him. Then they took another chain, padlocked it to the front of Johnny's waist cinch, draped it through his legs, and padlocked it to the back part of the chain, making a metal diaper.

They took the remainder of that chain and wrapped it around his neck and padlocked it in back, like a blunt sword across his Adam's apple. With the few feet of excess chain that draped from the neck lock, a guard—escorted by three other guards—led Johnny to the van to take him to court.

Johnny noticed that they had three or four police escorts, two or three highway patrol cars, and at least ten unmarked cars. He heard the whirl of a propeller and looked in the sky; there was also a helicopter shadowing them.

Once in the courtroom, Johnny was chained to a chair. He looked down. They weren't taking any chances. The chair was bolted to the floor.

"I want to represent myself," he told the judge. The assistant district attorney, Jerry Herman, advised him against it, saying, "This is a capital case."

"What do you mean?"

"We're going to be asking for the death penalty."

Johnny's stomach turned and his knees buckled slightly beneath his shackles. Now wait, he thought. They're not going to kill me. Not like this.

That night, back in the Adjustment Center, Johnny paced his cell. I'm twenty-two years old, he thought. I'm not ready to die.

He put a cigarette in his mouth, looking around him as if

for the first time. How the hell did it come to this? How did I get here?

Fuck, fuck, fuck, fuck, fuck, fuck, fuck! His hands gripped the bars, pulling on them with all his strength, trying to wrench a hole in his cage.

chapter
twenty-five

As a defendant in a criminal case, Johnny was entitled to find out what evidence the prosecutors would be presenting at trial. It was through this show-and-tell that he learned what had been found during the search of his cell. Officer B. D. Frye had moved aside the massive piles of books and papers and his organized collection of letters. Frye had picked up some wrapped bars of Dial soap. They seemed to be in their original packages, but they were heavier than usual. He took them over to a metal detector—and they triggered the alarm. Cutting them apart, he found eighteen bullets inside them—thirteen for a .38, four for a shotgun, and one for a .22 Magnum.

Johnny turned to the last page of the materials. It was a letter that made him feel a ghost had come alive. He recognized the blue ink as George Jackson's handwriting.

Nine months before George's breakout attempt, the letter had been found by a dry cleaner in a customer's pants. The customer was James Carr, George's former cellmate, who became one of Huey Newton's bodyguards when he was released. The dry cleaner turned the letter over to local police, who had shared it with the F.B.I. On January 15, 1971—more than eight months before the San Quentin breakout attempt—the F.B.I. turned over a copy to Sergeant

William Hankins of San Quentin. In blue ink, George had
written:

> *Deal with John Thorne or my father for money. X to prepare
> some chemical test tubes about 2/3 inch in diameter and one
> foot long and put some plastic explosives in each 10 of them the
> kind of plastic that can be worked into cracks, (that is not too
> unstable I mean). Get some of that K.Y. jelly that stretches the
> rectum. Frances and her husband and even Penny can be
> induced to bring them to me each visit, it's safe, just show them
> how to hide them on their person and don't stop the tubes up
> with lead, use rubber or cork. With 10 tubes of that a couple of
> .22 magnum Derringers I can get out if you'll knock out the
> electricity at the proper time. I'll let you know.*

In green ink, Carr had written a detailed response, talking
about explosives, weapons training, and other matters. In
closing, Carr asked, "Also what are your feelings concerning
the B.P.P taking over the Soledad Defensive matters? Fay has
refused to give me living expenses, have a talk with her, will
you? She also said she couldn't work with B.P.P."

Johnny's hands shook as he read the letter. They *knew*, he
thought in a rage. The prison pigs knew about George's
escape plan and used that knowledge to kill him. They were
aware he was trying to bring weapons in, but they didn't put
the screen down in the visiting room. They devised a way to
make George think he could get out so that they could use
that as an excuse to shoot him dead.

With this letter, the prosecution could prove that George
was plotting to escape. But there was no evidence that would
link Johnny to the plan. Nothing except his friendship to
George, and his own revolutionary aims.

As Johnny replayed the events of August 21 in his mind,
he kept thinking about his shoes. Because the hallway had
been so bloody, if he had walked down to the cells where the

guards had been held hostage, there would have been blood on his shoes. He hadn't—and his shoes could prove that. But when he asked about them, he learned that all the inmates' clothing had been buried in the dump.

This case was big, he realized, too big to handle on his own. He thought briefly about contacting Fay Stender, but he knew that after George had kicked her off the Soledad Brothers case, she'd gotten depressed and left prison law entirely. What a loss, thought Johnny. He smiled at the thought of Fay—relentless, brilliant. He thought of how she'd forced the prison to give in on so many things—not keeping prisoners in the hole for more than thirty days, getting them medical care and at least a brief chance to exercise. But now she'd given up.

With Fay out of the picture, Johnny wrote to the biggest gun he could think of—her old boss, Charles Garry, who had represented antiwar activists and Black Panther leaders. Garry was famous for putting the system on trial, and Johnny wanted to make the prison pay. Johnny was enraged that prison officials, aware of George's letter, had led him to his death. In George, Johnny had lost a brother, a father, a friend.

But Garry said he couldn't do it. He had pushed his firm into near bankruptcy with his lawyering for Huey Newton, Bobby Seale, Eldridge Cleaver, and other Black Panthers. He couldn't afford to take on an indigent defendant like Johnny, no matter what his heart was telling him about the merits of the case. So instead of the gnarled old warrior who understood the Panthers inside out, Johnny got as a court-appointed attorney a young, green, former army prosecutor.

Johnny complained to Fleeta, who had more ties to lawyers and radicals. He was still on trial in the Soledad Brothers case, and there was a whole cadre of black and white activists who stayed in touch with him. Someone gave

Fleeta the idea of filing a constitutional challenge claiming a right to a state-paid court-appointed attorney of his choice.

Months passed and Johnny still refused to work with the court-appointed attorney. How could someone who had always represented the oppressors do justice for him? As he tried to handle the case himself, Johnny handwrote briefs in microscopically small script to fit everything he wanted to say on the small allotment of paper the prison provided him.

He was in his cell trying to piece together the strands of a defense when Fleeta Drumgo returned from a visit with his legal investigator. "We can burn those court-appointed attorneys now," he told Johnny. "We got the lawyers of our choice."

When the judge refused to appoint Garry as Johnny's attorney, and refused to give Fleeta the lawyer he wanted, Fleeta had spearheaded an appeal to the court of appeals. That higher court granted them the right to have the state pay for the lawyers of their choice. Garry could now represent Johnny.

Fifty-eight-year-old Charles Garry wore loud plaid suits, and wound what seemed to be a single strand of hair around dozens of times to cover his bald head. He had studied law at a time when a college degree was not required. With only a high school education, Garry attended night classes at a San Francisco law school while he worked a day job at a cleaners.

Garry, with his contorted grammar, out-of-fashion suits, and distaste for brief-writing, did not fit the refined vision that many people had of a lawyer. He was like a pool hustler who only displayed his true talents in the end, when the stakes were highest. No matter what the facts or law of the case, Garry could reach the jury. When it came to his closing argument, he passionately, but plainly, called upon the jurors to use their common sense. His riveting summations pricked jurors' consciences. His piercing cross-examinations so rankled government witnesses that a cop on the stand in one case pulled his gun and aimed it at Garry. From then on, Garry asked judges to direct police witnesses to leave their firearms outside the courtroom.

Garry admitted to having a homicidal relationship with the English language, so he concentrated on courtroom tactics and used young intellectual lawyers to write his briefs. For the Huey Newton case, he'd relied on Fay Stender. Now he placed his trust in a young graduate of New York University School of Law, Dennis Riordan. While in law school, Dennis had served as part of the National Lawyers Guild defense team for the Attica prisoners who had rioted after George Jackson's death.

Johnny didn't have any hope he'd get a *fair* trial—if the system were fair, he wouldn't have been indicted in the first place. With Charles Garry and Dennis Riordan, though, he'd give the government a run for its money, directing his defense consistently with his political ideology.

When Garry first came to San Quentin to discuss the case, he knew it would be a tough battle in front of the jury. Blood had flooded the A.C. floor and showered the walls as inmates slit the throats of white guards and white inmates, and as George Jackson shot a white guard point-blank. The nauseating carnage that day had been documented in photos taken after guards had regained control of the Adjustment Center, photos which no doubt would be flaunted by the prosecution.

Garry had already begun to plot his strategy. "What happened on August 21," Garry said to Johnny in a tone that sounded like he was making a closing argument, "was a natural reaction of men brutally treated and existing under inhumane conditions."

He then explained to Johnny his three-pronged defense.

He would use pioneering legal tactics to introduce psychological witnesses to show how the conditions at San Quentin had dehumanized Johnny. He'd bring together people from Johnny's past to demonstrate how the system had failed Johnny from early on. And he'd show how the incident on August 21 was not part of a prisoner/Panther conspiracy, but a setup by law enforcement officials to give them an excuse to kill George Jackson.

As Johnny walked back to his cell after this first visit, he thought of the many cases that Garry had won involving Black Panthers and antiwar activists. He marveled at the compelling strategy that had served Garry so well so often—putting the system on trial, diverting attention away from the actual defendants. It was the lawyerly equivalent of Iron Palm.

Yet Johnny was surprised at how the meeting had turned out. Garry was so involved in the political aspects of the case he hadn't bothered to fashion a theory to show that Johnny was innocent. Not that it mattered. Johnny's only interest at that point was in having the world know that George Jackson had been murdered.

chapter
twenty-six

J ohnny hunched forward slightly, due to the way his wrists were cuffed to the waist chain. His ankles were bound together by the shackles. The guards led him into the prisoners' side of visiting room A.

There was a beautiful woman in an elegant pleated skirt, with red lipstick on. She smiled at the guards, like a queen thanking them for their service.

Once the guards departed, the smile disintegrated and her eyes sent out a flare of rage. "Assholes," she said.

Black Panther Elaine Brown sat back in the wooden visitor's chair for her first visit with Johnny. She came from the Los Angeles chapter, the roughest section of Panthers. It was a joke throughout the Party that if you violated one of the Party rules, the biggest punishment was you'd get sent to Los Angeles. The Panthers thought the LAPD was completely crazy. The chapter had had more people killed than all the other chapters. In one raid, eleven Panthers held off police for five and a half hours, even though the cops had military equipment.

Brown had also been at U.C.L.A. on January 17, 1969, when, egged on by the F.B.I., two members of a rival Black Power group had opened fire on Los Angeles Black Panther Party leaders Jon Huggins and Alprentice "Bunchy" Carter.

186

The Panthers had died, but instead of routing the rival group, the LAPD had dispatched over seventy-five SWAT team members to the home of Huggins's widow Ericka, ultimately arresting her and other Panthers. The purported rationale for the raid was that police wanted to prevent a violent retaliation by Panthers. In the process, an officer held a loaded gun to the head of Ericka's six-month-old daugher, Mai, saying, "You're next."

Elaine was now based in Oakland, where she had risen in the Panther hierarchy. She was an editor of *Black Panther* and had been the Panther liaison to George Jackson. The last time she'd seen him, he'd told her, "We always have outside thoughts, you know. Everything is outside. We live outside, you know. We try to envision what's happening out there. We think of ourselves as having another life even though we know we won't."

After George's death, Elaine had withdrawn from almost everything out of grief. Elaine decided that she was through with the prisoners. Because George was dead, she didn't care if they all died.

Elaine's unopened mail was stacking up on the dresser in her room. Then she got a letter written in what looked like George's handwriting. It was from Johnny. "Are you alright, Elaine?" he asked.

Here he is, half-dead, and he wants to make sure that I'm alright, thought Elaine. This was a sensitivity and unselfishness that she rarely saw in those she dealt with in prison, or, for that matter, out of prison. She read the closing of his letter: "The sky is dark, but there's still sunlight somewhere. Nothing's been assassinated inside of me."

She had written to him several times and begun to look forward to his responses. He reminded her of George's brother Jonathan; their actions seemed more born of love than of rage.

Elaine was impressed, as they corresponded, that Johnny was taking the high road. It would have been the easiest thing in the world for him to try to avoid indictment by smearing George's name and blaming everything on him. But keeping George a hero was as important to Johnny as it was to Elaine. They had much in common even before meeting.

Now Elaine was back in the room where she had last visited George, two days before his death. She was meeting Johnny for the first time.

"Tell me about the funeral," Johnny said to her. He couldn't rest until he knew.

"I had to buy his clothes," she said. "The thing that struck me the most about that moment of buying those clothes, was that in eleven years of his life he'd been in prison, a lot of it welded in his cell, in isolation most of the time, he had developed himself, had refused to lose his dignity as a human being. And, of course, he was off course in many ways. You can analyze it a hundred times over and I can always find a million things wrong. But I'm talking about the passion of a man. He wore prison clothes for eleven years, since he was eighteen years old. And here I'm buying clothes for this body that he could have never had in his life."

Johnny thought about how George had seemed to overpower everything. His well-built shoulders seemed to stretch the fabric of his shirts. His powerful hands seemed capable of bending back the bars so that he could step right outside. Even the coroner who had autopsied him had been impressed, saying George was the "most perfect example of a mesomorph" he'd ever seen.

"God, I miss him," said Johnny.

"Shit, so do I."

They looked at each other and laughed. Johnny couldn't

remember the last time he'd laughed like that, and neither could Elaine.

"I read a poem you wrote, about a year ago, in the *Black Panther,*" Johnny told Elaine on her second visit. "It was called something like 'One Time.'"

"It wasn't a poem, it was a song."

That's right, thought Johnny. He'd read about how she had released a few records on the Motown label. He'd expected her to be older. She couldn't be more than about twenty-eight.

"How long have you been a Panther?" he asked.

"Seems like my whole life. It's not something a mother wishes for her daughter."

"Heard you were at U.C.L.A. when Bunchy Carter and Jon Huggins got shot."

Elaine closed her eyes and remembered coming back down the stairs from the ladies' room, walking right into the panic, the blood, the screams. "Those days I didn't think I'd live to get this close to thirty. The pigs would show up with military weapons at the Panther headquarters and I'd grab a weapon and try not to cry or pee in my pants or do anything else to embarrass myself.

"It's a little smoother now. Bobby Seale's running for mayor and I'm up for a council seat in Oakland."

"Hey, maybe I could help you manage your campaign. I've got a little extra time on my hands."

"Well, good, I guess I'll have to come back next week to see you. Consult on campaign strategies and so forth."

Johnny smiled.

On her next visit, Johnny wondered where she was from; she didn't talk like the black women he knew from L.A. He learned later that she had grown up in Philadelphia, just her and her mother, not meeting her father until she was thirteen. Her mother had sacrificed to send her to a predominantly white private school, but that had only enhanced her sense of isolation. The Panthers gave her a sense of belonging; they became the family she'd never had.

Elaine was magical for Johnny. She gave him something to look forward to as the months passed in 1972 and 1973 while the prosecutors and defense attorneys prepared for trial. He didn't have to explain to her what prison was like; she'd been in jail because of her Panther activities. He didn't have to explain his politics; she'd already worked through the same social and economic analyses that he had. She accepted him unconditionally. He could open up to her about the pain of the chains—his backaches, the headaches—without her thinking he was weak.

"Things have gotten much worse in here," he told her. "It's like open warfare between us and the guards. They threaten us constantly, saying, 'You'll never get out of here alive.'"

The guards' hostility was palpable. Johnny was already guilty in their eyes. Johnny heard that one of the prison doctors felt that way as well, saying, "I'd like to get one of the Six under my knife."

The San Quentin Adjustment Center was now the battleground of a psychological war between the inmates and the guards. Johnny began to understand how George had felt in the months before his death. Would he live? It was agonizing to be so within the control of others. They could sneak up on him at any time. They could drug him and make it appear to be a suicide. They could lead him out in the yard alone and shoot him, and claim he was trying to escape. They could give someone from the Aryan Brotherhood a knife and leave him open for attack in the shower.

"Here, I'd like you to take this out for me," he told Elaine. He shoved a piece of paper through the open grate. She looked at his tiny scrawl:

> *I, johnny larry spain, being of sound mind, do make this last will and testament.*
>
> *I do hereby appoint Elaine Brown to be the executrix of my estate, to serve without bond.*
>
> *It is my intention to leave all of my estate, wherever situated to the Black Panther Party, the Party that I belong to along with Elaine Brown, Huey P. Newton, Bobby G. Seale and others.*
>
> *It is hereby requested . . . that I be buried according to the directions of the Black Panther Party. I wish to be dressed in guerrilla fatigues, beret, combat boots, an assault carbine with one round in it, and a "Gold Label" Dino cigar in my shirt pocket. I want no smile on my face. And, lastly, I want to be holding the carbine.*

"Don't give up now," she told him. "There're a lot of us on the outside pulling for you."

The longer he sat talking, the more the shackles dug into him. Each time he was chained, it was like a fresh blow; he still hadn't gotten used to it. He'd been filing legal motions like mad to get them removed—he was sure their use must be illegal.

The only thing that distracted Johnny from his plight was hearing about what the Panthers were planning. By now they were a strong political force, organizing black communities across the country. In Oakland, they had set up their own social services network—a medical clinic, a legal defense resource, a senior citizens' program, a free breakfast program, even a grammar school that taught history and culture from a black perspective.

Elaine explained to Johnny how guns in the streets were

not the only way to seed a revolution. "If we give the people food, they might want clothing," she told him. "If they are given clothing, they might want housing. If we give them housing, they might want land, and if they get land, they might want some abstract thing called freedom."

The Panthers had elevated Johnny to the position of field marshal, the role George had played before his death. They sought his advice on a number of matters, and even though he was still in solitary confinement in the Adjustment Center, he was able to conduct a great deal of business by having individual Panthers gain permission to visit him.

Elaine had a four-year-old daughter, Ericka, born around the time of the U.C.L.A. shootout. She went to the Panther school. In the mornings, at assembly, the students remembered their imprisoned brothers. An older second-grade class at the school wrote Johnny a letter, saying, "We're with you in your struggle." The schoolchildren did projects in Johnny's honor.

The children gave Johnny hope. "Even if something were to happen to me," he told Elaine, "these children are picking up the banner and holding it very high. If the government wants to stop the spirit, they'd have to kill all these children."

On one visit, Ericka accompanied her mother. She got a solemn look on her face when she saw Johnny's chains.

"Don't they hurt you?"

"Well, yeah, kinda."

For the entire hour, she couldn't get her eyes off the glimmering metal.

The next time they visited Johnny, little Ericka explained her plan. "Okay, what we're gonna do is get some ball peen hammers. And knock off the chains. And bring you home with us."

Johnny smiled at the thought. If only it were that simple.

. . .

The Panthers were not Johnny's only visitors. Some people were attracted to him initially for the same reason that he was on trial—because he had been close to George. The fact that George had been killed while running alongside him gave Johnny some sort of eerie cult status. But there was more to it than that. Johnny was bright enough, articulate enough, and, thanks to George, well-read enough to be able to communicate the prison experience to those on the outside, while making them feel that the vagaries of their own lives were worth addressing, too.

When local colleges assigned sociology students to attend the San Quentin hearings as part of their schoolwork, some of the students began corresponding with Johnny, launching relationships that would span decades. He was able to help them think through whatever was happening in their lives— fights with roommates or parents, a bum deal on a grade, an awakening sense of civil justice. Ironically, he was not able to apply that clear thinking to analyze his own past. He fled from revealing anything about himself and didn't acknowledge that he was half white. His identity was Johnny Spain, Black Panther.

In the summer of 1972, Johnny and his friends were hopeful about his future. The establishment had been shamed into releasing various of the other political prisoners. Charles Garry had gotten Bobby Seale off. Fleeta Drumgo and John Clutchette, the remaining Soledad Brothers after George Jackson's death, had been found not guilty of the murder of John Mills, the Soledad guard who was killed in the wake of W. L. Nolen's murder. A member of the Soledad Brothers jury told the press afterward: "Even those jurors who were initially very open to the D.A.'s charges were amazed. The government presented virtually no evidence

against these men. These men were held for two years awaiting a trial that could have cost them their lives, and when it
finally comes time for the government to present its evidence, it has none."

The week that the Soledad Brothers verdict came down,
the Angela Davis trial started. She was charged with helping
instigate Jonathan Jackson's Marin County Courthouse
shootout because Jonathan had used a gun that she had
bought.

On June 4, 1972, the jurors reached a decision in Angela's
case. On the murder charge, not guilty. On the kidnapping
charge, not guilty. On the conspiracy change, not guilty. All
the jurors hugged Angela as they left the courtroom.

For the past twenty-two months, Angela had been under a
court order not to address any groups. Now she was free. To
the crowd that had gathered outside the courthouse, she
said, "It is now time to deploy our forces for the freedom of
the San Quentin Six."

A multitude of people were willing to help. One, Cathy
Kornblith, had a particularly close relationship to Johnny.
She had met him at the Black Culture night he'd arranged
at Soledad and she had been writing to him for a long time,
before George had died and Johnny himself had become so
famous.

In Cathy, Johnny found a challenging intellectual. His letters to her were filled with pages of questions. She encouraged him to think about life beyond bars. She sent him
books and argued with him about the best way to achieve
social change. She loved it that he was like a sponge, soaking
in whatever she wrote to him about—from protest rallies to
ballet.

They wrote often—sometimes ten- or twenty-page letters
every few days. She was his eyes to the world outside, flooding him with diary-like chronicles of her own days. She told

him about the rallies she attended, about standing in the grocery line, about how her cramps felt when she got her period. At peace with who she was, Cathy was unafraid to let someone in on her most intimate thoughts. Johnny had never known anyone like her. She even liked to talk about sports.

Cathy was a founder of Connections, an organization to make connections between prisoners, their families, the streets, and services. She and the other volunteers provided emotional support for prisoners' families and provided child care and transportation so they could visit their loved ones behind bars.

Other prisoners wrote to her as well, sometimes addressing this twenty-three-year-old white woman as "My Beautiful African Queen." She tried to explain to them that there was more to social change than carrying a carbine. She wrote about the need for organizing, informing, folding newsletters and addressing envelopes.

One prisoner who favored guerrilla violence over community organizing wrote Cathy a letter saying "You're a prude. Things will be different when we're in the revolution and bathing together in the river."

"Where do you think we are?" she shot back. "This is not Vietnam. Where do you think we're going to be fighting this revolution—on the plains of Nebraska?"

When the San Quentin Six indictment came down, Cathy signed on as a legal investigator on the case. The position had an extra bonus. As a legal investigator, she could visit Johnny privately, plus she would be allowed in on the Wednesday meetings when all the defendants and their lawyers would meet at San Quentin.

Though now only twenty-four, Cathy had a strong sense of the kind of defense that the Six should get. She thought it was important for the jury not to be judging six prisoners, but six men. She decided to track down personal information about the defendants, their lives, and their loved ones. They were people who had been damaged, but she didn't want them discounted.

On a visit in spring 1973, Cathy Kornblith had a lot to report to Johnny. She had been traveling, collecting pieces of his life.

She had visited Helen Spain and slept in Johnny's boyhood bed on 23rd Street. When Cathy had walked into the living room, she'd noticed the worn-out stuffed dog that Johnny had carried with him from Mississippi to California, propped up on a pillow on the couch. But there was no other sign of Johnny—not even the recent photos she had convinced Johnny to send to Helen. All his trophies and other possessions were boxed up, imprisoned as tightly as he was. To Helen, Johnny was the failure she had always expected him to be.

Johnny grew quiet as Cathy explained about the visit. When she finished he said, "You've really made me feel like I was there—and it didn't feel good."

Cathy could see through Johnny's tough prisoner exterior to the damaged little boy inside. Until he came to grips with his past, Johnny would not get any relief. She wanted to tell him it would be okay to feel something again, to take a risk at being hurt. She remembered a book she'd read as a child, *The Velveteen Rabbit* by Margery Williams. It was about a little boy who loved his stuffed rabbit so much that the now-threadbare toy turned into a real rabbit. You had to take some risks, get a few knocks, to be real. Cathy mailed a copy of the book to Johnny at San Quentin.

The prison authorities confiscated the book, with its colorful sketches of the boy and his beloved stuffed toy. Giving it to Johnny, they said, would violate California Penal Code 2600 as potentially leading to escape. Perhaps they were afraid Johnny would hit someone with this thin hardcover volume. Cathy eventually tracked down a paperback copy which the prison allowed in. Johnny read it over and over, Ann's exuberant storytelling voice echoing in his mind.

Johnny pulled out a small piece of paper and in the darkened cell began composing a poem:

> i can't learn to love you
> there's no authentic course taught
> in school or church or even home.
>
> Oh sure, i've been to school before
> to church as well
> and i've been to many places i've called home
> but love wasn't taught
> (or at least i didn't learn it there),
> not like that;
> love grows,
> it is, and it reaches
> when it becomes
> with each child
> it is, and it gives
> when it becomes, you know
> life.

On Elaine Brown's next visit, he spoke to her about how Helen Spain would buy him presents instead of giving him a part of herself.

"That's very typical of people who have been poor," explained Elaine. "My mother gave me everything . . . everything but how to figure out how to deal with pain."

Elaine was anxious to tell him about some changes Huey Newton was planning for the Panthers.

"Huey wants to change the name and expand it and open

it to all races and become some other new vanguard organization," she said. "That will make it even more tense for us
with the black nationalist organizations.

"We are already the only black organization that has affil-
iations with white groups and an international perspective
and international connections. And changing our name
would make it clear that white people are not our enemy per
se. It happens that those people in power are white, but
they're also in power over other white people. So the color
of their skin does not define them for us."

Johnny looked at Elaine for a long time. She'd been his
friend for a while now; maybe it was time to open up to her.

"My mother is white," said Johnny, and then explained to
Elaine for the first time about Mississippi.

"What kind of cockamamie story is that?" demanded
Elaine.

"It's true," he said.

The minute that Johnny told her he had a white mother,
Elaine understood why he was in prison. She was a black person who had been through that identity crisis, too—as had
almost any lighter-skinned black, including Huey Newton,
whose grandfather was white. The kids in her neighborhood
as she was growing up would say, "Oh, you must think you're
cute" because she didn't look as black as the next person. So
then she had to fight to prove she was as black.

Elaine knew what it was like to go out in those streets and
try to be blacker than black. She moved her face closer to
Johnny's. "Have you seen her since you've been in prison?"
she asked.

He shook his head no.

"That is your *mo-ther!*" she said, raising her voice. "You
don't have to apologize to people because your mother is
white."

Johnny had been thinking about Ann more and more as

he watched Elaine and her daughter, Ericka. There were so many decisions Elaine faced as a mother about how to protect Ericka, while at the same time trying to give her the power and confidence to live in and change the world. Johnny had begun to long to ask Ann about the choices she'd made.

"Do you think I should contact my mom?" Johnny asked Cathy when she visited.

"Why don't you just stop talking about it and do it?"

He instinctively reached over to touch Cathy, but the gesture was short-circuited by his chains. "Will you do it?" he asked quietly. "Will you write the letter?"

Cathy agreed, but the letter was delayed in its journey. The post office box that Johnny carried around in his head all those years turned out to be a wrong number.

chapter
twenty-seven

I n the years 1972 through 1974, Elaine and Cathy formed the corners of Johnny's world. They were his family. They accepted him. They poured their love into him during their visits and their energies into his case. Although his life circumstances had led him to prison, he hadn't totally hardened or tuned out. He had the depth of character to move on to a better self. And both these women were willing to sacrifice a lot in their own lives to try to help him to do that. There were months when Elaine didn't have enough money to properly feed her daughter, but she still accepted collect calls from Johnny from San Quentin.

Elaine had a full plate. She became head of the Panthers after Huey Newton fled to Cuba to escape another murder indictment, but she used her contacts with the media to bring attention to the San Quentin Six case. Cathy did anything she could—tracking down witnesses and documents—to help get the case ready for trial.

As the pretrial hearings in the San Quentin case dragged on, the two women noticed that Johnny was getting increasingly irritable, picking verbal fights with them or tuning out entirely. He looked, and felt, terrible. The years of solitary confinement and the constant noise of his cement tomb were getting to be too much for him to bear. In 1973, Johnny filed a separate legal action in federal court protesting the conditions of his confinement.

Charles Garry asked Stanford University psychology professor Philip Zimbardo to be an expert witness in this other case. In the summer of 1971, Zimbardo had created a mock prison in the basement of the psychology department and incarcerated students as part of an experiment. To his horror, the students playing the guards became increasingly violent toward the student inmates. The "inmates" began plotting an escape. The tensions escalated, and on August 20, 1971, Zimbardo had called the experiment to a halt. In a deadly real-life parallel, the next day, George Jackson had been killed attempting to break out of San Quentin.

Zimbardo was allowed inside the Adjustment Center to interview Johnny. The regular cells were small, damp, cold, and poorly illuminated—and the strip cell that Zimbardo was allowed to enter was even worse. There was no toilet, sink, or bed, only a hole in the floor. Inmates were not allowed to take any personal possessions into the cell. Someone, though, had managed to etch REVOLUTION on the ceiling.

There was no sunlight in the Adjustment Center—in fact, there seemed to be nothing natural or human. Only the awful smells, the womb of concrete and steel, and the endless echoes of doors opening and slamming.

The cumulative pain of being chained every time he was out of his cell caused Johnny's voice to slur as he explained to Zimbardo how he had been trying to get out of solitary confinement in the Adjustment Center, back to the mainline.

"I went fourteen months without a write-up and that wasn't good enough for them," Johnny told Zimbardo. "How can you prove what you are by showing what you are not—by silence, by not doing anything to call attention to yourself, by not being noticed?

"I feel like a tamed animal, going through the gestures, but I don't know what are the right gestures, only what are the wrong ones that they will punish.

"Lately, I'm having problems with visitors. I find I'm unwilling to understand them, don't want to hear their problems and don't want any hassling. I look forward to visits, but now often get angry, act in inconsiderate ways; tune out of anyone else's problems. It bothers me because I know that's not like me, I'm a talker, I always dug talking to friends. But it doesn't mean much to me now.

"I'm wary of people. I can't let anyone walk up on me," Johnny continued. "The physical barriers are my protection. Survival is the only issue here. There is no pretense of rehabilitation or friendship or anything, only survival."

In his notes, Zimbardo wrote of how Johnny's mind wandered, how he was bothered by the constant noise, how he realized that he was becoming inconsiderate of visitors. "I can't show any feeling in any way," Johnny told him. "If the other prisoners or guards see emotion, they move on it. Emotions are a sign of weakness, so you suppress showing emotions, suppress showing compassion."

Zimbardo asked him how he saw his future. "I'm never going to get out of here," said Johnny. "It's hard to keep going with nothing to look forward to.

"Time," concluded Johnny, "is promises not kept."

Zimbardo's powers of psychological observation were focused not only on the prisoners, but also on the guards. They appeared tense, physically rigid, never smiling, not joking, no signs of friendship or friendliness among them. "The thing that struck me most was the fear," says

Zimbardo. "They were in some ultimate sense powerless, even though they were supposed to be in control. So they'd have to put on a macho performance to convey the sense that they were willing to die for their manhood."

Zimbardo's original prison study had sparked the interest of others in prisons. Research on Rhode Island guards in 1972 found that their violence potential was slightly higher than that of the inmates: the officer group actually had the potential for even more unexplained lashing-out than did the inmate group. Rather than being peacekeepers, the guards were as likely as the inmates to engage in assaultive behavior.

Afterward, Zimbardo explained to Charles Garry: "The total set of conditions creates, as far as I can see, virtually unbearable psychological and physical stress that men have to cope with in various ways in order to survive."

At the federal trial about the prison conditions, another witness, psychiatrist Lee Coleman, spoke about Johnny and the other men in the Adjustment Center: "Each of these men is really in a struggle that is overwhelming to him. Each is desperately striving to maintain some sense of self-worth and some hope for the future."

On January 14, 1976, the federal judge ruled that the treatment of the San Quentin Six constituted cruel and unusual punishment in violation of their federal constitutional rights. He required that the prison give the men regular showers and exercise. He prohibited prison officials from chaining the Six around the neck, waist, and groin while they were at San Quentin. His order, though, would not affect how the men were treated in conjunction with their criminal case. It would not affect the shackling of the defendants on the way to the courthouse, the use of elephant hooks in the court holding cell, and the chaining of the men into their chairs for the San Quentin Six trial.

The physical burden of Johnny's chaining was overshadowing everything else in his life. Each time he went to court, his right hand was connected to the belly chain by an eight-inch-long shackle, and his left hand was cuffed directly to his belly chain. It looked as if someone had sawed off his left arm and sewn that hand back onto his belt, like a handicapped puppet. Johnny had attempted to relieve the pressure of the handcuffs by taping his wrists, but that merely cut off circulation, producing swelling and damaging his nerves. There was even less he could do about his chains. In court each day, the chains caused excruciating pain in his sciatic nerve, as well as muscle cramps and spasms. If he tried to write, the movement of that hand would cause the waist cinch to dig into his back.

Through the haze of his pain, Johnny realized that he was changing. When inmates from the mainline smuggled questions in to him in the Adjustment Center, asking for advice about this beef or that, he no longer felt he had anything to say. Sometimes when Elaine or Cathy would visit, he would stay in his cell and refuse to meet them. The thought of them seeing him in the chains—and, more importantly, the thought of that cold metal around his neck, around his wrists, battering his penis through his pants, shortening his steps by connecting his ankles—he couldn't take it.

"You've got to do something about these chains," he said to Dennis Riordan.

The words came out in a torrent. "What animal has ever been chained like this before?" asked Johnny. "You can't imagine what it's like. Degrading. I can't reach far enough to wipe myself when I shit. Painful. My back is totally fucked up. How can they do this? If I'd been found guilty, they couldn't order a punishment as bad as this."

Dennis tried to discuss potential witnesses with Johnny, but Johnny couldn't get his mind off the chains. He couldn't concentrate on any aspect of the case until the chains were removed.

On March 7, 1975, Johnny's lawyers tried once again to unshackle him. They filed affidavits from several doctors who warned that the weight of the chains intensified Johnny's weight loss, rectal bleeding, and back problems and concluded that, medically speaking, Spain "should in no event be chained during his trial."

Johnny added his own memo to the judge: "These shackles and chains must be removed. I cannot endure the pain. If I were permitted to stand up and move my body for a moment or two every fifteen or twenty minutes, then I could endure the trial. Otherwise I am not able to do so.

"I make this promise to the Court that, if the chain and shackles were removed and I could sit in that courtroom as a human being instead of a wild animal, my conduct would be more than exemplary."

Judge Henry Broderick, a Governor Ronald Reagan appointee, turned down the request. Johnny remained bolted to the floor, despite the fact that between the San Quentin uprising and the trial, he had peacefully testified in the federal civil trial on prison conditions without any sort of restraints. By the time the trial began, one of his codefendants, Willie Tate, had finished his original San Quentin sentence and been released from prison, which meant that he stood trial with Johnny without any chains.

On March 18, when the pain was particularly great, Johnny filed an affidavit waiving his constitutional right to be present at the court due to his being in pain. On some other mornings, he would be teargassed into coming out of his cell to go to court. Later in the proceedings, the prison doctor would administer a pain shot in his back each day to make it bearable for him to attend his trial.

On March 25, 1975, jury selection began in the San Quentin Six case. For fifty-nine days, Johnny sat in his oppressive chains while potential jurors were selected. All those who made the final cut were white.

On the sixtieth day, the charge to the jury began. Judge Broderick cautioned them to judge the defendants fairly and to keep in mind the presumption of innocence.

This is ridiculous, thought Johnny. Every one of those people lied. They may not have had an ulterior motive, but they lied about being able to ignore the chains. With me chained like a rabid animal, the "presumption of innocence" is a farce.

He thought about the court victories in the cases of his friends. About how Angela Davis had been found not guilty and freed in the trial growing out of the Marin County Courthouse shooting. How Fleeta Drumgo had beat the rap on the Soledad Brothers case. But neither of them had been trussed up with metal, made to look like a wild and dangerous animal.

Rage poured through Johnny as he realized that the jurors would never see him, Johnny Spain. They would never be able to see past the chains. Look at me, he thought. Look at *me!*

With the eight inches of mobility he had from the chain on his right hand, Johnny picked up the file folder of legal papers he had in front of him. He reared back and threw the file directly at the jury. It landed with a frightening smack on the floor behind them, causing the youngest juror, twenty-year-old Susan Malerbi, to let out a short scream.

Judge Broderick ordered defendant Spain removed from

the courtroom—and subsequently changed Johnny's seat from the chair closest to the jury to the one next to Hugo Pinell, on the far side of the room.

The court recessed, and Cathy Kornblith rushed into the hallway. Tears were streaming down her face. The trial hasn't even started yet, she thought, and we've already lost the case.

chapter
twenty-eight

On the July day of opening statements in the trial, demonstrators crowded the courthouse grounds, carrying signs: "Free the San Quentin Six," "Justice for Jackson." Tom Hayden, a founder of Students for a Democratic Society, worked his way through the crowd to observe in the courtroom. The trial was costing the state $2.1 million, mostly for the security measures—the bullet-proof glass, the metal detectors, and the numerous deputies used to search everyone and patrol the corridors and courtroom.

The Marin County Sheriff's Department kept track of everyone who attended the trial. They regarded them as suspicious and distributed their names to law enforcers around the country as potential bombing suspects.

Angela Davis took out her driver's license for identification and signed her name. She was photographed, like everyone else who wanted to attend the trial, then passed through two metal detectors and frisked. The process was especially demeaning for her. The matrons poking their fingers in her Afro were the same women who had guarded her at the Marin County Jail.

On the fourth day of the trial, the prosecutors took the jury to the Adjustment Center at San Quentin. Susan Malerbi, the youngest juror, was petrified on the ride to San Quentin. The bus they were on had a police escort in front and back. She'd had no contact with the law before. She had never even been in a police station. So she had no idea what to expect of a maximum-security prison.

Once inside, her fear was replaced by revulsion. The place was filthy, with a disgusting smell. She hadn't expected it to look like the lap of luxury, but this was far worse than she had imagined. The place was in shambles and the cells were so small, she could hardly imagine how a man could live there for twenty-three or more hours a day. Fifteen years later, she would still be able to recount every detail of that visit, from the peeling paint to the wretched smell.

No matter what these guys have done, thought Susan, if they are put in this place, they are going to feel like caged animals. And when they come out, that's how they are going to act.

Back at the courthouse, prosecutor Jerry Herman began his parade of witnesses, giving the three surviving guards— McCray, Rubiaco, and Breckenridge—a chance to tell their stories.

Officer Kenneth McCray took the stand and described the horror of being placed on the floor, having his hands and feet bound with the inmates' radio earphone cords and his head covered by some light material. Then a figure he couldn't identify came close to him and, with a light and deadly touch, slit his throat.

The jurors sat rigidly in their seats as he described the dreadful acts that followed. The reporters hurriedly took notes as he described the atrocities and the courtroom artist drew sketches of McCray's drawn, frightened, solemn face.

He described how he was dragged into a cell and dumped between the bed and the toilet. Within moments, he could hear someone else being pulled in. He remained silent, listening to one of his companions in the cell, Officer Krasenes, pray, "May the Lord have mercy on my soul."

Someone in the corridor said, "One of the bastards is still alive." People entered the cell, stepping on McCray as they attempted to choke his praying companion. The man gasped and defecated.

McCray, bleeding through his neck wounds, continued to feign death. He strained to hear what another guard in the cell was saying, something like, "I have five children." Two louder voices, one of whom McCray thought he recognized as inmate Hugo Pinell, said in Spanish, "Tighten it up" or "Move it up."

McCray then could make out George's voice: "It's time I found out if this piece really works." McCray heard Sergeant Jere Graham say, "Good God man, no." The gun blasted, then McCray felt additional weight on his back, and blood running on him from above. A few minutes later, he heard another shot, elsewhere on the tier.

The jurors felt the story was almost too cruel to be true, but, if it was true, they were too afraid of the attackers to even look over at the defense table. McCray testified that other guards as well had been tied up with earphone cords from inmates' radios, and that he had seen Johnny rush out of his cell with his cords when George Jackson pressured Rubiaco into opening the locks.

Charles Garry approached the witness. "Look at this photo," he said. It was a photo of Johnny's cell, taken by prison authorities right after the incident. Johnny's earphone cords were in their place, undisturbed.

Other guards took the stand, followed by a stream of other prosecution witnesses. Each day, Johnny seemed to fade further away, his mouth set in a grimace of pain.

The prosecution called dozens of other witnesses. Month after month, Johnny came to court in chains. The weight of the shackles gave him hemorrhoids, forcing him to ask the court's permission to sit on a donut-shaped cushion, as if he were a pregnant woman. His headaches became more frequent. He lost his temper with visitors and often refused to see anyone at all.

When Charles Garry walked into the courtroom on April 30, 1976, Johnny was staring at the judge's empty chair. It's like he's not even here, thought Garry. I'm trying a case without a goddamn client.

Garry worried about what the jury thought about Johnny's total withdrawal. He hoped to God that Johnny would show some emotion today. He'd busted his balls to get this particular witness to testify. She was going to be the cornerstone of his case.

The bailiff swore in the new witness, a stout white woman.

"Do you know the defendant Johnny Spain?" Garry asked her.

"I do," she said, with a deep Southern drawl.

"In what way do you know him?"

The woman looked over at Johnny. "He is my son."

A buzz of surprise went through the audience.

"When was the last time you saw him?" asked Garry.

"It's been twenty years since I saw him."

As if to prove their unlikely connection, Ann showed photos—a two-year-old Johnny with an Easter basket, Johnny with his white half-brother opening presents.

"I think this is nothing but a blatant attempt to prejudice the jury," objected prosecutor Jerry Herman.

"Well, I don't think this jury is easily prejudiced," replied Judge Broderick.

Johnny looked over at the jury, trying to gauge their reaction. The young one, Susan Malerbi, is with me. And that woman from the bank, Patricia Fagan, seems sensitive enough. She looks at me a lot. So many white people in my life have been afraid to look at me.

Garry returned to his questioning of the witness.

"Your husband's name at the time was Fred Armstrong?"

"That's right."

"What was Armstrong's attitude towards you and your son Larry at the time?"

"Well, every time he got to drinking, which was very often, he would refer to my child as my 'nigger baby,' and he never beat the child because I stood between them, but I took the beating." She looked over at her son.

"He would get you instead?"

"Yes."

Johnny could feel tears forming at the back of his eyes. He sucked in deeply, trying to pull them back inside. He knew that her words were true—she had taken the blows for him. But he couldn't relate it to himself. It seemed as if all this sadness had happened to some other little boy.

"What effect did this have on Larry at the time that this was happening?"

"He was a nervous wreck."

"He was what?"

"He was nervous when he'd come in. Every time he'd come into the house, he would be very nervous, upset, for fear of what was going to happen."

The bulletproof glass that separated the courtroom from the spectators served as a blockade for emotion during much of the trial, preventing the feelings of the witnesses and defendants from touching the audience. It was like watching television, not a real life event. But this haggard Southern woman on the stand was getting through. A few spectators started weeping quietly, whether for Ann or for Johnny it wasn't clear. The simple way she told her story, and the way she had kept looking at Johnny, had more emotional impact than did the gruesome descriptions of the murders of the guards.

"And was there any problem with your taking Larry out on a group outing amongst the rest of the community?" Garry asked her.

"Yes, there was."

"What was the problem?"

"He was an exhibit. He was a different child in the group. Fingers were pointed and tongues were wagging, and they made no bones about it."

"What did you do in order to be able to keep Larry in your home and also be in the environment that he was living in at the time?"

"I attempted to stand between him and the world."

"In what way? What did you do?"

"I held him in my arms, I held him in my heart, and he knew this. He knew he was a loved child."

"Why was it necessary to send him away?"

"Are you familiar with Mississippi?" she asked. "And twenty years ago there were no integrated schools in Mississippi. There would have been no way that they would have accepted him in the white schools; no way."

Ann continued, "I even had a call from the Ku Klux Klan advising me not to attempt to enroll him."

"Then what did you do?"

"Well, I guess I cried a lot for a while, and then the opportunity came through friends, that Mrs. Spain would take him in Los Angeles and send him to school, and we—I—thought at the time that I was doing what was right for him—not because I loved him so little but because I loved him so much."

Elaine Brown listened to Ann's testimony. She had picked Ann up at the airport and found her to be much different than she had expected. She expected a woman who viewed herself as a victim, but Ann was a practical woman who did what had to be done and didn't bother with too much analysis about it.

Ann had almost backed out of testifying at the last minute. As it was, she used her maiden name on the stand, Ann Smith, rather than her new married name, Pitts. She had lost one husband over Larry, Fred Armstrong divorcing her soon after she'd sent Larry away. She didn't want to lose another.

Ann had told Elaine she understood why Johnny hated her and didn't want to write back to her. But she didn't feel sorry that she had done what she had done.

Johnny had been back in touch with Ann for over two years now. Cathy's letter had finally caught up with her, and in April 1973, Ann had written back.

Dear Cathy,

For weeks I have not known how to reply to your letter . . . I do trust that you understand that my son being in California in the first place was an act of love . . . I also trust that you know there is never even a part of one day that he's not in my heart and prayers. My way in life has been, and is, hard—very hard times, but I am not complaining. . . . Easter will soon be coming. What do I need to send him or do I send it to you or to Helen? I do not even have an address for him. Do you think he'd like pictures of his family here?

Write again, please....
Love and many thanks,
Ann

Johnny had read the letter dozens of times, but he avoided responding, just as he had as a child. Thirteen months later, he'd scribbled a few lines on a Mother's Day card and sent it to Ann. Her life had taken a number of twists and turns. She had married again and had two other children—Don and Nancy. She'd studied nursing and become supervisor of the night shift at a nursing home.

Cathy had sent her photos of Johnny and, although Ann had tried to keep them hidden under a lamp base in her bedroom, fourteen-year-old Nancy had discovered them. Ann had sat Nancy and Don down so they could hear from her lips the facts that had only been family innuendo until then. "You have another brother," she'd said. "He's in prison and he's black."

Ann had finally responded to Johnny's card.

6-3-74

5 a.m.

Dearest Larry—

—and this is what you'll always be to me—No words can tell you how very, very happy I was to get your card and your note. I've turned over a whole dictionary in my head trying to find the right words—none came so you'll just have to accept from my heart a reply. Your card and note are the answer to many prayers over the years. I do hope that since you have accepted the fact that "I am your mother" that we can go on from there. . . . There has never been any feeling of rejection on my part—every act of mine toward you—as any of my children, and you are all the same—has always been out of total love for you and anything I've ever done has been with the feeling in my heart that this was right for whichever one was involved for the moment—This includes letting you go to Helen to live when you were six. I sent all the love in this mother's heart with you and kept the tears and agony for myself.

I've made many mistakes, one of my biggest, I suppose, is loving too well and not wisely enough. . . .

I finally told Nancy the whole story. All the others have

known for a long time. All of them feel that you are their brother and that they'd like to write you and place the love we have for one another with you. . . .

Please do not wait years and years to write again—even though I'm slow answering I do care—maybe the next time will be easier for the both of us.

Love, always, Mama.

Johnny read the words so many times he had them memorized. But he didn't believe she knew the pain she had caused him.

Before Ann testified, Elaine Brown and Charles Garry had taken her to San Quentin to see Johnny. It was dubbed a "legal" visit—Johnny consulting with a witness—and so the prison was required to give them a little extra leeway. They were allowed to meet in the main visiting room, after all the other visits had finished.

When the guard came to handcuff him for his visit with his mother, Johnny thought of Mary's words to him when he was leaving Los Angeles with Johnny Sr. to meet his mother in Utica. Make your mama proud, or something to that effect.

His pace slowed as he and his escort neared the visiting room. Proud, indeed. He was an emaciated zoo animal, an old man whose long fingers combed through his food before he ate it, checking for cigarette butts and shards of glass.

Ann heard the approaching footsteps and turned toward the door. Johnny looked at his mother, her hair pulled back in a bun, her stomach heavy from years of Southern cooking, and thought about how much older she appeared than he'd thought she would. He had been carrying around in his mind the image of her on the porch in Utica, from that one visit back when he was ten.

She put her arms around him—a gesture he couldn't return because of the cuffs. He looked over at Elaine Brown. He had asked her to be there, thinking he would be more comfortable, but now he wondered if it was a mistake.

They sat and Ann spoke of the latest activities of everyone in the family. It didn't mean very much to Johnny. He had never met his brother Don or his sister Nancy, who had been born after he left Mississippi. And throughout her commentary, Ann couldn't take her eyes off his chains.

"I'm a member of the Black Panther Party, that's part of the reason for this," Johnny told her. "What the state is doing is making me appear to be more dangerous than any human being could possibly be. Or maybe they really are afraid of me. After you've mistreated a person for so long, you become afraid of them."

Thoughts of Ann had haunted him for months now, after he'd finally broken his silence and begun to talk to Cathy and Elaine about her. He wanted to open up to Ann, to have her pull her motherly magic and make things alright again, but his feelings for her were buried too deep, and he couldn't face the old pain of releasing them again.

As the minutes ticked by, Johnny felt torn between the older white woman from his past and the Black Panther leader with whom he was fashioning a new self. The contrast of having them both in the same room made him feel unsure of himself. He didn't feel that he could be man enough to impress Elaine, nor enough of a boy to get the comfort he needed from his mother.

For most of the visit he sat silently. He realized toward the end that he'd been pulling his wrists away from each other, as if trying to break the cuffs and free his hands. The next day, the outsides of his wrists were crimson from the gashes.

Elaine watched Ann closely during the visit. If Elaine had known the term "steel magnolia," she would have applied it to Ann. Ann wasn't ashamed of sleeping with a black man and she wasn't ashamed of her child. She'd sent him away because he would have died there. He didn't know that because he was too young. And she couldn't tell him, and that was the pain. You didn't see regret on her face. This, thought Elaine, was a full-grown woman.

After Ann returned to Mississippi, Elaine pressured Johnny, "Just go on and forgive her and give this shit up. If she hadn't done what she did, your ass would be dead. Given her poverty, given her resources, given her situation, she did the only thing that could be done. It certainly was no abandonment, which is what you've thought it was all those years. It was life-saving. It was what a slave mother does when she kills her child rather than have it be sent off to slavery. It's an act of absolute love."

But Johnny wasn't ready to think about Ann's actions in a context, in terms of a relationship, in the light of her needs and his needs and what was possible in Mississippi in 1955. He shut Ann out again, just as he'd done after the trip to Utica with Johnny Sr.

chapter
twenty-nine

Back in Mississippi, Ann returned to her job as head nurse on the night shift in a nursing home. She looked in on one of her charges, an elderly man who was tied into bed at night so he wouldn't fall. His eyes were like Larry's eyes—hollow, marching toward death.

For the first time, she wondered if she had done the wrong thing by sending Larry away. Her doubts deepened over the next few days as she watched her grandson Michael, whose mother Lissie had been shot to death a few years earlier. Michael was now six, the age that Larry was when he went to the Spains. Ann loved Michael and had taken him in after Lissie's death. But she could never provide enough comfort when he woke up screaming "Mommy" in the middle of the night.

The Wednesday after Ann returned home, Cathy Kornblith called her. "Charles Garry asked me to find Johnny's real father," she said. "He wants to call him as a witness on Friday."

Ann hoped she could help her son in some way. "His name is Arthur Cummings."

Ann said he worked with trucks, had even driven them, but when Cathy checked, the Mississippi Department of Motor Vehicles had no listing for him. She checked the

Jackson, Mississippi, phone directory. With such short notice, she had to report to Garry that she had hit a dead end.

Garry continued sculpting Johnny's past with a series of witnesses who had known Johnny in Los Angeles. Johnny's juvenile parole officer, Howard Lambert, testified at the trial that Johnny had been one of two boys of the thousands that he had counseled that he wanted to take into his home. Now ill, Lambert had to be assisted into the courtroom in a wheelchair. That man really cared, thought Johnny. He was one of the few. Until the Panthers, there was no place I really belonged.

Garry could sense that he was making some points. Some of the jurors had cried when Ann explained how Johnny had been jeered at and reviled as a child. Lambert had credibility and conviction, and gold medalist Ulis Williams's testimony was impressive, as he described how Johnny was one of the most gifted athletes he'd ever met. All Garry needed was to convince one juror that Johnny was worth saving. With a hung jury, Johnny would be cleared of these charges and might even be paroled as having served enough time on the original Long murder.

Garry knew that the jury would be empathetic if they could hear from Johnny. Garry thought about a poem that Johnny had written when he learned that his younger white sister had been killed.

lissie:

poem for my sister

I love you is often hard to say—
To see and feel and know and yet,
Sometimes,

Some people realize it is.
That it's warm,
That it's tender—yeah,
Some people realize and understand it is
Real.
Understanding
That it will grow strong, Sis,
                    Beautiful—
Like a newborn child is
                    Beautiful—
Like it is
Life itself
If it isn't torn to bits
Before it can see and feel and know
And live.

I've really wanted you to know that
For so long
I've longed
And tried to say it;
I've yelled, screamed and succeeded
Though silently, in my heart,
The reality and emotions echoed
From the canyon of my soul
Where I cut off all roads to the world
After I was cut off from the world
From you and your world . . .
I've really wanted you to know that
I love you, Lissie.
I know you understand
Why I am angry,
Why I will never accept this society;
It is strange—isn't it, Lissie,
That we could live in the same universe
On the same earth
And not be together (?)
We were born—given life together

By the same Mama . . .
But we were put in such different worlds
Because a deranged society deemed it so. . . .

I've never wanted us to be lonely
Or sad and unloved
I've always wanted us to be happy
Making the world happy—our world
Making a few dreams come true
(Or at least making the nightmares leave) . . .

We're together now, Sis,
And you live
Because I love
You
Try not to let them hurt you
             hurt me— . . .

The key to winning the jury over would be to put Johnny on the stand—to let them see his quiet intelligence, to let them hear from his own lips his agonizing past. That had been the deciding factor in the Angela Davis case—letting the jury hear Angela's story spoken as her own attorney, letting them see that she was no monster but a real human being, an intelligent woman with a conscience. But in this case, the patient, bright, charismatic Johnny that Garry had met at the beginning of the case had faded away once Garry had exhausted his legal appeals on the chaining issue. Johnny was in constant pain from the chains. He had lost almost fifty pounds over the course of the San Quentin Six proceedings, shrinking from 185 down to 138.

Putting Johnny on the stand now would be a wild card— Garry couldn't be sure how it would play. Although he still favored making Johnny a witness in his own behalf, the matter was taken out of his hands. Johnny refused to testify.

He felt that the chains sent a message to the jury: "He is not a human being."

Instead, psychiatrist Jane Oldden wove together the witnesses' testimonies into a fabric meant to represent Johnny. Oldden had first visited Johnny a year earlier, when he was in the hospital with one of his blinding headaches. He was chained to the hospital bed when she entered the room. He spent the first twenty minutes talking to her about how the chaining made him look like a savage animal.

"You could also say that it makes you look like a victim of oppression," she said.

Over the next ten months, Oldden had ten two-hour sessions with Johnny, first at the hospital, then later at the prison. She found it very difficult to get him to talk about himself. Later, she explained the difficulty to the court. "He was, in essence, surviving," said Oldden. "What I'm saying is it's hard, when somebody is holding on to a lifeboat, to ask him whether he was close to his mother or father. It seems irrelevant when they are surviving, so this did interfere with the usual taking of a history."

On their third session, Johnny had said to Oldden, "Did you ever read the book about children who are brought up in the wilderness by wolves or other animals, and don't have early social interaction with people so that they lose their ability to be socialized? I sometimes feel that I am one of those children."

"But—"

"Of course, I wasn't isolated from humanity, but I was so alienated from them that I think that alienation might be equivalent to the isolation."

Oldden formed a psychological picture of Johnny. "Emotionally, he is detached," she said at the trial. "He is very articulate, he is very engaging to talk to, but there was strange detachment from any feelings when I talked to him.

"I couldn't get much real sense of anger in his expression or his tone of voice and I couldn't get much of the pain that he, undoubtedly, had suffered."

She watched him act cooperatively with guards when it came to the chaining and unchaining, but Oldden found something abnormal about all this. She herself was getting enraged at the petty and damaging rules of San Quentin, the interminable delays when she would go to visit Johnny there. If she was angry at her feelings of powerlessness, how must he feel? Where was all of his anger going?

Part of the answer came to her as she read Johnny's poems. In their creativity, she knew, people were able to express feelings which they couldn't express directly to other people. She had kept a copy of one of Johnny's poems:

frankenstein's monster
a poem for those

i am frankenstein's monster
no matter how beautiful i may be
i am ugly
to those who created me

i am frankenstein's monster
i must die
for living
and not loving
those who hate me

i am frankenstein's monster
without fear or human emotion
i shed a tear
and the heart never given to me
skips a beat in sadness
for those masters of civilization

i am frankenstein's monster
i have strength
unknown and unintended
by those who really didn't know me

i am frankenstein's monster
because i've turned
on those who wanted me to turn
on myself

Oldden explained how traumatized Johnny had been by his initial abandonment, and how he had evolved into a borderline personality. Dr. Oldden, quoting a medical textbook, explained: "'The borderline patient in his daily existence attempts to cope with one repeated fear and conviction— that he has been and will be abandoned by important people in his life.'

"He was always trying to be a hero in somebody's eyes; I would say with wanting to be a great athlete and, then as I say, taking a certain amount of status from what he was in prison for."

Cathy Kornblith listened intently to Oldden's testimony. This woman has hit it right on the head, she thought.

On cross-examination, Oldden pointed out that the borderline personality syndrome was treatable, but that the prisons had provided no treatment for Johnny. Oldden testified that, ironically, a psychiatrist at San Quentin, Dr. Joyce Sutton, "does comment that many of his major conflicts have been, she says, resolved because of his active membership in the Black Panther Party and the fact that members of the Black Panther Party had visited him regularly and given him a sense of real belonging and real support for the first time in his life."

The prosecution tried to paint Johnny as a self-centered, manipulative sociopath who cared for no one but himself.

Charles Garry worried that the tactic might be working with the jury, since Johnny seemed increasingly leaden and withdrawn in the courtroom, in pain some days and shot through with painkillers on others. On redirect, Garry tried to regain his ground.

"What are some of the things that convince you that Johnny Larry Spain is not a sociopath and never was a sociopath?" Garry asked Oldden.

Oldden read from Johnny's poems. "He says things like, 'We have to keep questioning life to know where and who we are lest existence will be void of meaning.'

"And he says, 'I've been to many places I've called home, but love wasn't taught, or at least I didn't—'"

Jerry Herman broke in with an objection.

Judge Broderick turned to the witness. "I think you can get to where you want to be by saying what it is in his poetry that leads you to the conclusion that you expressed."

"The poem referred to his questioning of life, his anxiety about the meaning of life and his own meaning and his own identity.

"A sociopath is not interested in this. A sociopath, as I said before, is a person who is essentially self-centered, uninterested in other people, doesn't relate to other people except by manipulation, does not put any effort into becoming a great athlete, into reading and studying books.

"A sociopath uses other people to do these things, but never extends himself with that kind of effort. He doesn't stay awake at night when the Adjustment Center is quiet and read and write for hours. No sociopath has ever done that."

Charles Garry summed up: "When I say the story of Johnny Spain is the story of racism in America, I don't think I'm exaggerating or being overly dramatic. Here's a loving child and a loving mother who has to send her child away at the age of six to a land he has never heard of before or belonged to. Is it any wonder that Johnny Spain feels he is not wanted? Whose fault is it that when Johnny Spain entered prison at the age of seventeen, and was diagnosed as having serious mental problems, he did not receive any help? Johnny Spain's story, ladies and gentlemen, is the story of racism in America."

Garry's summation lasted three days, as he painted a picture of Johnny's life in prison and tried to show that the prisoners' actions were not the product of conspiracy, but an understandable reaction to their circumstances. "A famous writer once said that you can test the values of a nation by the type of prisons it has. Our prisons are hellholes. I wonder how many more San Quentins there are going to be, how many more Soledads, and how many more Atticas?

"You were told that the plan was to escape. Escape to where, pray tell? Assuming you went through the Adjustment Center door, assuming that to be a fact, you'd be shot down, mowed down; there are gun rails all over the place. And then after you get there, how are you going to hurdle that wall? We've got to use our common sense. We've got to use our natural feelings about things.

"I say that this was an emotional upheaval. It was like a cesspool that opened up, and many different people there had pent-up emotions and hatred toward the guards, hatred toward the system, and bore hatred toward the harassment and degradation they had to live in day in and day out. Remember that when the bodies of the three dead guards were being carried out, the entire cell block—three or four hundred men—let out a spontaneous series of rousing cheers."

The jurors went off to deliberate, trying to keep straight in their minds the complicated facts and fictions that had been presented about the multiple defendants. After a week passed with no decision, the lawyers on both sides began to feel that the waiting was almost as much of a strain as the seventeen-month trial itself. "It seems to me," Garry told Dennis, "as if I've spent my entire life waiting for juries to return with verdicts."

After fifteen days of deliberation, the jury sent a specific question to the judge: Could a defendant be convicted of conspiracy if there was no proof of a conspiracy between George Jackson and Stephen Bingham?

The judge answered later that day: No, there would be no conspiracy count unless they found a conspiracy between Bingham and Jackson. Johnny wondered how a jury could ever know the answer to that question, with George now dead and Bingham gone.

On August 12, 1976, the 226th day of the trial and the twenty-fourth day of deliberations, the jury in the San Quentin Six trial returned to the courtroom. The muscles in Johnny's arms tensed while he waited for the verdicts to be read.

The first verdict was Hugo Pinell's. The jury found him guilty of assaulting two guards, Urbano Rubiaco and Charles Breckenridge. He was found not guilty, though, of conspiracy.

Johnny breathed a small sigh of relief, feeling that the jury had not bought the prosecution's crazy argument about the six of them conspiring to break out. Then he realized that the foreman was about to read the verdicts about him.

For the murder of Frank DeLeon, GUILTY. For the murder of Paul Krasenes, NOT GUILTY. For the murder of Ronald Kane, NOT GUILTY. For the murder of Johnny

Lynn, NOT GUILTY. For the murder of Jere Graham, GUILTY. For the conspiracy, GUILTY.

Johnny turned around and saw the anguish on his friends' faces—the sadness around the corners of Cathy's mouth, the rage in Elaine's stare, the confusion in Dennis Riordan's eyes. Then he looked at the jury. One of the jurors, Susan Malerbi, was crying for him.

He barely noticed the other verdicts coming down. David Johnson was found guilty of assault, but would be released on the grounds that he had already served enough time. Willie Tate was acquitted, as were Fleeta Drumgo and Luis Talamantez.

Dennis Riordan was baffled. Conviction of all of the defendants of the most serious charges might have been expected, or none, but to single out Johnny? He felt the evidence against Johnny was among the weakest. After all, it wasn't his client who'd said "I love you, pigs" while slitting a guard's throat. And yet Johnny had got the stiffest conviction. It just didn't make sense.

Then the logic of the verdicts dawned on him. Johnny had been accused of little violence personally, but the evidence that he and George had been the only ones to run out the door was powerful. Johnny, the only Black Panther on trial, had alone been convicted of the conspiracy with George, his fellow Panther. As a result, he alone had been convicted of the murder of the two guards who had been shot by George. The other verdicts were a victory for the defense team—three complete acquittals, and Johnson convicted only of a minor charge.

Unlike Johnny, Fleeta Drumgo and Luis Talamantez had taken the stand and been acquitted. Lacking Johnny's own testimony explaining his run from the A.C., the jury had reserved its heaviest censure for him.

At the sentencing, Judge Broderick asked Johnny if he had anything to say. In response, Johnny formally addressed the court for the first time. He could not stand because he was still chained to the chair.

"I was chained like this for five years, for the duration of these proceedings," said Johnny. "This was a jury trial, and for 17 months I was forced to strain, contorted in my effort to turn and look at my peers through a warped barrier.

"The jury in this trial were not my peers. When we speak of my peers, you have to talk about a whole lot of people who have a history of slavery, who have been robbed of nearly all in life, and sometimes of life. You have to show me the people who have had their heads bashed, their ribs kicked, their faces and lives stomped for merely wanting to live."

Cathy sat on the edge of her chair, her hands grasping the seat. Elaine Brown sat quietly nearby, as if she were at a funeral.

"My peers are those who have been deprived of jobs, clothing, housing—the people who most of their lives have been hungry and cold and without. I'm talking about the people who have been lied on, hated and hung, and attacked by civilized dogs despite their prayers and pleas to God."

Several of the black spectators nodded. The bailiff listened more intently.

"You have to tell me about the people who have been sent to prisons, graveyards, and more than a few times to madness by rules and laws that they never had voice in creating; rules and laws that weren't created to serve their interests.

"You have to tell me about the people who have been plotted against and assassinated like Comrade George Jackson, and like Dr. Martin Luther King, and the people who were subjected to COINTELPRO, which was initiated by the FBI in an attempt to destroy the Black Panther Party.

"The jury in this trial were not my peers. And with that in mind, I would have to say if the goal was the administering of justice, and theoretically trials are supposed to represent a means by which justice is arrived at when issues are at variance, this trial fell far short in achieving it."

Johnny paused for a moment, thinking about the days upon days he had sat in this courtroom, grimacing in pain.

"There was an elaborate display of formality by the State during this trial," continued Johnny, "all of which was designed to conceal the truth about the assassination of George Jackson. You can sell half-truths and lies to middle- and upper-class people because their entire lives have been filled with nothing else, but formality, to me, means tradition, and I have as much respect for tradition as it has had for me, none. . . .

"I have all of history to support my position, and with the weapon of historical evidence, I have all of the future standing with me—the children—to resist what we as people are no longer willing to tolerate.

"This trial will not stop us, because it didn't start us. We are going to become, despite and because of this trial.

"And in closing, I would like to address this especially to the Court. It's a quotation from Comrade George Jackson:

" 'The strong can afford to be incompetent or wrong sometimes without loss of face. Even the mightiest and most capable of men are only human, but he who attributes to himself omnipotence must never be wrong. For once a weakness is found, no matter how small, in one who claims omnipotence, he is completely exposed. The fall from omnipotence ends only with insignificance.'

"That's all I have to say."

The judge looked over at Garry. "Mr. Garry," he asked, "do you desire to make a statement on behalf of Mr. Spain before sentence and judgment is pronounced?"

Garry had expected to bring the proceedings to a thundering close with a penetrating indictment of racism, but Johnny's own words had moved him too much.

"I was planning on saying some things," replied Garry quietly, "but after what he said, I have nothing to say."

Judge Broderick rendered Johnny's sentence. If Johnny had been tried in 1971, he would have been heading for the gas chamber. But the California Supreme Court had since ruled that the death penalty was unconstitutional. Broderick gave Johnny the maximum he could: two more life sentences for murder.

chapter
thirty

Mike Dufficy entered Galli's restaurant to meet Patricia Fagan and her husband. Dufficy had been the attorney for Fleeta Drumgo, and Patricia Fagan had been a juror in the San Quentin Six case. As an established criminal defense lawyer, Dufficy was interested in her observations about how to make his presentations more effective.

Dufficy and Fagan had not talked previously, but they shared the intimacy that occurs between people who interact in a courtroom over a long case. Outsiders find it hard to understand why jurors and lawyers feel that they have known each other forever when they end such a case. But there's a curiosity, one about the other, as they began their respective roles in determining the fate of the person on trial. Each, like a good lover, learns to read the slightest changes in the other's emotions.

"One of the toughest things for me was when Louis Tackwood took the stand and mentioned Elmer Pratt," revealed Fagan.

Dufficy took a sip of his drink and then asked Fagan, "Oh, why was that?"

"He was the Black Panther who killed a friend of mine in Los Angeles."

Dufficy choked on the drink. He looked at Fagan with interest, and urged her to continue her story.

"I went to Judge Broderick," said Fagan, "and told him that I didn't know if I could keep from crying in the courtroom."

Dufficy couldn't wait until the dinner was over so he could call Charles Garry. Patricia Fagan might have just handed Johnny Spain the grounds for a new trial.

Dufficy tracked Garry down at a California State Bar conference. When Garry got the news, he realized that his whole defense had been tainted. Because Jerry Herman had argued that the simple fact of Johnny's membership in the Black Panther Party could be used as evidence of guilt, no person biased against the Panthers would be qualified to judge Johnny fairly. There was even a statute in California saying that whenever evidence at trial will reveal links between a defendant and a controversial group of some kind, a duty exists to "ensure during voir dire that the jury selected be free from prejudice against the group." Fagan should have been disqualified from the beginning.

Since Garry hadn't known of Fagan's bad experience with the Panthers, he had presented a defense in which Johnny's membership in the Panthers was openly acknowledged. Jane Oldden had described the part Panther membership played in Johnny's intellectual and psychological development, and Garry had called prominent Panthers—Elaine Brown, Ericka Huggins—to testify on Johnny's behalf. Rather than helping Johnny, these witnesses had probably only reminded Fagan of the man responsible for her friend's death.

During the trial, Fagan had secretly met twice with the judge and revealed how upset she was when one of Johnny's defense witnesses mentioned Elmer 'Geronimo' Pratt, the

Black Panther who had been convicted of killing her friend. The judge had not shared the revelation with prosecutors or defense counsel. Perhaps the thought of starting the trial all over again, when they were over a year into it, to accommodate a new juror made him see the incident as less significant than it was. After the jury had been sent to deliberate, Fagan described her friend's murder by a Black Panther to the other jurors.

Garry and his assistant, Pat Richartz, drove out to Fagan's house to find out what had gone on. They talked to her about her friend's murder, and about other experiences that might have influenced her opinion. When Richartz asked Fagan whether she thought Johnny was violent, Fagan replied, "Well, he's a mulatto."

Richartz was stunned. She hadn't heard that term for years. She thought back over the questioning of the jurors during the voir dire. It hadn't dawned on her to suggest that Garry ask potential jurors, "Do you dislike mulattos?" "Do you have a problem with mulattos?" "Are you bothered by racial mixture?"

Richartz asked Fagan, "What's the matter with mulattos?"

Fagan explained that she had grown up in a neighborhood near Watts and that her high school had played sports against the one that Johnny later went to. Every football game, every basketball game, every game that was played with the schools from Johnny's community would end in violence, she told Richartz, and it was the mulattos who always started it.

Richartz later recounted the conversation for Dennis Riordan. "Fagan seemed to feel that, therefore, mulattos were violent and Johnny had to be," said Richartz. "Her reasoning was that if anybody started anything on August 21, it was a mulatto."

Between her friend's murder and her obvious prejudice,

thought Richartz, there was no way Fagan should have been allowed to sit on the jury.

Johnny turned the new facts over in his mind. Patricia Fagan had seemed such a conscientious juror. She'd paid close attention to the evidence and followed along when complicated events were explained. She had often looked over at Johnny. He had actually thought she might vote to acquit him.

A few days after Garry and Richartz met with Fagan, prosecutors Jerry Herman and Terry Boren got the shocking news that Johnny was requesting a new trial on the grounds of juror misconduct. On September 30, 1976, Garry and Boren were squaring off in Judge Broderick's courtroom.

During jury selection before the trial began, Garry had specifically asked Fagan whether she associated the Black Panther Party with violence and she had said no.

"The factual question is that she lied on the voir dire," Garry argued to Judge Broderick in the new hearing. "She deliberately, intentionally lied, wilfully lied, both as to her experience with violence and her attitude toward psychiatric defense.

"We know from the statement made by Mrs. Fagan that she told the jurors that she was sitting with exactly the kind of things that she told you," Garry told Judge Broderick, "that this man was a Panther and that a Panther had killed her close friend."

Judge Broderick considered the argument, then asked Garry, "How did you account for the fact that, out of the seven counts, your client was acquitted of four and convicted of only three if this is persuasive?"

"Very simply," replied Garry. "The only thing that he was

convicted of, Judge, was his relationship with George Jackson."

Garry pointed out that Johnny had been acquitted of all the counts charging that he had actually harmed anyone. At the same time, Spain was the only Black Panther, and the only defendant convicted of conspiracy—and, therefore, of two murders. Each potential juror had been quizzed extensively about bias toward the Black Panthers. None of the jurors who were seated had admitted any personal contact with the Panthers. But Fagan, whether consciously or unconsciously, had withheld the important fact that a Panther had been convicted of murdering her friend. When she later described the murder to the judge, he should have informed the attorneys. By not revealing Fagan's confession, Broderick had deprived Johnny of a fair trial.

Garry had raised enough issues to be able to put Fagan on the witness stand to ask her about her past contact with the Panthers. It was a sticky situation, though, because jurors were not allowed to "impeach" their verdict. They couldn't testify that they had arrived at an improper verdict. Otherwise, any case would be up for grabs so long as one juror could be cajoled or bribed into a later statement of impropriety. Garry's only hope of winning a new trial was to show either that Fagan had intentionally withheld information on the voir dire—or that Fagan's meeting with the judge was legally improper.

Judge Broderick agreed that Garry could bring Fagan to court and question her. In the courtroom, she confirmed that she had violated the judge's admonition and revealed to the other jurors that Black Panther Elmer Pratt had killed her friend.

Garry got Fagan to recount her high school experiences, and then said, "Isn't it correct, Mrs. Fagan, that at the time you were voir dired, that at that time your state of mind was such that a person who had lived in the ghetto area, the Watts area of Los Angeles, was used to violence?"

"Yes," she said, "I would have answered yes. The question wasn't asked of me."

After Fagan finished her testimony, Garry argued to the court, "I have never seen a more flagrant, more flagrant violation of a defendant's rights."

Terry Boren responded that Fagan had sworn that she associated the Black Panther Party with worthwhile activities. He denied that the jury was prejudiced by Fagan's information, because the fact that Pratt had killed a woman had been mentioned during the trial.

After the hearing, Judge Broderick ruled that, to his satisfaction, Patricia Fagan had proven that she was fair and impartial, even though she had not mentioned her personal knowledge of an apparent Black Panther murder. "She did not conceal it wilfully, but it passed her mind," said Broderick.

Dennis Riordan, the young lawyer working with Charles Garry, was incensed at the judge's ruling. How could he say that Fagan's hatred of the Panthers for killing her friend hadn't colored her feelings toward Johnny? Hell, she'd gone to the judge to get excused because she thought she'd cry in court.

Riordan immediately began writing the briefs for Johnny's appeal. Garry, who was a trial lawyer, not an appellate lawyer, had ceded the case entirely to him. Barney Dreyfus, Charles Garry's partner, reminded Dennis how much time and money the prosecution had spent in the initial trial. Getting a retrial would be no mean feat, no matter what the merits. Dreyfus mentioned the pending appeal of the seventeen-month trial to a friend of his, an appellate judge, who laughed and said, "That's affirmable per se. Who would reverse a seventeen-month trial?"

The remark proved prophetic. The state appellate court ruled in July 1980 that Fagan was not so prejudiced against Johnny as to render her verdict unfair. In 1982, however, a black federal trial judge in San Francisco, Thelton Henderson, held that Spain's right to a fair trial had been blatantly compromised by Judge Broderick's secret meeting with Fagan. A retrial was scheduled to begin in Marin when the U.S. Supreme Court stepped in. The Court dispatched the issue swiftly—without even asking the lawyers to make oral arguments. Fagan's actions were harmless, the majority said, over bitter dissents. Johnny's sentence would stand.

chapter
thirty-one

A few months after his sentencing, Johnny was transferred to Tracy prison. It had been seven years since he'd left the prison and most of the guards were new to him. But they'd already heard all about him. In the officer training academy, instructors used photos of the carnage at San Quentin to show new recruits what could happen if they didn't do a thorough search.

"Guard killer," one of them hissed at Johnny his first week there. The fine distinction that he had not pulled the trigger was lost on his captors.

"How do you feel about the California Department of Corrections not protecting guards?" Johnny asked him. Johnny pulled out the dog-eared court transcript, where the testimony of prison officials—and the text of the letter found at the cleaners—proved that the administration knew that George had been trying to escape, but did nothing to prevent it.

The guard read it silently, wide-eyed.

Johnny challenged, "Why weren't your administrators held accountable? Why weren't they forced to run through a double line of guards and hit with clubs?"

After a few months in Tracy's Adjustment Center, Johnny got permission to return to the mainline. It would be the first time he was out of solitary for almost seven years, since he'd been locked up on O Wing at Soledad.

His first day on the mainline, he spent every moment he could out of his cell. He walked, he ran, he visited every spot he remembered from his earlier stay at Tracy. He felt like Rip Van Winkle returning to the world. His body felt as rickety as the gray-bearded Van Winkle's.

As much as he wanted to, he wasn't able to blend back into the general prison population. His conviction for the murder of two guards had given him a sort of superhero status among inmates. It also meant that the guards were constantly testing him, taking him through more strip searches than any of the other inmates.

As weeks passed, Johnny learned how much the prison world had changed—and remained the same—since his last stint on the mainline six years earlier. There were more inmates in for drug-related crimes and much more drug use in the prison itself. And there was no longer any unity among prisoners. Blacks and whites were killing each other, just like in the old days of the race wars at Tracy and Soledad.

George Jackson's name was still spoken with reverence. He was known as a brother whose prison letters had made him famous around the world—and who'd lived every prisoner's fantasy by trying to blast his way out. But the new inmates had no interest in learning anything about George's political agenda. Instead, they evoked his name as a justification for violence against whites, blaming whites like Fay Stender for George's death, on the theory that they should have done more to break him out.

Johnny didn't know what he could do about all this. He didn't trust anyone inside. Someone might pretend to be his buddy, just to set him up. It had happened dozens of times to people he knew, not just in here, but with the Panthers and the F.B.I. He'd learned recently that the band of Black

Panther guerrillas George had been counting on from the Santa Cruz mountains had included a white SDS member who was an F.B.I. informant.

There was little reason for Johnny to dream of life on the outside anymore, either. The Panther Party was in shambles. Huey Newton had returned from Cuba, buried himself in crack, and was ruling the Party for his own self-interest rather than by principle. At first, Johnny took Huey's side whenever a Panther would complain. When Huey started expelling people from the Party, Johnny continued to believe there must be a valid reason for his actions.

Then Huey kicked Elaine Brown out of the Black Panther Party. She went into hiding, amidst rumors that Newton had beaten her as well. With that, the last piece of Johnny's dream of being on the outside, of reshaping the world, was extinguished.

Inside, the truce between black and white prisoners in 1970 and 1971 at Soledad and San Quentin was now a forgotten bit of history. Prisoner unity was a joke. The prison movement—the solidarity between black and white convicts—had totally dissipated.

Johnny saddened when he remembered the glorious days when they were starting to come together. He could have tried talking to the black and white leaders, like he had at Soledad, but he felt it was futile. Everywhere he looked, things were once again coming unglued.

Johnny had never seen anything like the race wars now going on at Tracy. Blacks had declared open season on whites. In the previous nine months, there had been over fifty stabbings—all by blacks of whites. Johnny was waiting for the other shoe to drop. The whites wouldn't just continue to take it.

On July 25, 1978, Johnny heard shouts in the yard and

ran to a window. A pulsating group of whites—hundreds strong—had surrounded fifty blacks in the yard. Johnny heard the gunshots outside as guards created a bullet dividing line between the blacks and the whites. A few seconds later he realized that there were about a dozen white prisoners in his wing, J Wing, who would soon be targeted and far outnumbered by the seventy blacks in that wing.

Johnny scoped out the situation. He could just look the other way, classic prison style, while God-knows-what happened to these whites. Or he could do something about it. Shit, some of these guys were just kids, no older than he'd been when he'd first come to Tracy.

He tilted his head to the left, motioning the whites over to the gate. If he could just get them safely to the grille gate, Murray, the guard, could open the gate and lock up the whites out of the blacks' reach.

But the whites, the "peckerwoods," had been spotted.

"We can't get to the yard to help the brothers, so let's kill these motherfuckers," cried one black, leading a mob into the television room, where Johnny had been rounding up the whites.

Johnny turned to the white prisoners. "Shut up," he said. "I'll handle it. Don't panic."

At that moment, he didn't have a plan. He didn't have a weapon. All he had was his reputation—as a mean, revolutionary guard killer.

"Where the fuck are you going?" Johnny asked the black leader.

"The brothers are being attacked by the 'woods. We're going to deal with these motherfuckers in here."

"We?" said Johnny. "I don't attack innocents. Every white guy who wanted to be part of this is out in the yard. These

guys chose not to be part of it—and that makes them innocents."

There was a moment of silence, while the outcome hung
in the balance.

From the middle of the mob, a young inmate stepped out.
He'd talked to Johnny a few days earlier, asking questions
about George Jackson and W. L. Nolen. "I don't know what
is happening here, but I'm riding with Johnny if anything
goes down." He was from a gang in L.A., which meant his
partners would support Johnny as well.

A couple of the other blacks shifted uneasily from foot to
foot. Then a few said they were with Johnny. Other members
of the pack began to move away.

Their leader, sensing the change in loyalties, backed off.
"Man, I got no beef with you."

The continued safety of the whites could not be assured if
they remained on the tier, though. Johnny turned to Murray,
and asked him to open the grille gates and get them off the
tier.

"The rules are clear, Spain. I can't open any gates during
an alarm."

"I won't be able to hold them off if they see any whites
draw blood in the yard," implored Johnny. "You're going to
have twelve lives on your conscience—thirteen, if you count
me. If you won't let them out, then at least come in and lock
the whites in the TV room."

Murray considered the request. They were in the middle
of a prison riot. Johnny Spain, a black inmate convicted of
killing two guards, was now asking him to come into the tier
where seventy angry blacks were on the loose.

"Will it be safe for me to walk the tier?"

"It will be okay," said Johnny soothingly. "It's the right
thing to do."

Hesitating, Murray pulled back the grille gate and entered the tier.

In the following months, Tracy prison oozed violence. The black gangs preached racist violence and virulent feuds infected the wings. It wasn't just the blacks and whites knifing each other. The Chicanos from northern California, many of whom belonged to a prison gang called Nuestra Familia, had a blood war on with the southern California Chicanos, who called themselves the Mexican Mafia. In the larger prison politics, Nuestra Familia sided with the whites, the Mexican Mafia with the blacks.

The only peaceful spot in the place was Johnny's wing. He'd been making some headway again at convincing blacks and whites that they weren't each other's enemies. He was able to cajole, inspire, and, if necessary, intimidate inmates to look beyond racial differences. Then, in February 1980, he got word that fifteen violence-prone southern Chicanos were scheduled to move in. Johnny went to see the assistant superintendent, Ray Walker.

"Don't do it," argued Johnny. "I've got the wing wired. You've had trouble everywhere else. It's not that way for no reason. I've got agreements, cross-agreements, and understandings from the people who are there. You change the mix and it will be out of control."

Walker agreed to look into it, but the following day the first group of Chicanos strode in, hard and together. The atmosphere in the wing changed radically. The prisoners on the wing had not previously been packing weapons, but now, thought Johnny, it was as if every inmate had gone back to his cell and shit himself a knife.

That afternoon, Johnny called a Panther friend, Jonina

Abron. Gone were his hopes of harmony. It was as if his efforts had never happened. "Get a hold of Dennis," he said. "I'm sure something's going to go down here."

As he spoke, he glanced down the corridor. Sixty paces away a black guy pulled a knife and stabbed a white to death.

Johnny hung up, went up to his third-tier cell, and locked himself in. He stomped back and forth across his cell, almost banging his head on the wall with the force of his anger. Fuck the prison, fuck Walker. That guy didn't have to die.

A few hours later, a guard came by.

"Spain, you in there?"

"Yeah, I'm in here."

"I've got orders to take you to the hole."

By then, the incident was on the news and Dennis Riordan was able to get a call in to Johnny. When he learned that Johnny was talking to Jonina when it happened, he thought he could get Johnny rapidly out of the hole. With telephone company records, he could prove that Johnny hadn't been the killer.

Riordan arranged to see the lieutenant who headed the security detail at the prison.

"Look," said Dennis, "I know that Johnny's been charged. I have evidence that he can't be involved."

"Oh, we know that Spain didn't do the stabbing," replied the lieutenant. "We've got a witness says he was on the phone at the time."

Dennis felt his stomach sink. There went his big Perry Mason proof.

The lieutenant continued. "Our information is that Spain is so respected and looked up to that something like this kind of killing couldn't go down without his approval."

. . .

After exchanging only a few sentences with Johnny, Riordan realized how upset his friend was. In the past few years Johnny had begun to open up with Dennis, but when he was really upset, like now, he re-erected his emotional barriers and started talking like the caricature of a nit-picking lawyer.

"They didn't give me the sheet with what they were charging me with until twenty hours after they sent me to the hole," said Johnny, puffing recklessly on a cigarette. "And they refuse to give me any of my property."

Johnny babbled on about procedures and precedents. Hanging around Riordan, Johnny had picked up some legal skills. He had written out a dozen writs—one to every court in a fifty-mile radius—to try to get sprung from the hole. "You know," he said, "the family of that white guy who died probably has a good cause of action against the prison for negligence."

A week later, the three-member disciplinary committee convened, headed by the security lieutenant Dennis had talked to. Johnny was escorted in, handcuffed. "Look, I know the way these things work," said Johnny. "The decision is already made before the person walks in. Just give me my property and send me back to the hole."

"The decision hasn't been made," said the lieutenant. "We want to hear your side of the story."

Johnny thought about the disciplinary sheet, which he had finally received that morning. It said that an unnamed informant claimed that Johnny was the most influential black in the prison and that nothing would go down behind his back. It labeled him as a member of a violent black gang and said he'd been part of a group running drugs and sexually pressuring young inmates. Johnny clenched his teeth as he thought about it.

"No, really," said the lieutenant. "We'll listen to you."

Johnny sat down. "I tried to *avoid* all this. I went to Walker to ask him not to shift those guys."

The lieutenant rocked back in his chair. It was the first he'd heard of it. He left the room briefly to call Walker.

When he returned, he told his colleagues, "The assistant superintendent confirms it."

"What's more," said Johnny, "the last thing in the world that a Panther would be is a member of that group. They hate Huey Newton and the Panthers. Man, I'm probably on some of their hit lists. The Panthers don't hate whites."

The lieutenant listened carefully as Johnny continued his civic lesson about the politics of prison movements. At the end, he said, "Okay, you're acquitted."

"When can I go back to my wing?"

"You can't. Once you've been accused, you'll be a target."

"I've been in prison fifteen years. I can take care of myself."

The correctional counselor on the panel was not happy that the lieutenant so readily acquitted Johnny. "We can't put you back on the mainline," he said. "We'll put you in Protective Custody."

In Protective Custody, Johnny would be with a group of inmates who had ratted on other prisoners. It would be like the Adjustment Center or O Wing all over again. He'd be locked up "for his protection." He would not be able to play sports, take classes, or hold down a job.

The next day, Johnny described the scene at the hearing to Dennis. "When he said he'd put me in P.C., it was as if they'd thrown a dead dog in the room. The tension was incredible. So I told them, 'Okay, put me in P.C. That way, I can kill all your snitches.'"

Dennis's face turned gray. Johnny would never get paroled with a comment like that in his record. But as Johnny described the meeting further, Dennis realized that his manhood had been sullied by the offer to put him in Protective Custody and that the committee knew that prison etiquette permitted such a response. No piece of paper from the prison ever contained a reference to his comment. But the Tracy committee did recommend a transfer to another prison.

chapter
thirty-two

A round the time of Johnny's transfer to yet another prison, in Vacaville, California, Fleeta Drumgo, who was out of prison on parole, had run into Fay Stender's daughter, Orianne. "Someone's looking for your mother," he told her.

Fleeta was having a hard time on the outside. For all his revolutionary talk about freedom and liberty, he was totally unprepared for the workaday world. He would hit up San Quentin Six supporters for money—asking Charles Garry's assistant, Pat Richartz, to pay for his gas bill, then conning two other people with the same bill. Fleeta stole one friend's checkbook, another's food stamps. He spent time with parolees from a new black prison gang that had spread throughout the penal system. He seemed so miserable that Richartz feared that he wanted to commit suicide. He was putting himself in dangerous conflicts with his friends, almost as if he wanted them to kill him.

Orianne Stender didn't think anything of Fleeta's comments. She thought it was just a bit of street jive.

Then, on May 28, 1979, Fay Stender was awakened by a black man with a gun.

"Sit down at the desk," he commanded. "I want you to write something."

He ordered her to pen the following message: "I, Fay Stender, admit I betrayed George Jackson and the prison movement when they needed me most."

She began to write, then said, "Now this isn't true and I would like to tell you why this isn't true. I'm just writing it because you are holding a gun at my head."

He moved the gun closer to her and forced her to write. Then he accompanied her downstairs to get some money.

"I didn't do it," she said quietly. "I didn't betray George or anyone." She passed him the forty dollars she had stashed in a kitchen drawer.

Money in hand, he started walking toward the door, then spun around and fired his .38. He hit Stender in the chest, both arms, the abdomen, and the side of the head. It gave the appearance of a bloody crucifixion.

Dennis Riordan called Johnny with the news of the shooting.

"Will she live?" Johnny asked, choking back tears.

"If she does make it, she'll never walk again."

I want to be there, thought Johnny. I want to be there when she wakes up. She did so much for all of us. She was a friend when no one else was interested. I look around and there are reminders everywhere. Books they wouldn't have allowed into prison were it not for attorney Stender. The right to send uncensored mail to attorneys. The chance for black prisoners to take classes like electrical shop that had previously been open only to whites. She had that passionate conviction that made even the wardens cower. What a force she was, and now it's come to this.

There was no way Johnny would be able to see Stender, but he could at least write. He went back to his cell after talking to Dennis and tried to put together his thoughts.

Dear Fay,

*I recall the times—many times—you came when the skies
were not very bright for me. I recall a long history of pain and
blood. So many loved ones/people we both knew have been
ripped off and their efforts obscured. . . . There are those who
obviously don't understand; those whose minds have been so
diseased, so tampered with, that they would commit such an
ugly, insane action; those who would strike a blow, not only
against you, but against some of the very ideals for which so
many loved ones fought so hard/gave so very much (for this?).
I wonder at the origins of such insanity . . . and are their
insane actions really any different from the insanity perpetrated
by those who control and benefit? . . .*

*I felt very sick with hurt upon hearing what happened. The
urge not to believe it persists, and yet you are there in a real
struggle for your life. Please be well, my dear friend. That is
more important than anything else I might wish for right now.
The only appropriate thing is your recovery, and no one can say
that. You must do it. Just refuse to accept any other alternatives.*

*love to you,
johnny*

When Stender awoke in the hospital, she was paralyzed
from the waist down. Fleeta Drumgo arrived at Charles
Garry's office to sell information about Stender's attacker,
but no one took him up on his offer. He had been there
before, bumming money under so many different guises,
that no one believed him.

On June 14, 1979, a former Folsom prisoner, Edward
Brooks, was arrested during a bank robbery attempt. Bullets
removed from one of Brooks's guns matched those removed
from Fay Stender during surgery. Stender identified Brooks
as the man who had shot her.

The court's first few attempts to appoint an attorney to
represent Brooks were rebuffed by the lawyers. Radical

criminal defense attorneys were in shock. Doron Weinberg, Stender's former law partner, recalls, "From the first reports, it seemed like a bad search. We were angry that the guy might get off on a technicality."

Police had seen Fleeta Drumgo with Brooks shortly before the attack on Stender. In December 1979, a month before Brooks's trial, Drumgo was murdered in a gangland-style shooting. Angela Davis gave the eulogy, calling him a "martyr."

When Brooks's trial began on January 16, 1980, more than a dozen criminal defense attorneys arrived to root for the victim. The defendant considered himself to be a hero in the image of the Soledad Brothers and the San Quentin Six. He was convicted and sentenced to seventeen years in prison.

"And so the railroad continues," Brooks told the court, "and you have successfully convicted another innocent man." Brooks filed a statement with the court comparing himself to Jonathan Jackson, George Jackson, Hugo Pinell. "All these strong, beautiful black men have been and are being framed-up, assassinated, and subjected to assassination attempts simply because they stand and fight as men against the racism, injustice, and humanity that is so embedded in the Amerikkkan society and its criminal justice system."

Johnny seethed that Brooks would dare invoke George's name to justify his acts. He had no association with the Black Panther Party, nor any understanding of what George stood for. I'd like to get my hands on him, Johnny thought.

Johnny settled into life at Vacaville. He started playing sports again, and challenged prisoners by trying out for both black and white teams. He had also started talking to other people about his own life, sharing his racial secret as a way to get people to be more tolerant. "I'm both black and white," he loved to say, just to watch the look of confusion in an inmate's eyes as he tried to come to terms with two such warring images in a single body. He had a new job, too, one he liked, as an electrician. He mentally thanked Fay for her battle to integrate the better prison jobs. Poor Fay.

After he'd been at Vacaville a few months, he got word that a cocky new black convict had entered the prison. He was Edward Brooks, Fay Stender's assailant. A young inmate brought the news to Johnny. He knew Johnny admired Fay Stender and credited her with the successes of the prison movement.

"Do you want me to kill him?" the young man asked. He watched Johnny closely, waiting for a nod.

Johnny remembered the grief and anger he'd felt at the news of the attack on Fay, and his immense sorrow when, after Brooks' trial, she had gone to Hong Kong and—to escape the ever-present physical pain—had taken her own life.

"Revenge," said Johnny, "is not a measure of correction. It wouldn't do any good in terms of Fay. And it wouldn't be a good message to people that killing each other is a solution.

"No," continued Johnny, "I don't want you to kill him. What goes around comes around."

The other man looked crestfallen. Then he said to Johnny, "You're a good brother."

Later, at Folsom prison, Edward Brooks was stabbed to death.

Brooks's death passed without any fanfare. It was like that in prison, thought Johnny. The corpses just piled up and nobody gave a shit. No one cared whether it was justice, vengeance, tragedy. The prison system just looked at it as one less troublemaker.

In Vacaville, the body count included not only those who were ambushed or bludgeoned or garroted to death, but also a growing number who took their own life. Johnny knew more about the latter than most, because he was the first one they called after the body was removed. Because prisoners were so closely watched, they couldn't get their hands on an easy way out—sleeping pills, razor blades. Instead, those wanting to end their lives tore a ribbon of sheet from their beds, tied it around their light fixture, and hung themselves.

As the prison's emergency electrician, Johnny was called in right after the deed, while the cell still stank of the defecation that accompanied death by strangulation. His job was to bolt the light fixture back to the wall.

The problem had been gnawing at him since he first arrived at Vacaville. For his first few weeks there, Johnny had been put in a locked cell on a solitary confinement tier, while the administration decided where to place him. Rather than housing the politically active prisoners, as at San Quentin, the solitary confinement tier at Vacaville housed a number of prisoners who were psychologically disturbed.

Johnny noticed that an inmate across the tier was nervously pacing his cell. He seemed to have made a rope out of a sheet, much like the one Johnny had made in other prisons to hurl messages, in a rolled-up magazine, to other inmates. But this inmate had other plans. He was attaching the rope to an electrical fixture, as if to hang himself.

Johnny started talking to the man as if he hadn't noticed what was going on. He asked the sort of questions that any new inmate would ask. The man let go of the rope and began to talk to Johnny. He seemed to be a little more calm.

Then he reared his head back with a start. "Hey, I know

what you're trying to do," he said to Johnny. He climbed on his bed, put the rope around his neck, and leaped to his death.

Over the next few months, other inmates tried to hang themselves in the psych wing. Some were successful, while others were thwarted when the light fixtures broke off the wall. Johnny went through the logs of the psych wing and learned that there had been seventy-two suicide attempts over a fifty-two-week period.

After a dozen repair jobs in which he used the concrete bolts in his tool kit to fix the lights, he realized that the better the job he did on the fixture, the more likely it was the next jumper would be successful. So he began to replace the front in a way that looked stable but wouldn't hold up if an inmate tried to hang himself on it. He no longer wanted to be responsible for anyone's death.

But the loose bolts were a stopgap measure, and might even lose him his job. Johnny thought about the problem during the nights, and began to design an alternative lighting system. In the shop, he took a piece of ten-inch-long, half-inch sheet metal, bent the edges under, and smoothed the ends. He ran a wire down the center of the bevel and gave the contraption a name—the "surface mount safety raceway." Since it would protrude from the wall less than half an inch, a prisoner would not be able to drape a sheet over it to hang himself.

Johnny told his civilian electrician boss about the idea, and was given the go-ahead to install it in one of the cells. The prison administrators saw how well it worked and asked him to transform the other psych cells. Because of his electrical skills, the guards were beginning to view him as an asset, albeit one they should keep their eyes on.

chapter
thirty-three

O n July 9, 1984, Johnny was in the television room, only
half watching as he talked to a buddy next to him.
Then he heard a phrase he hadn't expected coming from
the newscast: "the San Quentin Six."

He looked up to see photos of himself and his codefendants at the trial, along with a photo of George Jackson's last
visitor, Stephen Bingham. Then, as if in an enormous fast-
forward, the news focused in on the real Stephen Bingham
as he surrendered after thirteen years underground.

The surrender took place at the Glide Memorial Church
in San Francisco. Bingham told supporters there, many of
whom were wearing "Welcome Home, Steve" buttons, that
he was "a victim of a careful cover-up as to what really happened to George Jackson and/or a scapegoat of a prison system bent on discrediting lawyers."

Johnny stared at the image on the screen. At forty-four,
Bingham looked nothing like the angry radical with the
pointed Leninesque beard who had gone underground in
1971. He was now clean-shaven, with curly gray-streaked
hair. With his lean build and handsome face, he looked like
a television anchorman rather than a man accused of murder.

"I was afraid that day precisely because of my position as

a lawyer visiting a prisoner," Bingham said. "In the late sixties and early seventies the effort by prisoners organizing against medieval prison conditions had reached its peak. As national, even world, attention was spotlighted on California's prisons, lawyers became involved in helping to reform this inhuman system."

He recounted how lawyers had revealed to the world how the prisons conspired to kill inmates and how, both as governor and president, Reagan had retaliated against these attorneys.

"What has changed to encourage me to come back now?" Bingham said. "I believe today I *can* get an open, fair trial. I am convinced that most Americans reflecting back on the late sixties and early seventies are now willing to accept that the government has at times engaged in illegal, excessive, and immoral practices to discredit those who have been working actively for change.

"I am confident today that I will be acquitted."

Things were different now. The Vietnam war was long over. Watergate had felled a president. And a year earlier, in 1983, the California Department of Corrections had paid a fifty-thousand-dollar settlement to the families of W. L. Nolen, Cleveland Edwards, and Alvin Miller, the three black prisoners who had been killed at Soledad in the O Wing yard.

In the intervening years, the F.B.I.'s role in destroying the lives of Black Panthers and white activists had been well documented. A committee of eleven senators headed by Senator Frank Church of Idaho had been assembled to investigate abuses by the F.B.I. and C.I.A.

Chief counsel to the committee Frederick A. O. Schwarz Jr. described the F.B.I.'s COINTELPRO program as "an ugly little acronym which would have been at home in any police state in Eastern Europe or Latin America. It meant illegal investigations and secret punishment, administered not by a court but by the Government's chief law enforcement agency. And its aim was not to arrest, but to 'harass and disrupt,' dissidents and others deemed to be unacceptable. COINTELPRO'S tactics were designed, for example, to break up marriages of civil rights workers, to get teachers fired, to destroy reputations of lawyers, to sabotage political campaigns, and to encourage violent retribution by falsely and anonymously labeling intended victims as government informants."

The Church committee conducted hearings and a fifteen-month investigation, ultimately analyzing over 110,000 pages of documents. They learned that the F.B.I. had opened more than 500,000 domestic intelligence files, which often contained information on more than one person. At a public hearing, committee member Senator Philip Hart of Michigan observed, "As I'm sure others have, I have been told for years, by among others, some of my own family, that this is exactly what the Bureau was doing all of the time, and in my great wisdom and high office, I assured them that they were wrong—it wasn't true, it couldn't happen. They wouldn't do it. What you have described is a series of illegal actions intended squarely to deny First Amendment rights to some Americans. That is what my children have told me was going on. I did not believe it."

Now even establishment figures like Hart and Church were convinced. For fifteen years, wrote the committee in its report, "the Bureau conducted a sophisticated vigilante operation aimed squarely at preventing the exercise of First Amendment rights of speech and association, on the theory that preventing the growth of dangerous ideas would protect the national security and deter violence."

The F.B.I.'s tactics had violated the Constitution, and had destroyed the Black Panther Party. They had driven Huey

Newton over the edge by providing false documents and undercover agents to convince him that the people closest to him—people like Bobby Seale, David Hilliard, Elaine Brown, and Charles Garry—were actually government informants out to get him. His retaliation had smashed the Party into pieces.

In April 1986, the Bingham trial began in the same courthouse that Jonathan Jackson had tried to liberate. The same courthouse in which Johnny Spain had gained two life sentences for conspiring with Stephen Bingham.

Bingham was charged with the offenses that Johnny had been convicted of—conspiring with George Jackson and, as a result of that conspiracy, liability for the murders of Jere Graham and Frank DeLeon. He faced a maximum penalty of life imprisonment. But Bingham had numerous advantages over Johnny. He'd been to Yale. His father was a retired judge. And, most important, he was white. There wasn't even a hint that he should be shackled.

"George Jackson was one of the most closely watched prisoners in the annals of California prison history," Bingham told reporters. "It is simply not believable that a large 9-millimeter gun plus two clips of ammunition plus a wig could enter the prison, let alone be turned over to Jackson, without the knowledge and complicity of prison authorities."

The miniature San Quentin Six case took two and a half months to try and led to a mere six days of jury deliberations. When the foreman labeled him innocent on the first count, Bingham sighed. By the third innocent verdict, he and his attorneys, as well as several spectators, had tears running down their cheeks. A cheer of joy resounded in the courtroom.

With the acquittal of Bingham, Johnny was now being imprisoned for a conspiracy that the Bingham jury had decided had never existed. He was sure that meant that he could be released. After all, the jury in his case had asked Judge Broderick whether there had to be a conspiracy between Jackson and Bingham in order for them to find any of the San Quentin Six guilty of conspiracy—and Broderick had said that the defendants could not be found guilty unless Jackson and Bingham had conspired.

Johnny told Dennis Riordan to prepare the briefs to get him out. But Dennis explained that while Bingham's acquittal lent moral force to the argument Johnny should be released, it did not present sufficient grounds for a legal challenge.

Johnny had always looked forward to Riordan's visits. More a friend than just a lawyer, Dennis was really the only one Johnny could open up with these days. Certainly he couldn't show any weaknesses with the other prisoners by hinting at how he felt or what his doubts were. For Dennis, too, the times were special.

It was odd, thought Dennis—here he had never seen Johnny use a knife or fork in all those years, or run or throw a ball, or put on or take off a coat—all little things that one might share with the most casual of acquaintances. But he was closer to Johnny than to almost anyone else in his life. In all those awful green rooms they were able to conjure up the largest of worlds.

On one particular visit, Riordan talked briefly about the new legal strategy he was pursuing. For years he had been haunted by his image of Johnny Spain when they'd first met—the strong, proud black man chained like a slave at auction. He was now pursuing an appeal arguing that Johnny's shackling violated his right to be tried with a presumption of innocence.

He had impressive support for his approach. Amnesty International had written a report saying that Johnny's chaining during his trial was a clear violation of human rights and of international treaties to which the United States was a signatory.

"In this case," wrote Dennis in his brief, "Spain was charged with murder, assault, and conspiracy to escape. The jury knew that the courtroom was frighteningly secure— armed guards, bullet-proof barrier, metal detectors, body frisks, photographs, videotape system, etc. The jury also knew that despite all this, appellant Spain was chained, while sitting six feet from a guard, with belly chains, handcuffs, leg irons, and a restraint locking him into his chair. The jury well knew that other criminal defendants are not treated in that manner; in fact no other defendants in the history of California criminal law *ever* had been tried under such conditions. No intelligent human could do other than surmise that the reason the court imposed the chains on Spain was that he had proved himself so wildly volatile that to allow him the use of even his hands would threaten the life and limb of others. Rather than carrying a presumption of innocence into trial, Spain first confronted his jury wearing the visible manifestations of a judgment that he was inhuman, a fact obviously prejudicial to his case."

Dennis argued that the chains had caused Johnny severe pain, confused his mental faculties, made concentration on court proceedings impossible—and prevented him from testifying.

"Had Spain not been chained," wrote Dennis, "had he been able to testify, had the state begun its case against Spain carrying the burden of proof, had Spain been permitted to stand before the jury as the intelligent, controlled, and sensitive person that he is, his verdict of conviction could well have been different."

Dennis was angling to get a new trial. He had already mapped out what his strategy would be if they could begin again. He would use prosecution witnesses to make his case. He would call the state's fingerprint expert, Spiro Vasos, to make clear that none of Spain's prints had been on the Astra, nor on the soap in his cell, nor on the hidden ammunition. He would interrogate a state criminologist, Louis Maucieri, to show that no tests were given to Spain right after the incident to assess whether he had held a gun recently, and no attempt was made to examine his clothes for blood, even though Maucieri acknowledged that if Spain had been in the killing cell there would have been blood on his clothes. Dennis intended to argue that the failure to collect and to preserve potentially exculpatory evidence should be taken as evidence that there was no blood on Spain's clothes nor powder on his fingers.

Most importantly, the trial could go forward without Johnny in chains. Without the pain and distraction, Johnny would finally have the chance to tell his own story. He felt people were more prepared to listen now—and that, without the chains, there was a greater chance of a fair trial. Also, Johnny was now five years older than George had been when he died. The Panther Party was in ruins. He felt comfortable about being more true to himself than to people's view of him.

Dennis knew that things would be different if Johnny testified. No longer an angry, beaten-down prisoner, Johnny was now a person who was trying to get hold of his life. He was more comfortable with himself, more engaging when he talked, alive with resurgent idealism. Dennis had watched Johnny's transformation over the past ten years and he knew that Johnny deserved to be out on the street. Others recognized that, too.

Dr. Richard Delman, a court-appointed psychologist who had interviewed Johnny at length reported, "I did not administer psychological tests to Johnny, mostly because these instruments are largely pathology-based and are simply not useful in describing people who are as high-functioning as he is. He is articulate, intelligent, industrious, loving, considerate, respectful, energetic, aware, conscientious, empathetic and generous. He remains intensely remorseful about the life that he took as a teenager. Although one is always cautious in making predictions, I consider it almost impossible that Johnny could ever hurt another person. Having suffered through indignities that could embitter the strongest of men, he has matured into a unique kind of empathy."

Delman's report continued: "I have never been a particularly political person. I'm sure that I am closer to Ronald Reagan than to Huey Newton. . . . When I read some of Johnny's adolescent writings I had a hard time understanding them, and I'm certain that if I had been a prison administrator in the 1960's and early 70's they would have convinced me that this was a dangerous, angry, perhaps unbalanced adolescent, whose influence on other inmates needed to be isolated and minimized. However, it's been a long time since then, over a decade. We have all changed. . . ."

chapter
thirty-four

In many ways, Johnny felt that he was starting over. He was trying again to unify the prison, just as he had in his Soledad days. But he was coming at it from a much stronger personal position. He had finally come to a sense of unity about himself, a comfort with both his black side and white side, and a willingness to talk about it.

He was putting his initial focus into sports. Sports, to him, were a metaphor for life in general. If he could get blacks and whites together in sports, he felt the rest would begin to fall into place.

The teams—like the prison gangs—were divided along racial lines. Since coming to Vacaville, Johnny had tried to put together a mixed race football team. He was always rebuffed, since both black and white inmates saw sports as a way of demonstrating the superiority of their race over the other. Finally Johnny said, "Listen, I'm black and white, I could play on either side. But you've seen me coach and you know that, with the best team possible, of both races, we could win the championship." That year, blacks and whites joined together under his tutelage. Johnny drummed into them the importance of having a plan and executing it, rather than viewing sports as a chance to beat up on the other side. As a coach, he thought back to the old stolen playbook from the U.C.L.A. team and taught his team the audible system. They won the championship.

His team was a starting point for a political ideology group, just as the Iron Palm group had been. Johnny kept an inventory of the one hundred books he had in his cell, and started loaning them to his players and having discussions about them on the bleachers after practice. The scope of his readings had expanded in recent years. Not only were there the old standbys, like Marx and Che Guevara, which George Jackson had given him to read, but newer, feminist writers as well, partly due to Cathy Kornblith's influence. He urged his teammates to read Marge Piercy's *Woman on the Edge of Time*.

The women he'd known over the past decade had helped him transform his life. Cathy Kornblith and Elaine Brown in particular had taught him about the importance of small changes in the here and now, not just revolutionary ones in the future. He passed that message on to the young men who looked up to him now, and tried to lead them by example.

As a veteran of the prison system, Johnny acted as an adviser to younger prisoners. One told him, "Tomorrow, I'm going to get down on a guard who mouthed off at me."

"Why?" demanded Johnny. "You're getting released next month."

"Because I'm a man, and I don't take that shit from no-body."

"Don't be a fool. If you punch a guard, you'll get ten years. Five years from now you'll be willing to eat a truck-load of shit to avoid doing the second five, so stop acting like a moron and walk out of here in thirty days."

In 1986, Johnny met Huey Newton for the first time. Huey was sentenced to Vacaville for carrying a concealed weapon, in violation of his parole. He looked beleaguered, not at all like the strong, proud figure on the famous poster of the 1960s, where Huey sat guerrilla-like in a large wicker chair, a spear in one hand, shotgun in the other. Johnny wondered whether the wear and tear of his own life had similarly affected him. Sometimes he'd wake up and think he heard the sounds of birds, but it was just the squeak of rusty cell doors.

Johnny longed to talk politics with Huey, thinking what an incredible theorist Huey had been, how he'd taught himself to read looking at Plato's *Republic,* how he'd debated psychologist Erik Erickson at Yale with such a flourish that their conversation had been turned into a book, how he'd finally gone back to school and finished his doctorate. Now, though, Huey's attention wandered as he tried to size up the inmates around him.

When they were finally alone, Johnny told Huey, "It's an honor to meet you. You set in motion a political consciousness-raising throughout the country. You forced the country to look at some of its most glaring contradictions."

"We could do it again, you know," Huey said. "The world is ready."

"It wouldn't work yet," replied Johnny. "The left is too splintered. You'd need to do some work first on healing old wounds."

The COINTELPRO program had done its job. Decent people had been expelled from the Party. Elaine Brown was still in hiding. It would be hard to get people to trust again.

When Dennis Riordan had first heard about Johnny's new lighting system, it made him both proud and sad. Johnny had so much to offer the world, but it was like moving heaven and earth to try to get him free.

Dennis thought about how he had been drawn to Johnny's case because, to him, it illustrated America's obscene, obsessive history on the question of race. But now he could use the case not only to illustrate the damage racism does—God knows, you could walk around South Central Los Angeles and find a million instances of people who had been harmed by the social system of those years. He could now sound a second theme—that of Johnny's personal redemption. He could show how the events that had led Johnny to the Adjustment Center and away from his family had been transcended.

"The case," Dennis would tell anyone who would listen, "is about our system of apartheid and what allows somebody to overcome that. The central focus is on why he was what he was and how he came to be what he is today."

Riordan groped about for tactics to introduce information of his client's transformation into the barren record. Years earlier, Johnny had become eligible for parole on the original Long murder, but had not bothered to ask for a parole hearing because of the two additional life sentences. With a possibility that the conviction would be overturned because of the chaining, however, Dennis had Johnny ask the Board of Prison Terms for a parole hearing, for which he could ask people to write letters on Johnny's behalf.

"Johnny, could you see if there is a guard who is willing to write a letter in your behalf?" asked Dennis.

"I'll see if there is anyone here willing to stand for me," said Johnny.

At the same time, Riordan needed to find a way to get people on the outside to write letters endorsing Johnny's parole. He needed someone with a broad base of political support. He thought immediately of Elaine Brown.

Elaine had gone into hiding after she left the Black

Panther Party. She didn't know whom to trust. Two decades earlier, Elaine had been at the UCLA meeting where Panthers Jon Huggins and Bunchy Carter were murdered. Now she wondered nervously when she would meet a bullet meant for her.

Few people knew that she was living in Beverly Hills. But the previous year, Johnny had been determined to get back in touch with her, and he gave his letter to a friend of hers, who passed it to another friend, until, finally, it reached Elaine's hands. Elaine wondered whether she should reply. It could be a setup. Or, even if Johnny meant her well, letting her address make its way to the eyes of others in the prison system (the official censors, the other inmates) could be dangerous.

She wrote back, using the return address of a friend's production company. As the letters from Johnny mounted, praising her for her earlier work with the Panthers and describing his development of the antisuicide lighting system, she began to feel less fearful about getting into the public eye. If he was able to accomplish so much from prison, she could at least be doing as much on the outside.

When Elaine had fled from the Black Panthers in the last crazy days, she left virtually everything—her clothes, her daughter's toys. But she'd escaped with her Rolodex. The "Golden Rolodex," she called it. Her first foray back into public life would be to call people to request that they write letters on Johnny's behalf to get him out on parole.

When the letters started pouring in, Dennis was stunned by the response. Ninety guards and other correctional officials, including a friend of the guards who had died in the George Jackson incident, wrote letters supporting Johnny's parole. Some had been impressed by how Johnny handled the crisis when blacks and whites had been locked together in the Tracy wing during a riot. Others offered respect for his suicide-prevention lighting. Still others, who patroled the grounds at Vacaville, simply enjoyed talking to him.

Besides the guards, another two hundred people— including the speaker of the California Assembly, the president of Motown Productions, the mayor of Oakland, and several of the whites he had saved during the Tracy riot— also wrote support letters. A company that made glass display cases offered Johnny an electrical job upon release; a lawyer, Richard Zitrin, invited Johnny to live with his family.

"I could not imagine myself writing on the behalf of another inmate, simply because I do not know another inmate who demonstrates so clearly or consistently the qualities he has," wrote one guard.

A former guard recalled being told during his training that he should never "let Spain walk in back of me, to always be alert around him because he was an officer killer." Yet he had learned to trust and respect Johnny. His lengthy letter praised Johnny's work in prison and predicted that Johnny would succeed on the outside.

Sergeant D. C. Kitterman, who had been a close friend of Sergeant Jere Graham, one of the guards who had been killed on August 21, wrote that he had hated Spain for years after the murder and probably would never forgive him for whatever role he played in the deaths, but he described a "complete and incredible change in Johnny Spain's attitude."

"I do feel that he would make an excellent candidate for parole," wrote Kitterman.

Gonzalo Cano, Johnny's former coach, also recognized a profound change in Johnny. It came through in his letters. Now Johnny could write about more personal things, telling Cano, "You were one of only a few people who could really understand my aloneness. Not simply the fact of it, but in

many ways the necessity of it." In another letter, he wrote, "I
wish Lambert had lived to see these moments of change
and growth, though I'm not sure he didn't see them; it's
quite possible that my discoveries are not altogether new.
The road to recovery, as I like to think of it, is what I'm on
now, which doesn't even begin to describe what is changing
and growing inside of me. It has its moments of pain and, at
times, intolerableness, but I'm of the opinion that there is a
natural pain involved in healing and the growth that accom-
panies it."

When he received that letter, Cano looked through the
older letters that Johnny had penned in his angry and
demanding revolutionary days, the essays with titles like,
"Let White Blood Run." Then he took the pile of old correspondence and burned it in the garbage can. That part of
Johnny's life was over.

Johnny kept copies of all the support letters in his cell, sometimes thumbing through them late at night. It was like a
book about his life, laying out the details of his path to
prison, and the world he had created for himself inside. He
was reminded a little of his trial in the San Quentin Six case,
where his personal story was played out on the courtroom
stage. At that earlier time, though, he wasn't willing to try to
understand what it all meant.

In trying now to put his past in perspective, he kept coming back to that night in December 1966. The last day he'd
been free. The night he'd shot Joe Long.

Johnny couldn't believe how arrogant he'd been after the
murder, crowing first that it was self-defense, then that it was
some sort of bullshit revolutionary act. No way. It was the
action of an angry, mixed-up kid. Period. End of story.

The shooting was an intimate part of him. It had almost a

physical presence, like an arthritis in his bones. He'd never be able to shake it, just like he'd never be able to bring Long back. He thought of his days in L.A., before the shooting, when he felt like he had nothing, no matter what the Spains gave him, no matter how much he took. The hole in his life that had occurred when he was wrenched away from Ann had seemed too big to fill.

Now he knew he'd been wrong. He'd had something, and still did. He had himself.

There was one last detail, one last thing he had to put right before he could set aside the prison he made for himself.

He needed to see Ann.

Over the years, Cathy Kornblith had kept in touch with Ann, writing her and sending her Christmas presents on Johnny's behalf. Ann's health was failing. She had difficulty walking and needed insulin for her diabetes. But she was willing to fly to California. She wanted to see Johnny as much as he wanted to see her.

They sat in the visiting room in May 1987 on two round stools attached to a small round table. Ann fidgeted more than when she had visited Johnny at San Quentin at the time of his trial. She said she was sorry a dozen times.

"I've always struggled with the question of whether I did the right thing," she told Johnny. "I felt horrible for years after, and there was no one to talk to about it." Ann looked over at the prison guard patrolling the visiting room. "I thought you were going to a better thing. Had I known all this would happen, I just don't know what I would have done."

Johnny was seeing a different side of his mother than she had revealed in her letters. She'd always seemed so tough, so sure of her decision.

She bent her head down and whispered as she said the

next words. "I've often thought it would have been better to have killed you than let you go through all this," she confessed.

"Well," said Johnny slowly, "if I were your son and this kid Larry was another son, and you killed him, I would understand. But I would tell you that you didn't give him a chance.

"What you did was the only thing you saw as reasonable and safe," he continued. "Why would anyone keep their child in a situation where they were going to be killed, if they thought there was a safe avenue out like putting your kid in a basket and floating him down the river. That happened to Moses, you know. Who wants to float their kid down the river? There's a chance of death that way, but the other way is certain death. I think if you kept me, you were faced with certain death. If you did it, or if you allowed the Ku Klux Klan to do it, it was certain death. And rather than do that, you floated me down the river and that was the best thing you could do at the moment."

Johnny lit a cigarette, and pensively blew the smoke.

"How do you feel about what I did?" she asked.

"You've never asked me before," said Johnny. "I know this. I was very hurt and I went a lot of years very angry with you, because how can you give up your baby?"

Ann began crying quietly.

"It wasn't until I, myself, became aware of life and death decisions that I would be able to appreciate what you did for me," he said.

Johnny went on. "I think I understand better now. When I was a young man in Soledad, part of what later would come to be called the prison movement, people would come to me and say, We want to do this and, Mom, sometimes they were asking me, could they kill people. And, I put on my face like, Well, we need to consider this, but in my mind, I'm saying, Holy shit, what's going on here? And I knew that this thing was so real, it must have been how you felt when the Ku Klux Klan called. You know, it's not a game anymore, it's not something that happens and you read in the paper or hear on the news that somebody got killed in Soledad while you're in Tracy. It's a lot different when someone comes and says, 'I want permission to kill this person.'

"Ma, I can't order someone dead. That's what you're struggling over yourself, that you feel bad that you didn't order me dead, but I never could do it and I don't think I ever could. And maybe that's what you went through, not an easy decision, but, in fact, as we, you and I, sit here now and look back on it, it was the best decision."

"But, Larry, those chains, and living like an animal," she said.

"Mother, you are responsible for my birth, but you are not responsible for my life. I assume full responsibility for my own life."

"I hope you realize I've always loved you," Ann said through her tears.

At a nearby table, a little girl approached her imprisoned father. He swept her up in a giant hug and kissed her on top of the head.

"I love you, too, Ma. It's important to me to love you, because you're my mother, and not to hate you because society wouldn't allow you to be my mother. That's not your fault, it's not your problem. I think you committed a noble act, and just because I didn't understand it all my life doesn't make it any less noble."

Johnny was now ready to present himself to the parole board. A panel of three board members was convened to determine whether he should be allowed to leave prison. Johnny was quick to point out to them, "I don't come before the board as a new person. I come before the board as a person with a history. As I sit here today, though, I am capable of taking on responsibility in life. There was a time when I could not do that.

"I can't change history," said Johnny. "I can only change me and I think I have done that."

With a flourish, Dennis laid out the hundreds of letters for the board members to see. The board then took a break to make a decision.

Dennis and Johnny waited expectantly. They were sure they had presented a persuasive case.

The three panel members returned to the room. They had found Johnny unsuitable for parole. Panel chairman Paul Foster said Johnny had shown "exemplary adjustment" during the last six years but "needed more seasoning."

In a later hearing, Dennis argued, "The Board shouldn't be trying to keep him behind bars. It should be asking his help in trying to figure out how to keep other parolees from returning to prison. And that is important because who's going to tell the Crips and the Bloods that you may think you've been screwed over because of your race, you may think you've been screwed over because you're poor, but it's life and you only get one and you die in the gutter or you take a hold of your life and do something with it. Who's going to tell them that and have them listen? The prosecutor? Me? *John.* John can, he does, he has, and they listen—they listen."

The Board of Prison Terms pressed Johnny about when, exactly, his transformation had taken place. When had he first begun to feel remorse? When had he turned from a reprehensible killer to a responsible individual? They seemed to want him to give a particular day, to point to a single transforming experience.

But that wasn't how it happened at all, Johnny thought.

"It happened gradually," Johnny said quietly, "sort of like the Velveteen Rabbit."

Normally, Johnny would have had to wait a year before getting another chance at a parole hearing, but two months after the adverse parole decision, federal district court judge Thelton Henderson finally made his ruling on the chaining issue. Henderson was the judge who, in 1982, had ruled Johnny deserved a retrial for the San Quentin Six conviction because of Fagan's meetings with the judge, but his decision had been overturned by the Supreme Court. Henderson now held that the shackling had violated Johnny's constitutional right to a fair trial. He overturned Johnny's conviction and remanded the case for a new trial. That meant that Johnny could no longer be imprisoned for the San Quentin Six case. He was in prison only for the original Long murder.

As a result, Judge Henderson ordered the parole board to make a new assessment of whether Johnny was suitable for parole. The board could not consider the incidents involved in the San Quentin Six case in deciding whether Johnny was suitable for parole, since Henderson had reversed that conviction. The board could only consider whether Johnny had served enough time on the Long murder.

"There's a good chance you'll be home by Christmas," Dennis told Johnny.

At the December 1986 hearing, the Board of Prison Terms seemed impressed with the progress Johnny had made. But when it came time to render their opinion, they ruled that Johnny was unsuitable for parole. It would be another year before he would get another chance.

Dennis prepared for the December 1987 hearing as if it were a U.S. Supreme Court argument, spending hundreds of hours putting together materials for the hearing. He filed a petition in state court for a writ of habeas corpus to let the board know he would seek the court's help if the board ruled unfavorably.

Cathy put in long hours as well. In conjunction with the parole hearing and preparation for a new trial, she made her first trip to Mississippi. She wanted to visit Ann and track down various records about Johnny's family.

In the state records office, a black female clerk pointed to the shelf that Cathy should consult and said, "You're welcome to look in the books."

Cathy looked up at the shelf, at volumes marked "White" and "Colored." She shivered slightly.

"I'm not from here, but I'm involved in the civil rights movment," Cathy said to the clerk. "I've read about those books and I knew that they existed, but seeing them is like being slapped in the face."

The clerk's gaze seemed fixed on Cathy's pale skin. "You should have lived through it."

Back in California, Cathy tracked down information about the other people who had been sentenced for murder in 1967, when Johnny had been imprisoned for killing Joe Long. She found that virtually all of them had already been released, despite having committed more heinous initial crimes, including multiple murders, rape murders, and cop killings. Her findings would give Dennis the ammunition to look each of the three board members in the eye and bring up the names of more violent, less rehabilitated prisoners whom they had nonetheless released.

It was a terrible hearing. Unlike the December 1986 hearing, where there was some acknowledgment given to Johnny's transformation, now the board seemed not to believe that Johnny could fully overcome his past. At the end, they not only denied him parole, but said that their decision was justified because of the social circumstances surrounding Johnny's childhood.

The hearing ended on a Friday afternoon. Dennis went out and got drunk, then rose on Saturday morning and wrote a blistering challenge to the parole board decision. On Monday, he filed it in Judge Henderson's court, arguing that the board had violated Henderson's order not to consider the allegation in the San Quentin Six case when it ruled on parole. "Like Governor George Wallace standing in the schoolhouse door, the parole board has found a way to flaunt the action of this court," Dennis told reporters. Henderson, one of the few black federal judges, agreed, and the board was forced to schedule another parole hearing for February 1988.

Johnny was on the verge of giving up hope, of giving in to the depression about being in prison forever. He began to feel that his outside contacts, which had always sustained him, were just making things more painful.

While Cathy was in Mississippi, he had written in his journal, "Cathy will return today. I already feel better. She is the world to me. Not 'the world,' as an abstract, but my world, the person with whom I share my heart and love, my hopes and dreams, my fantasies and visions, my joys and sorrows." Now, as he waited for the inevitable disappointment of the February parole hearing, Johnny wondered if he should stop seeing her altogether.

"Cathy," he told her, "I've stretched as far as I can. You've opened all those windows and I can't go any further."

He was talking again about making one of those big changes in his life, like stopping all visitors again, trying to shake things up in his mind.

"I need a change," he told Cathy.

. . .

At the February 1988 parole hearing, two members of the board panel agreed to parole Johnny in two years, but the third member dissented—automatically sending the issue to full board review.

Dennis then requested a hearing before Judge Kathleen Parker in the Los Angeles court where Johnny had originally been imprisoned on the Long murder. He argued to Parker that Johnny's release date had been unconstitutionally determined by ex post facto application of a 1976 Board of Prison Terms rule that allowed disciplinary infractions to enhance an inmate's sentence.

Before the court hearing, Johnny had asked Dennis, "Are we going to win this? Shall I pack my bags?"

After so many false hopes, Dennis was cautious. "Don't pack your bags," he said. "But don't lend anybody any money."

Cathy was in the courtroom with Dennis and when the judge ruled, she ran to the phone.

"You're going to get out tomorrow or the next day," Cathy told him. "Think that will be change enough?"

Cathy explained Judge Parker's ruling that Johnny had served enough time.

"I gotta get off the phone," said Johnny softly.

"You don't need to," Cathy replied. "I already hear you crying."

chapter
thirty-five

On March 10, 1988, Johnny strode down the main corridor of the California Medical Facility, the state prison in Vacaville. He had spent the past twenty-one years—over half his life—in prison, his universe bounded by barbed wire, gun towers, and corridors such as this. Two days earlier, he had been told that he was free to leave, free to reenter the life he had left at age seventeen, as if heading back out into the sun after watching an afternoon movie.

One of the first people Johnny sought out was Angela Davis, who invited him to a dinner in honor of her mother, then visiting her from Birmingham. When he arrived, he hugged Angela warmly. Johnny realized he had never touched Angela before. When she had visited him at San Quentin, he'd been behind a glass barrier or a screen.

After they ate, Angela asked a friend of hers, a young Canadian folksinger, to play some music. She played a song about George Jackson, then asked Johnny what he would like to hear. Johnny stood to sing with her. He asked for song after song from the mid-1960s, the last time he had been on the streets. She didn't know "What Becomes of the Broken-hearted." She didn't know "You've Lost That Lovin' Feelin'." She didn't know a single song he named— they were all before her time.

Johnny lowered his head and sat back down on the couch.

Angela moved over next to him. "I can remember when I first got out," she said, facing him. "I had difficulty readapting myself. I had been in a year and a half or so, in solitary confinement most of the time [while awaiting trial], and I found it very difficult to be around people again. I couldn't make my own decisions—I had grown unaccustomed in that short period of time."

Johnny thought about his friends who'd been released. Fleeta Drumgo, shot on the streets. Even his friend Leroy "Hutch" Hutchinson had sometimes buckled under the weight of outside life.

"Angela, don't worry," he interrupted. "If I can survive in there, I can certainly survive out here."

The following weekend, Johnny and Cathy flew to Los Angeles for a court appearance. Cathy navigated the rental car up along Mulholland Drive, gifting Johnny with the panorama of a city he knew only from his bus trips with Mary, his long runs, and the joy rides he'd taken with the Slausons.

As they drove through Beverly Hills, he asked her to stop in front of a familiar-looking house. An older black woman answered the door and he asked to speak to her husband.

"He's sleeping," she replied. "Come back some other time."

Johnny and Cathy started walking back to the car, then he returned to the door to leave his name.

The woman opened it again. "Aren't you . . . ?"

"Johnny Spain," he said.

She disappeared down the hallway and returned with her husband in tow.

"I'm Johnny Spain," he told the man. "I've come back

after twenty-four years to apologize for stealing your guns."

Earl Broady waved them in. Broady was a judge now, one of the first blacks on the bench in southern California, and he'd followed the reports of Johnny's trials and appeals in the press. "Despite everything," he said, "I think Johnny Sr. would have been proud of you."

Johnny wanted to keep pressing into his past. When he returned to San Francisco, he asked his parole officer to give him permission to visit Ann. The parole board refused.

Five months of attempts to get permission to leave the state were rebuffed. Then Johnny got a call from Don Armstrong, his younger white half-brother.

"Mama's dead," said Don. "The funeral is in Jackson and you have every right to be there."

Johnny felt bitterness about not having been able to see her before her death. He wanted to be at the funeral, to bring it full circle, to acknowledge that he had forgiven her, just as others had now forgiven him.

After pressure from Dennis, the Board of Prison Terms relented, giving Johnny permission to leave immediately to see his mother buried two days hence. Johnny wanted Cathy with him. There was a stop he wanted to make on the way.

Six years earlier, long after the San Quentin Six trial, he'd put Cathy on a special mission—finding his father. She didn't have much to go on. All Ann had told her was Arthur's name, so picking up Arthur's trail after thirty years was a challenge. But Cathy was in a better position to do so than she had been years earlier, when Charles Garry had asked her to find Arthur in the middle of Johnny's trial. She was a private investigator and ran her own agency, The People's Eye, often dealing with political cases.

Months of dead ends went by before Cathy was able to track down the post office box of a Louisiana man named Arthur Cummings, who seemed to be about the right age.

On a subsequent visit, she handed Johnny the New Orleans address.

Johnny tried to get Cathy to write a letter, as she had with Ann. But Cathy felt that this was a bridge he'd have to cross on his own.

Johnny used every excuse he could think of to put off writing. He had to read a motion. He had to go to school. He had an electrical job to do.

"I'm frightened," he told Cathy. "All of a sudden here is Arthur, here is my father, here is a part of me—a part of what I might have been, things I secretly dreamed about. I don't want to face that part in my life where I will have to confront him and the possibility that he might not accept who I am."

Four years earlier, on July 19, 1984, while still inside prison, Johnny had finally broken down and written to Arthur for the first time.

Dear Arthur:

Writing this letter has been one of the really difficult tasks in my life. My name is John Spain. My mother's name in 1948 was Ann Armstrong. I was born July 30, 1949 in Jackson, Mississippi. I don't know that any of this means anything to you. What I do know is that writing to you, if you are my father, has taken many long years of painful searching, not only to find you, but searching within myself for the courage to touch a part of my past that proved to be one of the most damaging of my life. If you want to confirm whether or not I'm correct about you being my father, I would suggest that you call my mother. She has expressed a desire to talk with you, and for what it might be worth, I think you could bring some comfort in her life with a phone call.

I have a 35-year-old need to know who my father is. The knowledge would help calm some of the deep, pounding storms within me. I could finally have a piece of the connection I've longed for my whole life. That is important to me. . . . There is

much I still want to say, but I think it is necessary (that it <u>could</u>
be necessary) for you to inform me of how my presence might
influence your life. I will send my mother's phone number if you
wish me to. If you are my father but do not want to establish
communication on an ongoing basis, please inform me of that
fact. I am reaching out to you, or rather to my father, because I
want to know my father. I will not attempt to press for commu-
nication if you wish otherwise.

Thank you for listening/reading this.

> *Best regards,*
> *John Spain*

Johnny had spent the next week fantasizing about the
reply. He wanted Arthur to say, "I'm your father and I can go
back and give you all the things you didn't have, that you
didn't get from me as a father. I can make all that right. And
if not right, I can make it better."

On July 30, 1984, his son's birthday, Arthur had written
back about his surprise at hearing from someone he did not
know. Johnny had offered to send Arthur Ann's phone number and Arthur said he'd be happy to call, with Ann's permission. Although he empathized with Johnny's search, he
emphasized that it would be "awkward" for him to write to
Johnny.

It wasn't the sort of effusive, loving letter Johnny had
secretly wished for. In fact, it sounded like Arthur would be
happier to talk to Ann than to communicate with Johnny.
When Arthur said it was "awkward" to write, did he mean
that we shouldn't communicate? Johnny wondered. It
seemed like just another door slamming in his face.

Johnny had written back several times, and received
answers that seemed equally evasive. He was angry about
how distant and reserved Arthur was. He decided to try one
final letter, in January 1986, one which he worked on for

over a week to try to force Arthur to understand what his son's life had been like.

Dear Arthur:

. . . Being in prison may well have written off any chance I might have had of really knowing one of my parents. There is Ann, you say? Yes, there is Ann. She has enough of a time of things just staying above the surface of her own life. . . . I will never come to know Ann, or for that matter any of my brothers or my sister in Mississippi. Those people I can recognize as my family, love to the bitter end, but they cannot escape the harsh, cruel, southern conditioning that will not allow them to embrace any real measure of the child who was sent away thirty years ago. Hell, I can live well enough with that. Although it hurts like you could not imagine sometimes, I can live with that. . . .

You were the only real chance I had. You might not be able to understand what it means to me, what hideous creatures loom about me with the threat of you and I never meeting. What happened to you? What was your life like? What forces brought you to this point? I don't know.

. . . All and all, I really may have been the very best high school athlete in Los Angeles. Those were my greatest years Arthur. My greatest moments in my youth and you don't even know about them. You don't know that I cracked a bone and was told that I would not play for six months—but played in three weeks because sports was my only valid world when I was growing up. . . .

Anything that amounted to good in the Los Angeles years became a threat of some sort to me. I was a good kid in heart, though perhaps too angry at the many things that I did not understand. About life. About myself. I was running away from something—that awesome, fleeting, intangible something. I had no idea what it was or where to escape from "it." All I knew was that I had to keep running, faster, farther, and longer. There was no safety for me, no matter how/where I ran. There was only pain and running. Now having gone through so many

changes, having been through such an amazing sort of meta-
morphosis—namely, having grown up—I find myself squarely
facing another terrible pain. I know who I am. I want to know
who you are. If we don't meet . . . It's not fair. It's just not fair.

> *Please be well,*
> *John*

Arthur was still unwilling to give Johnny what he wanted.
He responded with a card for Johnny, with the printed message, "Happiness Always." The card folded out into three
sections. Ironically, across the tryptic was a picture of a moving train, like the one that had taken Johnny from his home
to the Spains in Los Angeles.

Now Johnny was ready to make one more attempt. He
and Cathy flew to New Orleans and arranged to meet
Arthur, his daughter Carol, and two of Carol's children at
Felix's restaurant in the French Quarter. Arthur sat quietly.
Cathy couldn't take her eyes off Arthur's long fingers, which
looked so much like Johnny's.

As they walked through the Quarter after dinner, the two
women dropped back to give Johnny and Arthur a chance to
talk. Johnny felt he'd learned a lot about Arthur during the
dinner. He'd realized how Arthur couldn't give him all the
things he'd hoped for, because that just wasn't the type of
person he was. It had nothing to do with Johnny. Arthur was
just as distant and reserved with his daughter Carol.

Johnny put his arm around Arthur's shoulder. "So, Dad,
this is where you live."

Arthur jerked his shoulder back as if burned by the touch.
"That's the first time that's ever happened," he said, referring to Johnny's use of the term "dad."

They walked a block in silence. "I do think about you a
lot," continued Arthur. "I think that you must have been
resentful."

"To tell the truth, I didn't focus on you much at first," said Johnny. "Then when I finally got back in touch with Ann, I got angry. I went through a whole series of things I was going to tell you like, Why didn't you go to bat for me? Why didn't you take me with you? You left me before she did, you know. At least she made the attempt to stay in touch with me, but there was nothing from you."

"I didn't know!" explained Arthur. "I left Mississippi for all sorts of personal reasons. I wasn't running from anything; I didn't know Fred was going to come looking for me. I didn't know you had been born."

Johnny saw in Arthur's eyes how difficult all this was, how shocking it must have been to have a full-grown son appear out of his past.

"I don't know you," continued Arthur. "Now what I mean by that is that we haven't had a chance. You go most of your life, you don't know about me and I don't know about you, and all of a sudden here's this person in your life and here you are.

"I don't know you," repeated Arthur, "but I am very impressed by you."

Johnny realized that this was the best he could do, a relationship where Arthur was interested in what he did, even if the interest was not paternal.

"I don't expect that you or I can bridge all the gaps of father and son," admitted Johnny. "Because we didn't have an opportunity to establish those bridges and those bonds. But it doesn't change the fact that you're my father. You're a person I can respect and that's something, whether you're related or not.

"Like I told Ann," concluded Johnny, "I've finally come to the point where I can say, 'You were responsible for my birth, but you're not responsible for my life.'"

Later that evening, when they parted, Johnny hugged

Arthur. "Are you sure you don't want to come with me to the funeral?" he asked Arthur.

Arthur's eyes were solemn as he shook his head.

Ann's sister, Margaret, had written the obituary for the Jackson newspaper. In listing surviving children, she mentioned Charles, Ray, Don, Nancy—and even Mandy, the daughter a youthful Ann had given up for adoption many years earlier, before her marriage to Fred. It listed all of Ann's white children. It did not mention Larry Armstrong, the little boy who had become Johnny Spain.

"I told Larry about the funeral," Don told Aunt Margaret on the morning Ann would be laid to rest.

The pink drained from Margaret's cheeks as she contemplated the colored man showing up at an all-white funeral. "Are you crazy? You're going to embarrass the whole family."

Margaret turned to Johnny's younger brother Ray. "Well, he's certainly not coming back to my house afterward."

When the word was passed through the funeral home that Johnny would be coming, Ann's other children went to the local library to read an *Esquire* article about Johnny that had appeared eight months before. When they read how he had been run out of Mississippi as a youth, Ray said, "I bet he's coming here to kill us all."

When Johnny arrived, he looked far from menacing. He walked through the funeral home doors not knowing what to expect on the other side. But that was no different than how he lived every day inside prison.

The first thing the funeral home guests noticed was the enormous dignity and peace of the handsome black man. He greeted each of them warmly, mentioning some fragment of their lives that Ann had described to him. This was Don's first face-to-face meeting with Johnny. He was amazed that Johnny had been able to put aside the past, not to dwell on it, not to be a bitter, hostile individual.

Johnny approached the coffin. Tears flooded his cheeks as he said softly, "You were my mother. No matter what, you were my mother." He composed himself and thought of a verse he'd read somewhere: "The bow is taut, mount up, it's a beautiful day to die."

There was a momentary confusion as the time came to be seated for the funeral service. The seat next to Aunt Margaret belonged to the oldest son, but Charles was in prison; the violence he had called upon to save his younger brother was still with him, despite the army's attempt to knock it out. The other sons, Ray and Don, stepped aside. Johnny was the oldest son present, and he took his rightful place.

Aunt Margaret looked at him, and then reached for his hand. "I held your hand when you were first born," she told him. "I'd like to hold it now."

Afterward, Margaret invited him back to her house. Johnny's younger brother Ray broke the ice there. "I remember you but I don't know you. That's not the way I wanted it, but that's how it turned out."

Just a few months earlier, Mississippi voters had finally repealed the 1890 state constitutional amendment prohibiting interracial marriage. Fifty-three percent of voters favored repeal, with 47 percent opposed.

Johnny returned to California and his electrical job. On the night of August 21, 1989, he lay awake, thinking back to the days right before George's death, exactly eighteen years earlier. It had been a wondrous, dangerous time, a time full of a sense that anything was possible. Sure, they'd gone off course in many ways, but some of the basic ideas rang true.

He thought back over the Panther ten-point program. The tenth point was: We want land, bread, housing, education, clothing, justice, and peace. It had been like asking for the world, but recognizing some of those rights back then might have been a small price for this country to pay to avoid the larger problems that existed in the ghettos today.

The same night, Huey Newton wandered the streets of Oakland not far from where he'd founded the Black Panther Party. Tyrone Robinson, an ex-convict half Newton's age, approached him. Moments later, Robinson shot Newton. Robinson claimed he did so in a dispute over drugs, but police suspected additionally that the kill would bring Robinson status within his gang.

"I remember him as a fighter for equality, humanity, equality of races, the dignity of black Americans, and I idolized him during those periods of time," Charles Garry told a reporter. "But the F.B.I. harassed him to the point where they killed him from an emotional standpoint. To me, Huey died ten years ago."

A few days later, Johnny, Angela Davis, Elaine Brown, and Bobby Seale filed into an Oakland church for the memorial service for Huey. The mourners were an amalgam of activists and revolutionaries who had enlivened the words "Black Power," "Off the Pigs," and "Power to the People." Panther David Hilliard commented, "Let Huey's death move us to action. That's where our focus should be. He understood that it was a long struggle and that he would not live to see it end."

Ten years earlier, Angela Davis had said, "I have marked my involvement in the movement by the funerals I have attended." Her own life had been threatened so many times that she had lost count. She had learned to check her car for bombs.

We are the survivors, thought Angela. As she looked

around the church, she wondered what combination of luck, determination and rage had allowed them to prevail.

"I didn't know if I could even bring myself to go to Huey's funeral," Elaine Brown would say later. "In the late 1970s, the Panthers had fallen apart wounded. But something magnificent happened at the funeral, a kind of healing as we all got together again. We realized that we had done a wonderful thing, we had set in motion our dreams and ideals. Even though we didn't get killed in the great revolution that we were still clinging to. That was all resurrected with the spirit of Huey. We were cheering and crying. We had a feeling of what we were and why we think there are things that still need to be done."

Elaine delivered her eulogy to Huey and then turned to introduce a man who offered a future to their ideas. "Here is a man who spent twenty-one years in prison, over a third of it in solitary confinement," she said. "He survived absolutely the worst physical and emotional torture of us all, other than those of us who were killed. And it wouldn't have happened to him if he hadn't been affiliated with the Black Panther Party."

Johnny approached the altar. He wore black slacks and a sports jacket, his first major purchase once he was released from his prison blue uniform.

He spoke in a quiet, reserved voice. "I visited Huey Newton's death site," said Johnny, "and people were gathered around it, as if it were a memorial. There were flowers and candles and food. A woman was explaining to her young daughter who the Black Panthers were, what they were about, and why it was such a sad thing that Huey Newton had been shot.

"The little girl turned to her and asked, 'Why would *anyone* be shot down in the street in front of our house?' And her mother had no answer.

"The little girl was right. It shouldn't matter whether it was Huey Newton or anyone else that had been shot. Why should *anyone* have been killed?

"Hers was a sad statement to which we had no answer. And it will be a sad statement for the rest of our lives if we never come up with an answer for that little girl.

"We need to direct our efforts toward the youth, toward those who are our future. These children will be better armed if we share with them our errors, our visions, so that they can use them to build their own world."

epilogue

Johnny's life on the outside of prison has not always been easy. After so many years of having the prison dictate his schedule, he initially had difficulty regulating his time and agreed to do too many things. He was perpetually late, often standing up long-time friends. He lived at first with a lawyer and his family, but he did not really know how to handle having other people around. He was so used to being alone in a small place that he moved out and began to sleep in his car. The first apartment he rented—two rooms in a dark, musty basement—had no refrigerator or stove, only a sink. The bedroom had no window and the small windows in the other room were tightly covered. Within a few weeks, he had bags, papers, and other belongings stacked everywhere. It looked exactly like a cell.

When Johnny was released from prison, he took a job as an electrician at a company that made glass display cases. But when the company hit a financial crunch, the owner cut his modest salary by a third. When a second reduction seemed imminent, Johnny quit. He took what little money he had saved, bought a computer, and had business cards printed up, listing him as a "Consultant." Since then, he has been able to put what he learned in prison to use. He taught prison courses at Berkeley and Stanford, advised a California city on how to handle racial strife, and taught a pre-release class at a San Francisco county jail.

Today, Johnny Spain is a community organizer with the nonprofit North of Market Association. His territory is the crack- and crime-infested Tenderloin District in San Francisco, where he strives each day to make life a little better for the neighborhood inhabitants. He has helped shut down liquor stores that were too close to the playgrounds and to build low-income housing that shows respect for the privacy and decency of the inhabitants. He lives in Oakland in a sun-drenched apartment with big windows.

Angela Davis still works in the prison rights movement and teaches. She was recently promoted to the prestigious presidential chair at the University of California, Santa Cruz, and was cited as a "great woman" in the Ms. Foundation's "Take Our Daughters to Work Day" literature. Elaine Brown's book on her days in the Panthers, *A Taste of Power: A Black Woman's Story,* was published in 1993 to critical acclaim.

In 1993, Cathy Kornblith sold her private investigation agency, The People's Eye. She continues to work on legal cases as a private investigator, but also devotes much of her time to volunteer work with children and young adults and to lecturing at colleges about the criminal justice system.

Since Johnny Spain's release, Dennis Riordan has continued to represent convicted and often notorious defendants on appeal. His clients have ranged from a Mexican Catholic priest charged by the Reagan administration with helping refugees escape to this country from war-torn El Salvador as part of the "Sanctuary" movement, to Frank LoCascio, alleged to have been the "underboss" of the Gambino crime family. Dennis consistently makes the organized bar's lists of the country's top appellate lawyers and has argued twice before the United States Supreme Court.

Dennis's fifteen-year battle to free Johnny helped establish the scope of the "presumption of innocence" in American law. In 1995, Dennis was awarded a Fulbright fellowship to go to Spain to help lawyers there begin to make use of the "presumption of innocence," which had recently been added to the Spanish constitution.

In 1990, a group called the New Black Panthers, with chapters in twelve cities, was formed by a twenty-eight-year-old Dallas radio producer. The members today include secretaries, lawyers, nurses, electricians, and other middle-class blacks who are carrying the torch, in the wake of incidents such as the Rodney King beating and the massive drug use in the black communities. At nights and on weekends, they don black berets, black ankle boots, and dark gray fatigues and patrol the streets to prevent police brutality and self-destruction in the black communities.

epilogue to the new edition
Understanding Johnny

Shortly after this book first came out, Johnny Spain and I appeared on *The Oprah Winfrey Show*. I steeled myself for the appearance, telling myself that I would not be emotionally manipulated by Oprah's plan to reunite Johnny with his white brother Charles. I had interviewed both Johnny and Charles for the book, but they hadn't seen each other for over thirty years. Oprah sprang the surprise reunion on Johnny and, much to my astonishment, when Charles hugged Johnny, I cried, Johnny cried, and Oprah cried. The moment was about forging bonds, black and white, both within oneself and in the outside world.

Oprah, as you probably know, chooses her studio audience based on the show's theme. The audience was teeming with people whose own lives had to accommodate for society's uneasy—no, hostile—reaction to the relationship of black and white. The white woman in her fifties sitting next to me said that her family disowned her when she fell in love with a black man. As we spoke, her black husband of many years revealed to her, for the first time, that her father had offered him a large sum of money to leave town and not marry her.

After the taping ended, a woman said to Johnny, "You say you have been harmed by your mother giving you up, but the grass is always greener. I had a black father and a white mother, and my mother kept me. When I went to my white brother's high school graduation, I asked her, 'Who is that woman hugging Danny?' and she said, 'That's your grandmother.'

"And then my grandmother walked by and spit on me."

What can we do for children like these, and the couples who break barriers around race? The question takes on increased urgency as we realize that there are now more than 600,000 interracial marriages each year. How will the children of these unions view themselves? How will others view them? What will be their political voice? While these children could be celebrated as the triumph over racial boundaries, many are instead shunned by each community in which they may claim membership.

Constructing Race

It seems obvious to most Americans that our goal is racial harmony—ideally, to synthesize identities not as "white," "black," "Hispanic," or "Asian," but to transcend race altogether. This seemed to be Johnny's goal to a large degree. He ultimately used his "split identity" as a means to form bonds with men of all races in prison. But even as Americans wonder why we can't "just get along," we also realize that simply ignoring racial differences is akin to ignoring one component of our identities. For most, if not all, people of color, regarding oneself as black, Asian, or Hispanic not determined by skin, but by experiences and how we choose to align ourselves. Sometimes these experiences tell us who we are. Sometimes we tell ourselves.

Johnny's more inspiring experiences teach us that at the individual level the lines that draw race are truly arbitrary and hence subject to change. Johnny reshaped his identity according to his circumstances. But on a broader level, few people of color feel their identities as so fluidly and easily manipulated. Ultimately, Johnny's race was more than a matter of skin color, but less than the totality of both white and black experiences. He was neither fully black nor fully white. Johnny was that rare coin that, when flipped, landed standing up.

For others, race is largely about sociological conditions of class, education, or cultural norms that lock people into specific racial categories. Or it is about difficult negotiations between several determining factors of race. Does a person who finds herself wealthy, educated, and prosperous also find that she is regarded as less "black" than her poor, inner-city counterpart? Does she think of herself in that way?

On *Oprah*, Johnny said that whenever he gets a form that has a blank for race, he fills in "Human."

A woman in the audience said, "That's all well and good, but when I tried that, all that happened is that my employer refused to pay me until I listed myself as either black or white."

This woman's critique of Johnny is poignant, revealing the rigid, unforgiving aspect of racial construction in this country. As moved as we may feel by Johnny's story, we should acknowledge that racial categories generally immobilize or even prevent people from resisting labels in the way Johnny does now. To make matters more complex, some Critical Race theorists would contend that Johnny's appeal to color blindness serves to support hierarchies of racial power. They argue that when modern institutions insist on taking race out of consideration, they are able to obscure the biases and practices that sustain racial discrimination.

Most blacks in this country are similarly "entitled" to transcend racial boundaries. America is already largely multiracial—up to 80 percent of all blacks have white ancestry. Hundreds of thousands of people thought to be solely white have some black ancestors as well.

The question arises as to where the children of cross-racial parents fit in. If most blacks are to some degree white, then why are people trying to create a biracial category on the 2000 census? Why are there support groups for biracial children? The answer is that perhaps race still depends largely on experience, which in turn is balanced between internal choices of identity and external factors such as economics and/or physical appearance.

Johnny Spain's life demonstrates the exhausting personal journey that is required of individuals for whom categories fail. Too black for Mississippi, he was, in turn, too white for L.A. There were two separate cultures for him as a child, and he couldn't adjust to the rules of either. When he was in the South, "nigger" was a fighting word, but in California it was a homeboy term of solidarity.

Most of his life was a matter of taking sides, of either/or. In prison, initially, he was viewed as black and went to great lengths to avoid any mention of his "dirty" white heritage. When his white brother visited him when he was first jailed, he did not reveal to fellow inmates the family connection. Choosing to be black in those years probably saved his sanity, if not his life.

"Biracial children quickly figured out which way to identify," writes Yale law professor Harlon Dalton in *Racial Healing*. "Although they might occasionally catch grief from the Black community, they had little if any chance of acceptance by Whites. Often, biracial folks were among the most militant members of the Black community, perhaps to foreclose any concern that their mixed heritage made their race loyalty suspect."

The ascendancy of the Black Panther Party gave Johnny pride in the black part of his heritage as its leaders claimed a better way of knowing and being than did the current white political structure. Africans were a communal people, he was told, unlike the commodifying selfish hysterics running this country. Politics—in the form of the antiwar movement—gave him the chance to form relationships with white radicals around causes. For some of Johnny's black brothers in prison, this was the first time they had talked to whites as equals.

In later life, when Johnny was comfortable enough to disclose his heritage, he used his racial mix as a trump card to gain trust from warring sides in prison. His argument was that if black and white could exist more or less peacefully within him, they should be able to do so in the outside world. He integrated prison sports and, more important, helped curb race riots in prison by claiming entitlement to a voice for both sides.

But in prison, men's differences were not as demographically determined as in the outside world. There was no wide gap in economics or education among prison inmates. They were mostly the same, differing marginally in their skin colors, their neighborhoods, and their manners of speech. But half the battle of overcoming racial differences had already been won—they were all prisoners, and most were poor and uneducated; as those who believe in a purely social criterion for race might hold, all these men were "black" to some degree.

American race rules are cut-and-dried, based in large part on the amount of "racial blood" one possesses—a notion that carries from slavery times. Race calculated by blood percentage was a way to ensure the purity of whiteness. The current U.S. classification is still an artifact of slavery, resulting from the "one-drop" rule (hypodescent), a legal construction that assured that all the offspring and other descendants of blackwhite matings would be considered slaves themselves. During slavery, a person who possessed one-eighth "black blood," but seven-eighths "white blood," was not white, but "octoroon"—a different shade of black from, say, "mulatto."

In modern times, people have abandoned such racist terms, but still follow the rule of hypodescent, requiring a person to choose the "lesser" in status of two racial identities. Thus, a person who is half-black and half-white is essentially black. At the same time, few racially mixed people are willing to accept only half their racial identities.

"An African American today could fly to Brazil and be classified into one of about forty divisions, from black to white," notes University of Chicago professor emeritus James Bowman. "In Brazil, if a black person is educated or is wealthy, he or she is categorized as white. There is an old Brazilian aphorism, 'Money whitens.' The African American could then fly to South Africa and be classified as Colored, or Black, or one of many tribal groupings, or even white. The African American could then fly to the Middle East and be categorized as Iranian, Lebanese, Saudi Arabian, Iraqi, etc., and then fly home and be African American once more."

But in America, blacks may be suspicious of others who try to excuse themselves from "blackness" by asserting a white heritage, or by using wealth as a means of shedding "blackness." Many blacks find methods of redefining a person's race dubious. Aside from historical determinations of blackness, current measures of blackness range from a person's class to a person's genes.

No matter that anthropologists, sociologists, and even the World Health Organization now say that race is socially constructed, and not a preordained fact of nature. New technologies are turning back to blood as the oracle of race. British researchers claim that they have discovered three genes that can indicate, through genetic testing, whether a person is black. American scientists similarly claim to have found a gene on the Y chromosome that indicates whether or not someone is a "true" Native American.

In his essay, "Handle with Care: Race, Class, and

Genetics," University of Pennsylvania bioethicist Arthur Caplan asks, "Will the information generated by the genome project be used to draw new, more 'precise' boundaries concerning membership in existing groups? Will individuals who have tried to break their ties with ethnic or racial groups be forced to confront their biological ancestry and lineage in ways that clash with their own self-perception and the lives they have built with others?" And will people who want to identify with a minority group find themselves victims of the ultimate exclusion—being considered genetically unable to meet the profile of black or Native American?

Does genetic evidence suggest that a person with one-half "white" blood is half as likely to live and identify as white as someone with only "white" blood? Of course not. Instead, blacks' contemporary adherence to lineage and bloodline is perhaps a way of objectively identifying one's experiences through a single expression. Blackness is not about the presence of black genes or the percentage of black ancestry. Blackness has multiple dimensions. But what terms could adequately describe the web of sociological, economic, cultural, and even psychological factors that constitute one's race better than words like "black" or "white"? My instinctive answer is that no term could do a better job—unless we begin questioning what we mean when we say "black" or "white."

Courts, for example, have often assumed that their goals should be color-blind analysis. This, notes Professor Neil Gotanda, professor of law at Western State University College of Law, "ignores the ordinary lived experience of race as a highly charged concept with complex historical and social implications." In the instances of substandard housing, education, and employment, "race-neutrality" has had the effect of substantiating inequalities between people of color and whites. While Johnny's ultimate goal was to transcend race, a more current goal might be to explore the diversity among races and come to a general understanding of their social contexts and constraints before trying to go beyond racial categories.

Many of the forces that helped Johnny to overcome pigeonholing are no longer prominent in our society. The Black Power movement has weakened, massive political changes seem far less possible, and notions of individual responsibility have replaced the collective social conscience of the 1960s and 1970s. With the tutelage of the Black Panthers, Johnny's blackness, an otherwise "monstrous" condition, now became beautiful. The "one-drop" rule made it appear that black was a contaminant, while white was pure. But under a black pride analysis, says attorney Julie C. Lythcott-Haims, black blood could be viewed as "powerful, strong, and superior." In such an environment, Johnny could not escape his race, he could only redefine its meaning.

Along with the disappearance of massive social movements, a wave of neoconservatism today has tried to essentialize race and turn all social issues into racial ones. Welfare is seen as a "black" problem, even though more recipients are white. Yet, if people think of black synonymously with poverty, crime, and lack of education, we invariably construct the world around us to match that ideology. Richard Herrnstein and Charles Murray's book, *The Bell Curve: Intelligence and Class Structure in American Life* (The Free Press, 1994), sold 400,000 copies, sending its message that blacks are inherently inferior. This assertion is still used as a rationale to deny funding to programs such as Head Start or college affirmative action programs on the grounds that blacks' potential achievements are biologically limited.

Elaine Brown, the former head of the Black Panthers, identifies a "New Age Racism" coming not only from the Right, as before, but from liberal quarters as well. "New Age ideas of personal responsibility," she says, "allow the powerful to write off blacks and other poor and oppressed."

Stereotypes about race can actually cause poor performance. Stanford social psychologist Claude Steele's work on race indicates that students do more poorly if they know they are part of a group that traditionally has not been as strong academically. He studied why blacks do less well on standardized tests than whites. He discovered a phenomenon known as "stereotype vulnerability." When black and white college students were given a test that was described as simple problem solving, they did equally well. When similar groups of black and white college students were given the *same* test, but told it measured their intellectual potential, blacks performed significantly less well than whites. Steele postulates that blacks have to contend with the stereotype of intellectual inferiority at the moment they undertake such tests. They try harder, perhaps as a result working too quickly or inefficiently. Steele's research reached similar conclusions with women—and even white males were affected when told that Asians did better on a particular exam.

And no matter what level of education and social class blacks attain, *de facto* discrimination based on essentialized race continues to exist. The black middle class has quadrupled since 1968 when Dr. Martin Luther King Jr. was shot, but, as Henry Louis Gates Jr. and Cornel West in *The Future of the Race* note, "fully one-third of the members of the African American community are *worse off* than they were the day that King was killed."

Blacks find it three times as difficult to find service jobs, even when they have the same training and experience as whites. Blacks find it twice as hard to get a mortgage as whites with comparable income. Even medical care is delivered discriminatorily. Blacks who can afford medical care are still less likely to get needed surgeries and treatments; they receive fewer appendectomies, cardiac valve replacements, lumbar disk procedures, and tonsillectomies. The only categories in which they receive more medical procedures than whites are those that relate to their reproductive organs (hysterectomies and prostatectomies), a trend that further underscores stereotypes about race, sexuality, and reproduction.

"In 1993, 2.3 million black men were sent to jail or prison while 23,000 received a college diploma—a ratio of a hundred to one," writes Henry Louis Gates Jr. Our country's criminal laws have long been applied in discriminatory ways. During the time of slavery, slaves were punished for acts that were legal if performed by whites. After the Emancipation Proclamation, southern legislators passed laws that imprisoned freed slaves on minor offenses. Various studies show that even today blacks are treated more harshly in the criminal justice system. Black individuals are more likely to be prosecuted than white individuals, and black individuals receive harsher sentences than whites for similar crimes. For example, white pregnant women are slightly more likely to abuse drugs than black pregnant women, but black women are ten times more likely to be reported for substance abuse during pregnancy. Moreover, offenses that are seen as primarily black are punished more harshly than white offenses—for example, users of crack cocaine are subject by statute to longer prison sentences than are users of powder cocaine. In addition, the stereotype of the violent criminal as a black has fueled erroneous manhunts, such as when, after drowning her children, Susan Smith claimed a black man was responsible. More generally, surveillance has been used discriminatorily against men of color, to the point where it has been found justifiable to detain black or Hispanic men and search them if they are found in primarily white neighborhoods.

A new wrinkle in the management of prisons—privatized, commercialized penal institutions—exacerbates the problems that Johnny encountered in prison. As Eric Schlosser points out in "The Prison-Industrial Complex" in the December 1998 *Atlantic Monthly*, prison has become big business. Across the country, companies such as Corrections Corporation of America, Turner Construction, Brown & Root, and KMD Architects are building, designing, and managing dozens of new prisons a year. Rural areas experiencing economic downturns compete for new prisons. This means increasingly that men of color from cities are sent to remote prisons—sometimes even in other states—making it difficult for their families to visit. It also means that the guards tend to have little previous interaction with nonwhites.

The commercial companies behind the prison-industrial complex are lobbying successfully for new law enforcement measures to fill those new cells. In the past twenty years, the prison population in California has grown eightfold. This is largely due to an increase in prison time for nonviolent offenders, who in countries other than the United States would be sentenced to community service, fines, or drug treatment. Often, the arrests are for drug use. Schlosser points out that while white men and black men are equally likely to abuse drugs, blacks are five times as likely to be arrested for a drug offense. One in four black men will spend part of his life in prison.

In order to reevaluate the positions of people of color in our society, it is vital to question first the criteria by which we construct race. Whether it is through class, education, or the perpetuation of stereotypes, both social and scientific, the racial dimension of our social fabric can be resewn. But only if we understand how essentialized notions of race can limit us all.

Letting the Children Redefine Race

Until quite recently, sexual relations between a black man and a white woman were legally forbidden in most states (and, for the man, often punishable by death), but the converse was not true—in antebellum times, black women did not have the legal volition to refuse sex and thus could not be legally raped. Historically, then, multiracial identity has had one of two results: it either defined a person as black (as in slave black) or as illegitimate and estranged. Neither of these connotations fosters a welcoming environment for multiracial children.

Alabama's state constitution still frowns upon interracial marriage. As I was writing this epilogue, a vote was being taken on this very issue in South Carolina—the second-to-last state to forbid such marriages. In February 1999, voters elected to remove that section of their state constitution. Of course, any anti-miscegenation law is clearly unenforceable. In 1967, the U.S. Supreme Court, in *Loving v. Virginia*, declared unconstitutional the laws banning marriage between blacks and whites. By the beginning of the 1990s, such marriages had increased fourfold.

The number of blacks and whites who feel cross-racial marriages are wrong has dramatically decreased over twenty-five years. A 1997 Gallup poll showed that 60 percent of white Americans approved of interracial marriages, while twenty-five years earlier, only 25 percent approved. Indeed, 80 percent of the blacks interviewed in the 1997 Gallup poll approved of interracial marriages.

But both whites and blacks sometimes shun the children of these unions, viewing them with suspicion. The discrimination faced by blacks has been similarly—and, in some instances, more intensely—faced by the offspring of cross-racial parents. Multiracial children are often excluded from membership in both black and white communities. Since some blacks are suspicious about others' attempts to escape "blackness" by adhering to a "white identity," and since these children are unlikely to be accepted as white, the children often find themselves struggling to construct their own identities at the risk of alienating part of their heritage.

Biracial children not only lack a community, but also are subjected to a particular brand of racism. In 1994, an Alabama high school principal prohibited students from bringing a date of another race to the prom. When a biracial student asked him whom she could bring, the principal said, "That's the problem. Your mom and dad shouldn't have had you. You were a mistake."

"Just when I thought they were getting a little soft," comments one multiracial woman on her website, "*National Alliance* comes through again with a pseudo-scientific argument that biracials/multiracials are the result of 'sexual warfare' against whites. What's next? Biracials the cause of global warming AND the lackluster box-office receipts for this summer's blockbuster movies?"

Today, as more biracial children are beginning to acknowledge their multiple heritages, attempts to construct a unique racial identity for biracial children have increased. Support groups established in several states have fostered greater awareness of biracial children and mobilized such individuals for political and social movements. The Interracial Voice website, www.webcom.com/~intvoice/advocacy.html, lists over seventy interracial support and advocacy groups around the country. The emerging norms for "biraciality" are, for some, creating the conditions to actively challenge the stereotypes about race—as Johnny Spain did in prison. Johnny Spain himself has been active with teenagers in "I-PRIDE," an interracial support group in the Bay area.

Psychologist Agneta Mitchell, in a study of children of

interracial unions, found that those who identified as biracial had a higher level of anxiety than those who called themselves black, but also had a stronger sense of who they were. "They came out feeling they belonged in both worlds rather than feeling they belonged to neither," says Mitchell.

The upcoming 2000 census has given rise to a political movement for biracial offspring. Children of mixed-race couples say they are reluctant to check black or white on a form since either choice erases one of their parents. The 1990 census seemed to accommodate these concerns by letting people check "other" and then write in their racial classification, such as mother white/father black. Nearly ten million people checked "other" on the last census. They labeled themselves as being from almost 300 different "races," 600 Indian tribes, 70 Hispanic groups, and 75 multiracial combinations. Unbeknownst to those filling in the forms, the United States Census Bureau reclassified individuals by assigning them the race of their mothers—eerily suggestive of hypodescent, where a female slave's children were always considered black, no matter who the father was.

Schools that allow parents to check "other" for their children sometimes allow teachers to reclassify children based on skin color, hair texture, and facial features. Susan Graham, executive director of Project RACE (Reclassify All Children Equally), Inc., is a white mother of multiracial children. She told Congress, "Ironically, my child has been White in the United States Census, Black at school, and Multiracial at home, all at the same time."

The issue of racial mix has become even more relevant due to immigration trends. "We've had this large group of people coming from parts of Latin America . . . who don't consider themselves white or black," Harvard sociologist Orlando Patterson told *Newsweek*. "They don't want to play the binary game."

"Recognition of racial mixture," says Yale African American Studies professor Lewis R. Gordon, "dilutes identities premised upon conceptions of 'purity' and can therefore be an important stage on the road to a raceless or more racially free future."

Others are more skeptical about the impact. "The idea of a 'multiracial' category on the census fills us with ambivalence," says Lisa Jones in *Bulletproof Diva: Tales of Race, Sex, and Hair*. "Is this just one more polite, largely academic game of identity hopscotch folks are playing while Los Angeles burns?" Or, worse yet, "would 'multiracial' be akin to South Africa's 'colored' caste created under apartheid?"

Essentialized race also plagues minorities culturally. "Is black identity so problematic that one is to be judged as an 'anti-Negro Negro' for being critical of Baldwin or Jesse Jackson?" questions Julius Lester, professor of Judaic studies at the University of Massachusetts at Amherst. "Having been involved in the civil rights movement, I didn't fight against whites trying to limit and define me to turn around and have blacks try to limit and define me."

But it is this very cultural essentialism that has been voiced by the National Association of Black Social Workers (NABSW), which takes the adamant position that transracial adoption cannot work. Fearing that transracial adoption would result in the "cultural genocide" of the black community, the NABSW advocates placing black children in foster care rather than putting them with white families. The resulting pressure has pushed many states to adopt a presumption against transracial placement even though there has been (and still is) a dearth of adopting black families.

As Julie Lythcott-Haims points out, the NABSW perspective becomes more troublesome when we consider the adoptability of multiracial children. The NABSW perspective holds that most multiracial children in the social welfare system are considered black. According to Lythcott-Haims, the NABSW has, over twenty years, convinced social workers, adoption workers, and many state legislatures that: (1) a multiracial child loses his/her cultural identity by being reared in a white home, and (2) a black family can be found for multiracial children, so transracial adoption is unnecessary.

In the case of *Palmore v. Sidoti,* the U.S. Supreme Court unanimously rejected a Florida trial court's decision to modify a white mother's custody of her child after she married a black man. While the court ultimately felt it could not constitutionally consider any racial biases, it did articulate "a risk that a child living with a stepparent of a different race may be subject to a variety of pressures and stresses not present if the child were living with parents of the same racial or ethnic origin." But, as Professor Gotanda has pointed out, the court failed to realize that being raised in a biracial environment could benefit the child. Indeed, if increasing diversity can be used as a criteria for school admissions or for securing broadcast opportunities for racial minority viewpoints, why is it not seen as equally beneficial in the domestic sphere?

In fact, there is substantial evidence that children who are transracially adopted develop a strong connection to their racial identities. Harvard law professor Elizabeth Bartholet reports that transracial adoptees develop as strong a sense of black identity as black children adopted by black families. "They see themselves as black and they think well of blackness," writes Bartholet. "The difference is that they feel more comfortable with the white community than blacks raised inracially."

Lythcott-Haims urges that, at the very least, multiracial children be allowed "to be adopted by parents who represent at least one of the heritages in the child's ancestry which would create many more parental options for Multiracial children." *Washington Post* columnist William Raspberry recounts the haunting case of a black six-year-old who was not allowed to be adopted by a white couple and instead spent the next six years under state care until, at age twelve, the agency declared him unadoptable, saying he was fit only for the ministry, the military, or prison. In another case, a child with a white birth mother and a black father was classified as black and not allowed to be adopted by his white foster mother and her black husband because that family was classified as white. As Professor Bartholet points out, there is almost no evidence or research regarding transracial adoption that suggests that it harms children. But "there is extensive, unrefuted, and overwhelmingly powerful evidence that delays in permanent placement do devastating damage to children."

What does the disquiet between black and white communities mean for multiracial children? Many biracial children are tired of waiting—they've begun defining things for themselves. But a larger question may be what this disquiet means for race at large. As statistics show, more Americans favor interracial marriage, yet our true acceptance of such relationships will not come until we stop trying to hide the offspring.

Bartholet shares a story in which her three-and-a-half-year-old son asks why his mother does not look like him. He expresses sadness by this alienation, even after being told that it makes no difference that there is a disparity in the appearance of mother and son. But she examines his pain, ultimately asking herself if it "is a signal that living as part of a multiracial, multiethnic, multicultural family will force us to confront racial and other differences on a regular basis." Perhaps it is this very fear of pain that strengthens and cripples multiracial children like Johnny Spain.

The ground that biracial children are breaking in regard

to essentialized race may similarly expand the ways in which black, white, Asian, and Hispanic communities will construct race in the future. It is these steps that may build the painstaking bridge between black and white. The newfound "biracial movement" emphasizes acknowledging our commonalities—and continuing to fight against prejudice and discrimination, hate crimes, and ignorance, in all their guises.

acknowledgments

Dozens of people contributed untold hours of interviews in the six years that I worked on this book, most particularly, Dennis Riordan, Cathy Kornblith, Elaine Brown, and, of course, Johnny Spain himself. I interviewed Johnny on seventy-two separate occasions, with some interviews lasting several days. Jonina Abron, Earl Andre, Charles Armstrong, Don Armstrong, Charles Bates, Richard Beban, Stephen Bingham, Terry Boren, Charles Breckenridge, Gonzalo Cano, Fred Castillo, Angela Davis, Mike Dufficy, Dino Fulgoni Jr., Charles Garry, Kate Grissom, Ericka Huggins, Leroy Hutchinson, Mama Jennings, William Kunstler, James Menard Jr., Susan Malerbi, Ron Niver, Pat Richartz, Gerald Schwartzbach, Judge Richard Silver, Pinkey Spain, Elisabeth Sunday, and Philip Zimbardo opened their lives, file cabinets, and hearts to me, as did many other lawyers, prison rights activists, revolutionaries, guards, judges, prosecutors, and friends and neighbors of Johnny throughout his life.

The interview process was much more than just a means of obtaining information. It was a dramatic, transformative process where I learned as much from the events surrounding the interviews as I did from the interviews themselves. I am haunted by several of those moments: Watching the pain on Johnny's face as we walked from the street corner where he shot Joe Long into the building in which he had tried to flee. Meeting his brother Charles Armstrong at Shoney's in Jackson, Mississippi (so that I could identify him, he told me, "I look like a big bear and I'm wearing a Bad to the Bone T-shirt"), and crying as I realized that this white man's life had been just as destroyed by the racism against blacks as his black brother's life had been. Chanting and meditating with Ericka Huggins, the Black Panther who had been on trial with Bobby Seale in New Haven, and realizing that the search for a more perfect world she had started in the Panthers in the 1970s had evolved in the 1990s to an analogous quest that took place in ashrams with incense rather than at the barricades with automatic weapons. Hearing the choppers overhead and watching the drug dealers in the South Central neighborhood where Johnny had grown up—and realizing how much worse things are today. Meeting Charles Bates, the F.B.I. agent who spent the first part of his career overseeing the arrests of Bobby Seale, Angela Davis, and other prominent revolutionaries, and then was transformed himself to the point that he testified on behalf of a black boy shot by cops.

I had no lack of material for any number of books, and for that reason I am especially grateful to those people who helped me turn a mound of facts and feelings into this publication. Special thanks go to Amanda Urban, Clements Ripley, Michelle Baker Richardson, Erroll McDonald, James Lindgren, John Jacob, Eric Goodman, Bryant Garth, Zeshan Khan, and, above all, Lesa Andrews.

index

about the author

Lori Andrews, a Chicago lawyer and writer, is one of the 100 Most Influential Lawyers in America, according to the *National Law Journal.* A graduate of Yale College and Yale Law School, she is an internationally recognized expert on the civil rights issues raised by new technologies. A recipient of several journalism awards, she has written for a wide variety of publications including *The New York Times Magazine, The Washington Post, New York, Vogue,* and *Psychology Today.* She has discussed her work on *The Oprah Winfrey Show, Good Morning America, Today, CBS Morning News, Prime Time Live, Dateline,* and other shows. She is a professor at Chicago-Kent College of Law and director of the Institute for Science, Law, and Technology at the Illinois Institute of Technology.